Great Thinkers in Economics Series

Series Editor: **A.P. Thirlwall**, Emeritus Professor of Applied Economics, University of Kent, UK.

Great Thinkers in Economics is designed to illuminate the economics of some of the great historical and contemporary economists by exploring the interactions between their lives and work, and the events surrounding them. The books will be brief and written in a style that makes them not only of interest to professional economists, but also intelligible for students of economics and the interested lay person.

Titles include:

William J. Barber
GUNNAR MYRDAL

Paul Davidson
JOHN MAYNARD KEYNES

Peter D. Groenewegen
ALFRED MARSHALL

Michael Szenberg and Lall Ramrattan
FRANCO MODIGLIANI

Forthcoming titles include:

Esben Sloth Andersen
JOSEPH A. SCHUMPETER

Charles Rowley
JAMES McGILL BUCHANAN

Michael A. Lebowitz
KARL MARX

John King
NICOLAS KALDOR

Alessandro Roncaglia
PIERO SRAFFA

Julio Lopez and Michaël Samuel Assous
KALECKI'S THEORY OF CAPITALIST ECONOMIES

Gerhard Michael Ambrosi
ARTHUR C. PIGOU

J. R. Stanfield
JOHN KENNETH GALBRAITH

Warren Young and Esteban Perez
ROY HARROD

G. C. Harcourt and Prue Kerr
JOAN ROBINSON AND HER CIRCLE

Roger Middleton
ROBERT SOLOW

Gavin Kennedy
ADAM SMITH

Gordon Fletcher
SIR DENNIS HOLME ROBERTSON

Great Thinkers in Economics
Series Standing Order ISBN 978–1–4039–8555–2 (Hardback)
Series Standing Order ISBN 978–1–4039–8556–9 (Paperback)
(outside North America only)

You can receive future titles in this series as they are published by placing a standing order. Please contact your bookseller or, in case of difficulty, write to us at the address below with your name and address, the titles of the series and one of the ISBNs quoted above.

Customer Services Department, Macmillan Distribution Ltd, Houndmills, Basingstoke, Hampshire RG21 6XS, England

Franco Modigliani

A Mind That Never Rests

Michael Szenberg
Pace University, New York, USA

and

Lall Ramrattan
University of California, Berkeley Extension, USA

Foreword by
Robert M. Solow

palgrave
macmillan

First published in 2008 by
PALGRAVE MACMILLAN
Houndmills, Basingstoke, Hampshire RG21 6XS and
175 Fifth Avenue, New York, N.Y. 10010
Companies and representatives throughout the world.

PALGRAVE MACMILLAN is the global academic imprint of the Palgrave Macmillan division of St. Martin's Press, LLC and of Palgrave Macmillan Ltd. Macmillan® is a registered trademark in the United States, United Kingdom and other countries. Palgrave is a registered trademark in the European Union and other countries.

ISBN-13: 978–0–230–00789–5 hardback
ISBN-10: 0–230–00789–9 hardback

This book is printed on paper suitable for recycling and made from fully managed and sustained forest sources. Logging, pulping and manufacturing processes are expected to conform to the environmental regulations of the country of origin.

A catalogue record for this book is available from the British Library.

A catalog record for this book is available from the Library of Congress.

10 9 8 7 6 5 4 3 2 1
17 16 15 14 13 12 11 10 09 08

Printed and bound in Great Britain by
CPI Antony Rowe, Chippenham and Eastbourne

B'H
Dedicated to the memory of my sister, Esther;
to the memory of my parents, Henoch and Sara
to my children Naomi and Avi and
their spouses Marc and Tova;
to my grandchildren
Elki, Batya, Chanoch, Devorah, Ephraim, Ayala, and Jacob;
And to my wife, Miriam;

And to that Righteous Austrian-German Officer who took my immediate family to a hiding place just days before the last transport to Auschwitz, where most of my family perished

–M.S.

To my wife Noreena,
to my children Devi, Shanti, Hari, and Rani;
and to my grandchildren Soham and Lakshmi

–L.R.

Contents

Acknowledgements

In bringing this manuscript to fruition, we have benefited greatly from the support and assistance of many individuals. First and foremost, we wish to thank Paul A. Samuelson for borrowing the subtitle to this volume and Robert M. Solow, who extended to us many kindnesses in the past and who unhesitatingly agreed to pen the foreword to this biography. Along the way, we have benefited from Jim Hall, the Associate Dean of Lubin School of Business, for unfailing support, and encouragement in ways too numerous to list.

We are very grateful to Serena Modigliani, the wife of Franco, for granting us a lengthy interview and phone access recalling her husband and his milieu, which brought him alive. Also we are thankful to Leah Modigliani, Franco's granddaughter, for providing us with personal vignettes.

Marina Slavina and Lesley Sejdak, our devoted and caring assistants deserve special thanks for their ever cheerful mood and patience with the many revisions during the last year. Another assistant, Iva Juric, generously extended herself to me in constructing the index.

We are grateful to Diana Ward, the Assistant Director of the Lubin's Center for Applied Research, for being helpful in providing encouragement in our research efforts, and to Carmen Urma, the Coordinator of the Finance and Economics department, for lightening my administrative burden with aplomb. They do it with remarkable devotion and efficiency. Kudos to them.

The Pace's library is a superbly run unit where efficiency and kindness dwell together. We are grateful to the librarians of Pace University – Adele Artola, Elizabeth Birnbaum, Amerne Denton, Michelle Fanelli, Alicia Joseph and Sanda Petre, who are unfailingly enthusiastic and extraordinarily supportive.

Deep gratitude and thanks are owed to the members of the Executive Board of Omicron Delta Epsilon and the Honor Society in Economics for being an important source of support: Professors Mary Ellen Benedict, Kristine L. Chase, James Bradley, Robert R. Ebert, William D. Gunther, Robert S. Rycroft, Kathryn A. Nantz, Farhang Niroomand and Charles F. Phillips, Jr.

And we thank our MBA and doctoral students who have sustained us for decades in this and all our work. We are in awe of Raizel Kaufman, for her accomplishments in the face of great obstacles. All of them are really the dessert of our life.

The collegiality at Lubin of Lew Altfest, Bill Freund, Matt Morey, and Berry Wilson was a constant source of affection and encouragement. My immense gratitude goes to P. Viswanath, a most treasured, creative and energetic colleague in my department who never tires of assisting others when asked. He accomplishes his mission with remarkable, humbling skill.

Abundant thanks go to William Dewald and Robert Brazelton for their comments on the manuscript.

Special thanks to the editor of the "Great Thinkers in Economics" series, Tony Thirlwall, who potently combed through the text providing insightful and critical comments on an earlier version of the manuscript. We owe an enormous debt of appreciation to him.

Turning to the publishing end of the book, we are grateful to Amanda Hamilton, economics publisher at Palgrave Macmillan for her encouragement and efficient support. She incorporates the best publishing virtues of high standards, precision and empathy.

Finally, we dedicate the book to our grandchildren. They are a joyous gift and blessing. We thank them for urging us to "Get it done already!" But I will ask them to be sympathetic, because another book project is moving from the back to the front burner.

And now welcome to the world of Franco Modigliani.

Preface

The theologian Abraham Joshua Heschel tells of a failing blacksmith whose customers were dwindling away. The blacksmith sought advice from the rabbi who told him, "My child, you have learned your trade well. You can forge the metal, place the anvil, strike a smart blow with the hammer. But, alas, you have not learned to kindle the spark."[1] The purpose of this book is to explore the life and the intellectual harvest of a Keynesian economist, a writer of intellect and brilliance whose ideas found prolific expression in 14 books and 200 articles, assembled in six volumes of Collected Papers, a lecturer who spellbound his students and whose creative spark never dimmed even as he advanced in age. He was the only person elected as president of the American Economic Association (1976) and the American Finance Association (1981). Modigliani was also elected as President of The Econometric Society (1962) and was honorary President of the International Economic Association. He had three loves that pervaded his life: Serena, his wife,[2] economics, and two countries: the United States and his country of birth, Italy. As for Modigliani's love for Italy, the last words of his namesake (no relation), Amedeo Modigliani, the painter come to mind: "Italia! Cara, cara Italia!"

Modigliani never faced the problem that plagues scientists and writers – lack of inspiration and imagination. In the poem "The Circus Animal's Desertion," William Butler Yeats describes his loss of creativity, which limits him to rehashing old themes. "I sought a theme and sought for it in vain, I sought it daily," and in the closing stanza Yeats resigns himself to his barren state. "Now that my ladder's gone, I must lie down where all the ladders start."

Joseph Ben Halafta once famously remarked that since creation God is busy constructing ladders for some to ascend and others to descend.[3] For Modigliani, a free thinker that he was, the ladder was delivered by Jacob Marschak, his mentor, who took him under his wing at the New School for Social Research (now known as the New School University) in New York.

Howard Gardner[4] argues that for breakthroughs to occur, creative minds must have emotional and cognitive support. In Modigliani's case, the remarkable warmth radiated to him from his family, especially his wife and children. Contrast this with Victor de Riqueti, Marquis de Mirabeau, the

French economist of the Physiocratic school, nicknamed "Friend of Man," (after his work "L'Amides Hommes,") whose son, the famous revolutionary leader, lamented "The friend of man was friend to neither wife nor children."

In terms of work habits, Modigliani loved comradeship and since he did not particularly itch to write, he took on many collaborators – about 40 of them.[5] As Elhanan Helpman remarks, "collaboration is like a Ping-Pong game, where ideas are tossed back and forth. Except no matter who scores, you end up winning."[6]

His formidable scientific virtuosity was as keenly honed as his wit. To a Texas audience he relayed how economics can be chaotic.

> An engineer, an economist, and a surgeon argued over whose profession was the oldest: The surgeon spoke first and said, "Remember at the beginning when God took a rib of Adam and made Eve? Who do you think did that? Obviously, a surgeon." The engineer, however, was undaunted by all this and said, "Just a moment. You remember that God made the world before that. He separated the land from the sea. Who do you think did that, except an engineer?" "Just a moment," protested the economist, "Before God made the world, what was there? Chaos. Who do you think was responsible for that?"[7]

Modigliani gave us a firsthand account of his life and works in *Adventures of an Economist* (2001). The book's three chapter headings: "My Story and America," "Europe and the Monetary Adventure," and "Italy and Me" outline Modigliani's life. Modigliani consistently kept one foot on theory and the other on applications with equal zest, and continued to expand and articulate Keynesian economics when it was not fashionable to do so. In Keynes, he found permanence and invariability that he would fiercely defend against the classical school. This intellectual biography traces the initial conceptions and evolution of Modigliani's seminal contributions, which are characterized by depth, unity and scope. Franco Modigliani died at 85 years old on 25 September, 2003 in Cambridge, Massachusetts, while working. He requested that his body be cremated and have his ashes spread over the Atlantic Ocean near Cape Cod. He is survived by his wife, two sons, Andre' and Sergio, four grandchildren, and three great-grandchildren.

Foreword

Robert M. Solow

Reading some more about Franco Modigliani and his work will be good for you, and for two reasons. The first is that you will learn about Franco, a real, non-bland person, and an excellent economist. (I can not bring myself to refer to him simply as "Modigliani," even though I know how to pronounce it.) I have said on other occasions that being Franco's friend was not for sissies. He was always engaged, passionately devoted to his work, especially to whatever he was doing right now. If Franco was interested in some piece of theory or practice, he took it as a sign of inexplicable personal deficiency on your part if you were not as intensely interested as he was, or if you made the obvious error of thinking that your hot topic was hotter than his. He would try to set you right with great kindness and an encouraging smile.

There was also the discouraging certainty that, while you were watching a ball game or mowing the grass, Franco was working at his hot topic, and finding something new to tell you about next time.

The very same characteristics made Franco a wonderful colleague and a brilliant economist. There was never a dull moment where he was involved. Nobody ever described Franco as non-judgmental. He had a well-developed sense of right and wrong – in which Serena's opinion played an important role – and he was as much of a bulldog on moral issues as he was on intellectual ones.

This part of his intellectual and moral life took up an extra amount of space because he had two countries to worry about and two sets of policy issues to think through and evaluate. It could be exhausting, but it was always lively and fascinating and, above all, involved.

The second reason why you should want to read about Franco and his work is that doing so will put before you an idea of what macroeconomics can be, an idea that you would not absorb from studying the rather desiccated reality-resistant discipline that modern macroeconomics seems to be intent on becoming. This is not the place for me to expand on this contrast. It is not a matter of theory versus empirical work, or of narrow methodological and epistemological disputes. It is more relevant to say that Franco' s vision of the macroeconomy is populated by consumers and their families, investment committees and their bankers, wage-earners and their organizations, and not by one lone representative agent who sweeps under the Ramsey integral all the conflicting preferences, varying expectations, incompatible beliefs, and different statuses that seem to be in play in the economy at large as it fluctuates.

Macroeconomics Modigliani-style – or Modigliani-and-friends-style – is not necessarily informed by careful psychology and sociology. Maybe it would be better if it were. But at least it avoids terminal blandness by allowing for the interaction of recognizable interest groups with their own theories about the economy around them.

Franco Modigliani was a Keynesian, his own kind of Keynesian, not exactly the same kind of Keynesian as James Tobin, say, or others I could name. It is important to understand, however, that the contrast I am drawing between Modigliani-style macroeconomics and optimizing-representative-agent-based macroeconomics has little or nothing to do with that old textbook warhorse, the Keynesian-Classical (or New Classical) dichotomy. I like to use the examples of A.C. Pigou and D.H. Robertson, economists whose beliefs were the direct objects of Keynes's attack, but whose general approach to macroeconomics was, in style if not in content, not so different from Modigliani's.

Neither is the distinction I am making related in any way to slogans about "micro-foundations." There are many ways to incorporate any restrictions imposed by micro-behavior on an aggregative model. The life-cycle hypothesis does that in its way with respect to aggregate saving; the Modigliani-Miller theorem does it in its way with respect to aggregative investment behavior. In truth the shoe is on the other foot: the notion that the extreme and tendentious representative-agent version of the Ramsey model is a useful embodiment of the wish for micro-foundations will hardly stand up to sober reflection. The less formal but more accurate approach of Modigliani (and Tobin and others) seems more likely to yield a macroeconomics with meaning and verisimilitude.

Franco was not much given to purely methodological disputation. He simply chose to do macroeconomics in a way that seemed appropriate to the world he observed around him in Italy, the U.S. and elsewhere. In the course of doing it, he produced a distinguished group of students, and a large body of work that you can read about in this book and in his own writing.

They teach a lesson about macroeconomics that badly needs learning or relearning because it is a piece of simple wisdom that is in danger of extinction in a blaze of implausible Euler equations. Reading about Modigliani offers you an exemplary story that will help to preserve the memory of one good way of being a macroeconomist and of one extraordinary economist who chose it and lived by it.

1
Modigliani's Early Life and Influences

Introduction

Modigliani penned an autobiography relating his experiences in Italy, America and other European countries.[1] For each country, he presents his major works like a meal consisting of graphs, symbols, data, and explanations for general readers to digest. A "scientific autobiography" written by "a ferocious Galileo," says Samuelson. "His memoirs are just like him. Any reader will get to know a delightful person and learn some economics besides,"[2] echoes Solow. *Adventures* stands besides other biographical pieces Modigliani had written, one for his Nobel Prize in 1985,[3] and a chapter in a book.[4] Why should we have another record of his life and works?

To know Modigliani is to know a genius

How many ways can we know a genius? Aristotle said that a wise person could grasp things that are further removed from the senses.[5] Modigliani was a wise man because his works reach beyond common sense. Striving for perfection, his works appear timeless and fresh. He insisted on numerous refinements, amendments and revisions during the publication of his 2003 "The Keynesian Gospel According to Modigliani" in *The American Economist*, a journal we edit. The liquidity preference theory written in 1944 had its last revision in 2003. The Modigliani-Miller theory of the cost of capital, written in 1958, was revisited in 1988,[6] and he had expressed his intention to further revisit it. He expounded his saving paradigm in the late 1940s, and applied it to China in a 2004 article,[7] published posthumously.

At Modigliani's memorial service at MIT's Sloan School of Management, his colleague, Paul Samuelson, referred to Modigliani's thought process as D-E-E-P. As an example he pointed to the way Modigliani penetrated into the intricate Dual Pasinetti theorem that they both formulated. During the collaboration Modigliani called Samuelson incessantly, demonstrating an exceptionally concentrated mind on the subject which shortly thereafter, led to the illumination.

A die-hard Keynesian

Modigliani took pride and delight in developing Keynesian economics, but he appeared to be a thorn in the flesh of the classical economists. From the publication of the *General Theory* in 1936, Keynes' teachings steered the direction of economics into the 1970s, when stagflation started to appear. Economists who share Modigliani's macroeconomic paradigm would view the main part of Keynes' theories as the "Gospel" truth. Others not only reject it, but try to overthrow it. The result is a constant tug-of-war between ideas from both sides. Ultimately, scientific progress is made "funeral by funeral."[8]

Modigliani's work is built around "hard-core" Keynesian thought. That hard-core element took birth in his 1944 dissertation from which he built a long lasting research program, as far as new theories of macroeconomics go. Modigliani's frequent revisions of his major works were an attempt to integrate new ideas, respond to and accommodate critics, and to articulate the models in different ways. The adjustments, however, occurred only in the protective belt around his hard-core model of Keynesian thought.

If Modigliani is seen as a committed Keynesian, then it is because of an unshakable belief in his scientific program. All scientific endeavors need repeated rounds of shaking up. Think what science would have been like had scientists adopted Greek philosopher Epicurus' notion that atoms are hooked. His atoms are motionless, as though they are nailed to a wall. The scientist, however, mobilizes and shakes-up ideas. As Henri Poincare compares ideas to the hooked atoms, "the mobilized atoms undergo impacts which make them enter into combinations among themselves or with other atoms at rest, which they struck against in their course. In those new combinations ... lie ... spontaneous inspirations."[9] Modigliani's meticulous attitude and the multiple revisions of his works made it possible to shake up ideas.

Difficulty of the subject matter

Modigliani first embraced macroeconomics through his mentor, Jacob Marschak, at the now New School University in New York. The concern at that time was to crack the secret codes in Keynes' newly published book, *The General Theory of Employment, Interest and Money*. The text lacks serious mathematics, yet Marschak advised him to study the subject. Modigliani went to R. G. D. Allen's, *Mathematical Analysis for Economists* text. Moreover, he studied statistics by attending the well-known Abraham Wald's seminars at Columbia University and participated in an informal seminar, at the invitation of Marschak, whose members included, besides Wald, Tjalling C. Koopmans and Oscar Lange.[10] A glance at Modigliani's scientific writings confirms that Marschak predicted well. The general reader will appreciate Modigliani's contributions if they are not averse to the use of symbols, graphs, and data.

The area of macroeconomics developed rapidly after Modigliani and others had insisted on direct applications. Just after graduation, Modigliani joined Hans Neisser at the New School University in producing a quantitative macro model. One of the highlights of the model was the establishment of the relationship between foreign trade and domestic economic activities in a multi-country setting.[11] Subsequently, Modigliani continued to alter and improve the validity and compactness of the model.[12]

Formative years: A developmental profile of Franco Modigliani

We embark upon this journey with Modigliani's early days. The sources of information are from Modigliani's own works, general reports, and our interviews with Modigliani's family members, collaborators and colleagues. In his *Adventures*, Modigliani tells us that he had a happy childhood.[13] Psychologists urge us to look at the external and internal factors of any protagonist. When we look at the environment surrounding Modigliani's birth, we find a mixture of positive and negative experiences. On the good side, we find that he had loving and caring parents. He describes holiday trips with his cousins as though he were never home alone. If there is any hurrying at all in his school days, it seems self-imposed.

Born into fascism

The dark environment surrounding Modigliani's childhood began around the time of his birth. He was born when WWI ended. Italy at that time was not as developed as France and England. Its industrialized, forward-looking northern regions were affluent, while the southern regions were impoverished and therefore more resentful of the ruling powers.[14] Social tensions started to emerge as the fascist regime began to place its emphasis on nationalistic issues. The Italian fascism that Modigliani confronted during his childhood was the doings of Benito Mussolini, who began in politics as a Marxist. But he did not bond with socialism. A split with the Italian Socialist party brought Mussolini national recognition.[15] When he was expelled, he declared in his last speech to the party: "You think to sign my death warrant, but you are mistaken ... you have not seen the last of me!"[16] As he urged Italy to enter the war, he added, "every epoch and every people has had its wars."[17] After WWI, Mussolini remarked, "The war has been a jet of pure water for our nation."[18]

Italy did not fare badly immediately after the war relative to other European countries, even though it came under the rule of Mussolini's fascist dictatorship. Germany became a Republic. And in Russia, renamed the Soviet Union, central planning was introduced subsequent to the communist revolution in 1917. What ensued were years of Stalinist terror and deprivation. Stalin's favorite phrase was, "No man, no problem." In Germany, "the year before the end of inflation in November 1923. ... Everybody was a billionaire, but a billion marks would not buy a loaf of bread."[19]

Mussolini had three aims for Italy: nationalism, production, and protection of the working classes.[20] He began his drive for power by organizing "paramilitary, black-shirted units (*fasci de combattimento* – hence the name *fascist*)."[21] He gathered support from the Catholic Church by declaring: "I maintain that Catholicism is a great spiritual power, and I trust that the relation between Church and State will henceforward be friendlier."[22] He also had the support of the army and the press. In 1922, he organized a massive "March on Rome," and the Italian King, Victor Emmanuel III, invited him to become the new parliamentary leader, the prime minister, "Il Duce." Two years later his party won approximately 70 per cent of the vote, and Italy soon turned into a fascist country.

Italian fascism opposed "liberalism, democracy, rationalism, socialism, and pacifism."[23] It had shared elements in common with Hitler's Nazism that were developing in Germany, such as an "organic state, the importance of struggle and will, the glorification of militarism, and insistence on authority and discipline, rule by an elite, and a mystic faith in the leader."[24] But the Nazis were also known for their racist beliefs which Mussolini adopted. When Modigliani was about 20 years old, he wrote:

> ... we were surprised by the publication of the race laws that were to degrade the life of any Italian Jew who wished to remain in Italy.

> It was no longer possible for Jews to attend public schools or to hold public office, including university teaching, and, what probably affected the Italian Jewish middle class more than anything else, it was forbidden to employ a non-Jewish domestic.[25]

Modigliani, being from "an old Roman family of Jewish ancestry," felt the discriminatory laws directly. This proved to be a turning point for him and led him to flee Europe. At Modigliani's memorial service at MIT, it was suggested that such an experience had made him fearless. Modigliani was therefore not only prepared for his conferences and meetings – during which he never showed anxiety – and delivered his talks without notes, but he was uncompromising in the pursuit of truth. It is clear that his experiences with the brutality and degradation of fascism and anti-Semitism created indelible memories in his mind, and were to define how he approached new subjects. There is nothing like suffering to sharpen the social sense. As Ernest Hemingway once remarked, he understood Cezanne's paintings far better when he was poor.

Modigliani's relations with his parents, siblings, and cousins

Modigliani was "an obstinate child, with occasional wild tantrums."[26] He communicated well with his father, whom he referred to as Papa. Modigliani's mother, Olga Flaschel, was a voluntary social worker. Her father, Emilio Flaschel was from Krakow, Poland, and her mother Ernestin Cagil was from Florence. Olga Flaschel was born in Florence, and had attended the University of Rome, attaining a degree in pedagogy in the 1930s. After graduation, she managed her family's business, trading in real pearls, but soon the competition with cultured pearls dominated the real pearls market causing their family's business to close down in the 1930s. Modigliani observed "arbitrage" at work in his young days as his grandfather bartered pearls against coral between Italy and Poland.

Modigliani's father, Enrico, was a famous pediatrician. He showed great dedication for illegitimate children for whom the law provided little protection at that time.[27] He met these children while serving at some of the institutions which cared for abandoned children. From his observations, he developed the theory that "the very high death rate of foundlings in the orphanages was due to lack of maternal love in the first weeks of life." Franco Modigliani was thus exposed to two major economic influences: arbitrage through his mother, and demographic analysis and social concerns through his father.

Childhood memories

Modigliani was born on 18 June, 1918 in Rome, Italy. In *Adventures*, Modigliani tells us of three indelible childhood memories. The first is about a nickname his father gave him: "comfort spider." The other two occurred at about the age of four. One occurred on a holiday when his cousin Maria fell into a lake while stepping into a boat. He remembered everyone in the party laughing. The other was a feeling captured by his Papa's poem: "But by golly, That's enough, We want bread, And we want stuff! We will call in, with hand grenades, all the fascist Black Brigades."[28] These stories mixed fun with serious times.

His own words relay that his childhood was happy even though he admits that he had "the most awful tantrums and kicked out wildly." He had few memories of his Papa, who died when he was 14, which he considered to be his childhood tragedy. He had an elder brother, Giorgio, to whom he was attached. In *Adventures*, Modigliani relates Giorgio's struggle to survive during the Holocaust. A major reason for Franco's continued attachment to Italy was because Giorgio's family was saved by other Italians, most of them strangers.

Might Modigliani's memory of his father calling him a "comfort spider" be a fantasy and not a reality? Freud wrote that childhood memories are like the history of antiquity.[29] Early history has heroes; later history, reflections. In *Adventures*, Modigliani offers an explanation for his reflection: "when I was a young boy I was very thin, bony, and fidgety, and maybe also because I was wiry like a spider."[30] The reality is that the spider image is a popular symbol for creativity, since the spider spins its web from the inside. Also, a person needs comfort in order to create. We find it interesting that Modigliani mentioned his "comfort spider" childhood memory when he was at the pinnacle of his career. If he was not creating a history by reflecting back to his formative years, then might he have repressed his creativity instinct in childhood? The environmental factors – a bad teacher, attempts at other careers, such as medicine and law, and fascist and anti-Semitic sentiments favor repression. Yet, it appears that these factors became drivers for Modigliani. Whether his childhood memories were fantasy or reality, in our opinion they produced a well-rounded character.

Modigliani's school days

At elementary school, Modigliani skipped the fifth grade. He spent two years at the upper secondary school skipping the third year. When he was 14 and in his first term at Regio Ginnasio Umberto I, his father died from a duodenal ulcer operation. Perhaps because he was grieving the loss of his father whom he dearly loved, he showed a lack of discipline for schoolwork. His grades deteriorated and he was disciplined by one of his teachers. For this reason he chose not to continue at that school.

Modigliani entered the second term of the prestigious Liceo Ennio Quirino Visconti in 1934. The school boasted that it had turned out several future bishops, cardinals and popes. Being Jewish, he would leave the classroom with a protestant student during instruction in the Catholic religion. Two subjects were of special interest to him: literature and classical studies. The literature teacher, Carlos Graber, read Dante's *Divine Comedy* in class and other Italian poems, with "wisdom and passion," says Modigliani. Don Vannutelli, a priest, who taught Latin and Greek, and was well versed in Sanskrit, addressed his students in rhyme. Vannutelli was also a man of exceptionally good deeds; he saved many of his Jewish students from arrest or deportation during war time.

After graduating from the Liceo in 1935, Modigliani vacationed for two weeks in England. Besides improving his English, the trip to England helped him to "appreciate the strong critical attitude that prevailed in Britain toward the war in Abyssinia."[31] Mussolini invaded Ethiopia, then known as Abyssinia, in October 1935. In order to settle the conflict Samuel Hoare, British Foreign Secretary, and Pierre Laval, French Prime Minister, proposed to hand over large areas of Ethiopia to Italy. Mussolini agreed to the plan, but British public opinion vociferously opposed it, and so Hoare had to resign, shelving the plan. Mussolini continued his aggression causing a break with England and France, and leading him to seek alliance with Germany.[32]

The war with Ethiopia ended in 1936, followed thereafter by the Italy-Germany alliance in 1936 that was to gain in strength. In September 1937 Mussolini visited Germany, and was greeted with a magnificent display of Germany's military power. In May 1938, Hitler visited Italy, but the Italian people did not extend to him a warm welcome. "Italian police were ordered to lock up local Jews or expel them from towns which Hitler was visiting."[33] The introduction of the anti-Jewish "Racial Manifesto" in 1938 in Italy paralleled the introduction of the Nuremberg laws of 1935 in Germany.[34] The 45,000 Italian Jews were excluded from "the military, education, banking and insurance, the bureaucracy and Party, and any but small-scale business and agriculture."[35] Consequently, about 10,000 Jews were deported, and thousands emigrated to other countries. Modigliani was among them. Afterwards, a tit-for-tat game of invasion of European countries ensued – Hitler invaded Czechoslovakia in March 1939; Mussolini took Albania on Good Friday that year. The so-called Pact of Steel cemented the partnership of Fascism and Nazism in 1939.

And the Second World War erupted with the invasion of Poland by Germany in September 1939.

Some may assume that by skipping the third year at primary school and the fifth year at the upper division makes for an unusual student. Modigliani thought it was an achievement, for it allowed him to enroll at the University of Rome in 1935, at the age of 17, two years ahead of the norm.

Modigliani's father wanted him to follow in his footsteps and study medicine. However, the sight of blood frightened him and he decided to study law instead. Modigliani found "The curriculum in law was really very easy, and [he] had a lot of time."[36] What was he to do with his free-time? The mid-1930s was a stressful time for the Italian economy. Both the Depression and the war with Ethiopia were on. The stock market lost a third of its value during 1929–1932, unemployment remained high and real wages declined.[37] By chance, Modigliani found a job translating German articles into Italian. About 20 of those articles dealt with price controls in Italy that were occasioned by the Ethiopian war in 1935. Modigliani transferred that experience into an essay on price controls for a competition among university students. He won the competition. But more importantly, he began to think like an economist.[38] He was encouraged by the fact that economics was also taught at the Faculty of Law. At that time, he had access only to the works of the classical economists. Keynes' works, which were to steer his later life, were not yet available to him. He mainly studied the writings of Italian economists and the British classical school, especially Alfred Marshall.[39] This first brush with economics was soon interrupted by the fascist discrimination against Jews. Modigliani expresses this when he says,

> After the Ethiopian war and the fascist intervention in the Spanish Civil War, I began to develop a strong antifascist sentiment and the intent to leave Italy, but the final step was the close alliance of Mussolini with Hitler, which resulted in anti-Semitic laws, which made it impossible to live in Italy in a dignified way.[40]

With the encouragement from his future father-in-law, Giulio Calabi, Modigliani left Italy for France in 1939, expecting to continue his study of economics. He found that "the French university was even worse than the Italian. People did go to class in large numbers, but as far as I could tell, their only purpose was to make noises of various kinds – very effectively so that you could not hear what was going on."[41]

He made some progress studying in the quiet environment of the *Bibliotheque St. Genevieve* library. But his mind then veered in the direction of the United States. In May 1939, he married Serena Calabi,[42] a childhood friend, returned to Italy in July 1939 to defend his thesis for the Doctor Juris degree, and set off for the United States in August 1939, just days prior to the onset of WWII.

Modigliani did not have prior arrangement for studies in New York. With the help of a well-known refugee, Max Ascoli, and a friend, Paolo Contini who held a research position at the New School, Modigliani obtained a scholarship. The New School, nicknamed "University in Exile," was a refuge for anti-fascist intellectuals fleeing Europe. Now, at the age of 21, his economic studies were to take off. The popular subjects at that time were Schumpeter on business cycles, and Keynes on macroeconomics. Reading Keynes' *General Theory* left an indelible mark. He had several teachers – Fritz Lehman, Adolph Lowe, Kurt Wertheimer and Jacob Marschak, who became his mentor. Modigliani wrote:

> Jacob Marschak was at once a great economist, a magnificent teacher, and an exceptional and warm human being. He took me in hand and persuaded me first of all that if I wanted to get anywhere as an economist, I had to study mathematics.[43]

At the New School, "Modigliani's training as an economist can be said to have diminished in 1941 when Marschak left to join the University of Chicago."[44] In 1942, Modigliani taught at the New Jersey College for Women (then part of Rutgers University) in the areas of economics and statistics, and also taught at Bard College, which was then part of Columbia University. In 1944 he published his first article in *Econometrica*, which he adapted into the dissertation titled, "Liquidity Preference and the Theory of Interest and Money." The paper was the milestone that set his lifetime research work in economics.

In 1944, Modigliani returned to the New School as a Lecturer. Collaborating with Neisser, they published a book on *National Income and International Trade*. He also published on the theory of savings, starting his journey towards his breakthrough contribution on the life-cycle hypothesis.

Following the publication of the liquidity preference article, Modigliani received a prestigious fellowship in political economy at the University of Chicago in 1948. Shortly thereafter, in 1948, he was asked to join the College of Commerce of the University of Illinois where he researched expectations and business fluctuations and co-authored the first version of the life-cycle model of saving with a brilliant graduate student, Richard Brumberg. During this time he was invited to join the Cowles Commission then attached to the University of Chicago. At the Commission, aside from Marschak, Modigliani interacted with three future Nobel laureates: Kenneth J. Arrow (1972), Tjalling Koopmans (1975) and Herbert Simon (1978).

In the early 1950s, as the reactionary atmosphere created by Senator Joseph McCarthy swept across the United States, the administration of the University of Illinois replaced the liberal faculty members along with the Dean, Howard Bowen, who hired them. Modigliani was the last holdout. The new Dean summoned and addressed Modigliani, who hilariously describes the scene:

> Dear Modigliani, in the past you taught two subjects. One was macroeconomics, but you are evidently quite incompetent in that subject. There are plenty of old professors here that can teach it better than you. The other subject you have taught is mathematical economics, and I have to admit you are competent in that subject. But, you know, I'm afraid this subject, for which I personally have great admiration, can no longer be taught because it doesn't agree with the trustees. ...[45]

This reminded Modigliani of the early stages of the fascist regime in Italy. Since the Dean could not dismiss Modigliani, given that he was a full professor with tenure, he wanted Modigliani to take offence at his words and resign. Indeed he succeeded. Decades later, the University of Illinois recognized its error and made amends by bestowing upon Modigliani an honorary doctoral degree.

A similar discriminatory encounter occurred in 1957, when Modigliani was offered a permanent position at Harvard by the economics department, but the anti-Semitic chairman, Harold Burbank, dissuaded him from accepting it.[46] Modigliani charmingly describes Burbank's argument.

> Look Modigliani, if you have any common sense you won't accept this job we are offering you, because you know ... we have people here of the caliber of James Duesenberry, Sidney Alexander, Richard Goodwin, and many others. ... You'll never make it. Why don't you go back to the New School where you'll be a big fish in a little pond? Don't try being a big fish in this pond where there are plenty enough big fish already. ...[47]

From Illinois, Modigliani moved to Carnegie-Mellon University where he spent eight very fruitful years until 1960. There, he did more work on the life-cycle hypothesis, but this time alone, for Brumberg died in 1955. He began to build his reputation in other sub-disciplines. He wrote on optimal production scheduling, with Charles Holt, John Muth and Herbert Simon, and began his work on what later became the famous Modigliani-Miller (M&M) theorem. Last, but not least, he had something to say about what has become the precursor of the now famous rational expectations hypothesis in a paper, "Predictability of Social Events," co-authored with Emile Grunberg. In 1960, he left Carnegie-Mellon for MIT to be a visiting professor, and at the same time to occupy a permanent chair at Northwestern University. He returned to MIT permanently in 1962, joining forces with Paul A. Samuelson, Robert M. Solow and others, making it at that time, the premier economics department in the world. Modigliani was named MIT Institute Professor in 1970, a title bestowed upon scholars of exceptional distinction, and received several honorary degrees from the University of Chicago, Bard College, University of Illinois, the Universite Catholique de Louvain and the Institute Universitario di Bergame. In October 1985, he was awarded the Nobel Prize for his work on the life-cycle of consumption theory, and the M&M hypothesis. In 1988, he became Professor Emeritus.

Development assessment

Studying social scientists involves exploring the relationship between a person's environment and his/her consciousness. As we look briefly at these aspects and how they correlate with Modigliani, we are guided by one principle: while argumentative, "Modigliani is also known as one who never argues for victory, but rather for truth."[48] Sigmund Freud gave us the psychoanalytic view, where parent and sibling relationships are significant in explaining a person's developmental stage. Arnold Gesell tackled maturational stages, Watson talked about the environment, and Piaget talked about cognition. Their works have formed a springboard for many current approaches to a person's development.[49] We are not even providing a "lay" analysis in the sense that Freud[50] has defined the term. Therefore, we can only offer observations about the character of our protagonist.

Character portrayal

Generally, Modigliani was warm to both strangers and friends. He took scientific research seriously, and since scientists can cast doubt even on their own paradigms, we expect even more discord with rival paradigms. "Before he had even heard of Karl Popper, Modigliani was already practicing the advice that a scholar should be his own most stringent critic."[51] On the one hand, he demonstrated his ability to build bridges among rival paradigms as he did between the Monetarists and Keynesians in the 1970s. On the other hand, he openly disagreed with collaborators and colleagues. Suffice to mention that he differed with Merton Miller on the M&M hypothesis, particularly in the area of taxes to the extent that he wondered whether two Nobel Prizes should be awarded on the subject. He disagreed with Robert Barro that the M&M hypothesis is linked to Ricardo's theorem through the way savings and debt are handled in the Ricardian Equivalence theorem. From the inception of his scientific career, he disagreed with his colleague, Abba Lerner, over the functional finance interpretation of Keynes' work.[52] Robert Hall of the Hoover Institution and an MIT student of Modigliani tells us that in a "public academic interaction ... in a meeting of the Brookings Panel on Economic Activity ... [Modigliani argued that Hall's] MIT Ph.D. should be revoked, on account of some heterodox opinions" that he expressed in support of Chicago's Robert Lucas, who questioned the basic methodology of Modigliani's FRB-Penn-MIT- econometric model of the US economy. Most likely, Modigliani's harsh reaction to Hall was ignited by the fact that Hall had been his student. Furthermore, Hall states that Modigliani "liked originality, but wanted it to stay within the framework of modern Keynesianism."[53]

That is the nature of scientific honesty. But he got along well with his companions, which is not paradoxical. Not surprisingly, the Keynesian revolution allowed a tug-of-war among practitioners that has more agreeable than disagreeable elements. He had sowed the seed of that agreeable element, according to Samuelson, when he "wrote a seminal article setting Model-T Keynesianism on its modern evolutionary path and probing its microfoundations in rigid, nonmarket-clearing prices."[54] His early foundation works bred widespread collaborations with his colleagues, where his name is mostly suffixed by Ando, Brumberg, Dreze, Grunberg, Miller, Papedemos, and Samuelson.

We see then that his character was multifaceted. We know he had something important to say, but it appears we cannot predict the manner in which he would have communicated it. And we are told several times that one didn't want to give Modigliani the chalk. He had that overpowering presence that tended to dominate a conversation or discussion. For this reason, Serena Modigliani decided to send their two children to boarding school, so that their independence could fully develop. Robert Solow, the 1987 Nobel laureate, tells us about a seminar that he gave at the Carnegie Institute of Technology:

> Someone – I can't remember who it was – warned me that there was this Modigliani person and said that, sometime during my talk, he would come to the blackboard and ask for the chalk. At that point, I would be dead. Sure enough, Franco came to the front with something on his mind: "May I have the chalk, please." So I replied: "No." It had apparently never happened before.

Robert Solow also shares an insightful experience he and Modigliani encountered while their families vacationed together in Martha's Vineyard, in which Solow invited Modigliani to race with him on his 17-foot dinghy:

> In the course of the race, [Modigliani] was explaining some fine point about the life-cycle model to me. I pointed out to him that we were on a collision course with another boat in the race, and it had the right of way. Franco kept telling me more about the life-cycle model ... I reminded him that the other boat was still bearing down on us ... He continued to explain. A few seconds after my third warning, the other boat banged squarely into us. Franco was still explaining. The other boat was being steered by the wife of the chairman of the race committee. We were disqualified, but I learned a lot about the life-cycle model.[55]

Modigliani had a phenomenal capacity to work coupled with an extraordinary concentration of mind. He was able to block out his surroundings and stay with the task at hand, oblivious to anything else. Ben Friedman tells us, "if he [Modigliani] engaged in a conversation and it touched upon a certain topic, he didn't let go. Even though others veered to other topics, he continued dwelling on the initial topic." Friedman also recounts a particular phone call he once received from Modigliani on a Saturday morning at 6:30 a.m., in which Modigliani stated, "I am going to New Hampshire." Friedman did not understand what this had to do with him. When he inquired about Modigliani's purpose for calling, he told him that they had a meeting scheduled to discuss the non-linearity of the Phillips Curve, and since his wife Serena convinced him to go to New Hampshire, he was calling Friedman to cancel the meeting. This meeting that Modigliani referred to was actually never arranged.[56] This anecdote reflects how Modigliani's mind was so focused on the problem, he did not realize that a meeting was not even scheduled.

Dennis Snower, a collaborator with Modigliani, tells of a time when they were working on the Manifesto and were staying at the same hotel. Some of the major problems for the European Monetary Union (EMU) are summarized in a manifesto published by Franco Modigliani and others (Modigliani et al., 1998). The manifesto claims that demand side management with limited supply side policies have resulted in high unemployment rates in the EMU. Snower relates that after a long day of working together well into the night, Modigliani saw him early the next morning and said that he had had an idea occur to him at 3:00 a.m. and had continued to work on it throughout the night. Snower notes that Modigliani was inspirational in his ability to work for such lengthy periods of time.[57]

2
Modigliani and Keynesian Economics

Introduction

Modigliani built a Keynesian macroeconomic model that has attracted research for over 60 years. It started with his dissertation in 1944, which he revised just several months before his death in 2003. Some hold that the model revived classical thought, others say it betrayed the tools and thoughts of classical economics. But the model performed well overall in the sense that it solved problems and predicted macroeconomic events. In this chapter, we present Modigliani as a model builder who has one foot on theory and the other on application, extending the Keynesian paradigm.

We contrast Modigliani with some major classical and Keynesian protagonists as we proceed. The Boolean grid (Table 2.1) marks the 12 relationships to be investigated. Besides the 12 combinations, we can also study an author's earlier versus later views on a subject. Pigou, for instance, provided an early defense of the classical school, but later accepted some of Keynes' views. Don Patinkin, who followed the classical line of Pigou on the "real balance" effect, had some major disagreements with Modigliani's revival of classical economics. But while Patinkin and Modigliani reached some convergence in thought, their disciples disagreed over who had the better model. Last but not least, Hicks, upon whom Modigliani relied, altered his versions of Keynesian economics. After Hicks reviewed Keynes' book, he "beat a retreat" on several issues, and in his latter days, had second thoughts on the IS-LM framework. Modigliani's model framed the debate on these issues with deep imagination.

Mathematical and statistical tools and laws of macroeconomics have been significant factors in the development of Modigliani's model.

Table 2.1 Authors' writings that link Modigliani's ideas of Keynes

	Pigou	**Keynes**	**Hicks**	**Modigliani**
Pigou		1	1	1
Keynes	1		1	1
Hicks	1	1		1
Modigliani	1	1	1	

Although Say's Law, Walras' Law, and the homogeneity postulate are touched upon, the focus is on comparisons that bring out Modigliani's essential contributions to the modeling of macroeconomics.

This study follows the central ideas of the four authors cited in Table 2.1, to show how Modigliani weaved his contributions. A 1 in a cell represents that the idea between two authors say Pigou and Keynes can be described back and forth – what Pigou said of Keynes and vice versa. In cases where for instance Keynes did not say anything about Modigliani's view, we can investigate what Keynes's followers have said instead. We, of course, will not investigate all the possible back and forth ideas, but will paint the landscapes of classical versus Keynesian views that are not completely clear in the literature. Modigliani's model is not only easy to perceive, but provides the seeds for the post-Keynesian research programs.

Keynes as a model builder

Keynes built macroeconomics from what he thought were the defects of the classical school. Keynes describes his thoughts as follows: "The outstanding faults of the economic society in which we live are its failure to provide for *full employment* and its arbitrary and *inequitable distribution* of wealth and income,"[1] [Italics added]. Elsewhere, he exclaims, "But heavens, my doctrine of full employment is what the whole of my book is about! Everything else is a side issue to that."[2] Unemployment became the top issue during the 20th century as banking and other issues were of the 19th century.[3] The Great Depression of the 1930s captured Keynes' mind. Reminiscing about the Depression, Modigliani says the following:

> I think that a major fact that got my interest in the subject was the experience of the Depression and the high unemployment rates of the '30s ... And then there was Keynes, who said that it should not have happened. His paradigm swept the profession because it provided a simple and unified explanation for the occurrence of the

Depression. There was a great need at the time for an assurance that it would never happen again. And that fascinated me.[4]

Keynes' mindset was that "Economics is a science of thinking in terms of models joined to the art of choosing models which are relevant to the contemporary world." A good model should "segregate the semi-permanent or relative constant factors from those which are transitory and fluctuating."[5] He was skeptical about the quantitative aspects of a model. He thought that to "convert a model into a quantitative formula is to destroy its usefulness as an instrument of thought."[6] However, during his time, econometrics was in its infancy, and as it evolved Modigliani was able to utilize it in both the theoretical and applied arenas.

Today, a good model still has the virtues that Keynes expected and Modigliani valued. A good model must meet the following criteria: it should either explain and predict economic events, or provide solutions to problems posed. Our goal is to explain economic reality with all its deep a priori thoughts. We should also ascertain that our goal gives proper attention to the size and signs of our estimates. Old anomalies should disappear or be resolved, and some novelties should emerge. If the model that Keynes advanced can be said to meet these requirements, then economists such as Modigliani have given it the necessary retooling over time to attain its goal.

Modigliani as a model builder

In the U. S., two names tower high in the development of such high quality Keynesian models. One name is Paul A. Samuelson, who built the *Neoclassical-Keynesian Synthesis* that gives Keynes' model a classical backbone. The other is Franco Modigliani, who in Samuelson's words, "wrote a seminal article setting Model-T Keynesianism on its modern evolutionary path and prob[ed] the microfoundations in rigid, nonmarket clearing prices."[7] The metaphor is apt because just as Henry Ford made cars the popular means of transport in the U. S., Franco Modigliani made Keynes' model the domain of macroeconomic research.

Modigliani's Model-T Keynesian economics runs on four wheels, which he lists as "the consumption function, the investment function, the demand for and supply of money and other deposits, and the mechanism determining wages and prices."[8] He designed the engine of his Model-T macro model in his dissertation at the New School University, *The General Theory of Employment Interest and Money Under the*

Assumptions of Flexible Prices and Fixed Prices (1944). The title is identical to that of Keynes' masterpiece, with the addition of his two assumptions on prices that became Modigliani's research province for the rest of his life. He published his dissertation as *Liquidity Preference* in 1944.[9] This study became the chassis of his model that went through two major overhauls in 1963[10] and 1976.[11]

After he published his 1944 model, Modigliani felt compelled to revise it, given the significant economic changes that took place in the mid-1950s when new theories in the areas of asset management and portfolio analysis took root in Keynesian economics. Other significant changes followed the stable expansion period from 1950 to 1970 when the U.S. economy suffered major shocks – starting with the OPEC crisis in 1973–1974, which challenged Keynesian economics to explain simultaneous inflation and unemployment or stagflation as it is now called. In his presidential address to the American Economic Association (AEA) meetings in Atlantic City, New Jersey in 1976, Modigliani declared that his interpretation of the *General Theory* in 1944, as well as the interpretation by others such as John Hicks, could be made more relevant with some expansion and refinements. He advanced the central idea that because of interactions between the liquidity preference and wage rigidity concepts, stabilization policies "should be made more effective in the future than they have been in the past."[12] Loosely speaking, stabilization refers to policy measures that would counteract the tendency for the economy to move in cycles. In his last published article[13] while still alive, Modigliani continued his consistent strand of thought, slowly adopting different tools to express his model of Keynesian economics. In an interview with Barnett and Solow, he described the new basis of his presentation as follows:

> I am revising that paper [Modigliani 1944] completely and starting from an approach which I think is much more useful, I am starting from the notion that both the classics and Keynes take their departure from the classical demand for money, which is one of the oldest and best-established paradigms in economics. The demand for money is proportional to the value of transactions, which at any point can be approximated as proportional to nominal income (real income multiplied by the price level).[14]

The final classical demand approach that Modigliani took diverged in presentation, but not in substance, from his original work. The model maintained the hard core concepts of the Model-T Keynesian version he laid out in 1944. At the beginning of his research program, the general form of money that includes transaction as well as speculative demand formed the hard-core. At the end of his research, speculative demand plays less of a role, chipping away part of the hard-core. To foreshadow what is to come, we will start out with Modigliani's assumption that the wage rate is fixed. Then we shall explore how he combines that assumption with other assumptions during the various revisions of his model. We acquire another view when he combines flexible wages with the general demand for money equation where liquidity preference is central to the model, and another view when it is not.

In the rest of this chapter, we portray the stages of the progressive approach Modigliani made over time, starting with his 1944 model. Modigliani reported his progress in scientific terms. His policy prescriptions addressed mostly policy makers, not students or general audiences. Our task ahead is to distill his thoughts with a sufficiently graded filter for the general audience. Among the problems that abound, we shall ignore the frequent disagreements as to what the classics said, who the classics were, and whether Keynes' model is superior to that of the classics', or vice versa. The focus in this chapter is on the Keynes' model and Modigliani's contributions.

Keynes' model

Keynes provides a summary of his model in Chapter 18 of the *General Theory*. We will divide this summary into three parts. First, the production side includes capital, labor, and technology. Second, the consumption side includes tastes, preferences, and the disutility of labor; and lastly the social side includes supervision, organization, social structure, and the forces that distribute income. Keynes emphasized the marginal propensity to consume (MPC), the marginal efficiency of capital (MEK), the rate of interest, r, the liquidity preference (LP), and expectations of yield on capital assets. The wage-unit was determined by collective bargaining and the quantity of money. Two dependent variables were central to Keynes' thought: employment (N) and national income (Y).

Keynes claimed that the above elements of his model would make a general theory. Logically, a general theory would be one that provides the necessary and sufficient conditions to attain a desired result. In Keynes' case it is full employment, while a special theory would be one that concentrates on attaining statistical values. To show how the above elements can be arranged to provide a general theory of full employment, we have to link them in a schematic way. Keynes presented the first schema that used the production and consumption functions above to obtain national income, which depends on employment.[15] The hallmark of this outcome is that it appeals to experience. Practical economists, in the field of urban economics, are always trying to empirically find a direct relationship between output and employment, the so-called economic base multiplier, and to assess the influence of various industries on job growth.[16] Keynes found that experience reveals "severe fluctuation of output and employment."[17] The objective is to arrive at a paradigm that links these fluctuations to its sources, such as savings and investment.

Keynes discussed a second schema about the relationship between the rate of interest and the marginal efficiency of capital (MEK). This concept is to link the expected yield with the supply price of capital goods. Keynes defined it as " ... equal to the rate of discount which would make the present value of the series of annuities given by the returns expected from the capital asset during its life just equal to its supply price."[18] Obviously, investors borrow money to invest. If the yield from investment exceeds the rate at which they can borrow, the investment would be profitable. Therefore, profits will continue until $r = MEK$.[19] In post-Keynesian representation, this schedule is known as the demand for investment schedule.

Keynes' third schema is that a change in investment, I, would affect changes in income, Y, through the investment multiplier.[20] If we assume that the employment multiplier is approximately equal to the investment multiplier, then a change in I can also result in a change in employment. Finally, we can say increments in employment will raise liquidity preference when the demand for money is increased. Keynes concluded, "if we examine any actual problem along the lines of the above schematism, we shall find it more manageable."[21]

Early interpretations of Keynes' model

Gerald Shove, a friend of Keynes, praised the "system as a whole," particularly the inclusion of "expectation" into the analysis, but he desired more explanation on the relationship between liquidity preference and the rate of interest.[22] R. G. Hawtrey, a colleague of Keynes, wanted to accept that "the rate of interest is wholly determined by the amount of money in M_2 ... The monetary system determines M. Economic activities determine M_1, Given $M\text{-}M_1$ or M_2, the liquidity preference function determines the rate of interest, and the rate of interest determines investment."[23] He also thought that the classical system corresponded to the case where M_2, the speculative demand for cash, is negligible. Although Hawtrey's characterization of the demand for money had some modern foresight, he was not clear how it explained the "goal" that Keynes had in mind, namely, full employment. Hawtrey wrote to Keynes: "Your doctrine of involuntary unemployment or full employment I must confess I do not understand."[24]

Keynes took the opportunity in responding to Hawtrey to set out his views of the classical positions. He listed a common element between him and the classics, namely that: "All the classical economists, including Marshall and Pigou, have always held precisely the view that I hold, that savings and investment are necessarily and at all times equal."[25] By this he meant that S = Y − C, and Y = C + I, where S is savings, and C is consumption.[26] Keynes also considered the concept of *exante* vs. *expost* for equating saving and investment, but settled on the more logical concept of national income identity. Using the symbols defined thus far, Keynes represented the classical way of fixing the rate of interest as follows: S = f(MPC, r); I = f(MEK, r), and r = f(MPC, MEK). In this model the rate of interest was set where I = S. Keynes declared, "This is the opinion against which mine should be contrasted."[27]

Pigou's influence on Keynes' model

Arthur Cecil Pigou's latter writings rendered praises for the Keynesian system. After filtering through many iterations of comments, Pigou wrote that "a set of interrelated problems which bear on the behaviour, not of particular parts of the economic system, but of economic systems as wholes ... Many of these problems were brought into the forefront of economic discussion by the late Lord Keynes' book on *The General Theory of Employment, Interest and Money* ... that book rendered a great service to economics by asking important questions ... Keynes was a true pioneer."[28] Pigou too had as one of his major goals to explain full employment. He wrote that "a [person] is only unemployed when he is both not employed and also desires to be employed."[29] Keynes was able to identify a category of the unemployed, namely "involuntary" unemployment[30] that the classics have ignored. This concept requires a special form of the supply of labor curve.

During the debate between Keynes and Hawtrey, Keynes asked Pigou to explain the nature of the supply of labor function. Pigou responded that the supply of labor curve is a reverse "L-shape" or kinked curve with the x-axis representing the "number of employable persons in the population," (not the "number of unit hours worked"). Out of that came the significant point that the number of "would-be wage earners" does not respond to wages on the vertical section of the kinked labor supply curve.[31] This point sealed the position of the classics to be interpreted as saying that the supply of labor is the number of people employed at a given wage rate. To emphasize, if wages change, the supply of labor would not change because we are looking only at the vertical range of the kinked supply curve. This curve also underscores the importance of "involuntary unemployment" as Keynes proposed,[32] which is located on the horizontal segment before the kink. These concepts are now understood as saying that the classical labor supply curve depends on real wages; the Keynesian labor supply curve, on money wages. The possibility therefore exists for involuntary unemployment to occur as workers cannot determine their real wages, and they are off the classical supply curve frequently. In his 1944 presentation, Modigliani singled out this kinked demand curve as a novel hard-core element in Keynesian economics. He actually led off his research program with that rigid wage concept, embellishing it with unique aesthetic and algebraic symbols for scientific analysis as shown below.

Keynes used Pigou's characterization of the classical economic doctrine to build his system. According to Hicks,"Mr. Keynes takes as typical of 'Classical economics'; the latter writings of Professor Pigou."[33] Pigou was Keynes' teacher, and Keynes explicitly adopted his definition.[34] Pigou is relevant because he has laid out the parameters and equations of an employment system. Some may dispute whether Pigou's model is classical or neoclassical. Both place the dividing line between those schools at 1870, the birth of the marginal revolution.[35] While Keynes referred to Pigou's work as representing the classical school, we should not think that Pigou's model is beyond controversy, for Hicks has said that Pigou's work was relatively new and difficult, and "has not yet made much impression on the ordinary teaching of economics."[36]

Pigou's writings on employment are scattered over time. His very early book, *Unemployment* (1914), targeted students and general readers. His later book, *The Theory of Unemployment* (1933) is considered difficult, and Keynes summarized it in an appendix to chapter 19 of the *General Theory*. Pigou's *Employment and Equilibrium – A Theoretical Discussion* (1941) is less difficult, and according to Samuelson, "more important." It has sound methodology and comparative static and dynamic analysis.[37] Pigou's *Lapses from Full Employment* (1945) expands on the causes of unemployment. One underlying thread of Pigou's works is that a fall in money wage rate would lead to increased employment. However, as Harrod asserted, Pigou's claim of "wage-reduction is not established by his reasoning."[38] In his 1952 *Employment and Equilibrium,* Pigou incorporated some of the objections Keynes made to his ideas.

Table 2.2 below displays the equations that we will be referring to in the subsequent discussions in comparing Modigliani's model with that of Keynes, and the Classics. The first column displays seven equations from Pigou's works, followed by Keynes, Hicks, and Modigliani's model in columns 2 through 4, respectively. We will be explaining these equations when we compare the authors' views in subsequent sections.

Pigou's equations, even now, have a liquidity preference dimension. Equations one and two parallel the MPC and MEK concepts. Equations five and six define the labor market. The heart of the Pigou-Keynes debate is about how wage cuts can cause unemployment. Broadly speaking, the classics and Keynes differ about what determines the rate of interest. Table 2.2, (1c) indicates that according to Keynes, the liquidity preference schedules depend on the rate of interest. He hypothesized about the classics that "If traditional theory merely said that given 'Y' and the 'I' and 'S' schedules, then the rate of interest is thus determined, that would be okay ... The only way out is to assume that income is given, for example, full employment – it will tell you what the rate of interest is at full employment, but not what determines the rate of interest."[39] Given the expectation, W, the rate of interest equates M with the liquidity preference, A. This is determined from the outside of the model. To observe the way this is determined externally, one could fix M, then determine the rate of interest. And one could fix r, and then determine the quantity of money.

Hicks' interpretation of Keynes' model (from Keynes to a simple Walrasian model)

Before we get to the heart of Modigliani's contributions, one more model, constructed by John Hicks, attracted Keynes' attention, and requires some consideration. When the *General Theory* was published, Hicks[40] published a review that toed the line of Keynes' summary which we presented earlier with the three parts assumptions. Hicks' review is significant for another reason. It initiated Keynes' correspondence with him, which came across with the sentiment that Keynes was largely in agreement with Hicks' presentation, except on some minor point on which Hicks had to "beat a retreat." Hicks agreed with Keynes that a theory of employment was of paramount importance, but he broadened his review over other vintage theories to include "a theory of 'output in general' ... a theory of 'shifting equilibrium' ... a theory of money."[41] These developments are a foundation on which Modigliani built his model and need to be visited before we can get the full picture of his contribution.

Table 2.2 Comparison of macro models

A. C. Pigou	J. M. Keynes	J. R. Hicks	F. Modigliani
7 Quantity of money income. MV = g(r) Pigou, 1941, p. 65	1. $M = L(r)$ Keynes, 1936, p. 168 1a. $M = M_1 + M_2 = L_1(Y) + L_2(r)$ Keynes, 1936, p. 199 1b. $M = A(\omega,r)$ Rymes, 1989, p. 125 1c. $r = L(M)$ Rymes, 1989, p. 155	1. $M = L(r)$ Hicks, 1937, p. 191 1a. $M = L(Y, r)$ Hicks, 1937, p. 192	1. $M = L(r, Y)$ 1.a $M = kY$ Modigliani, 1944, p. 66 1b. $M^d = k(r)P_oPX$ Modigliani, 2005, p. 343.
2. Output of net Investment goods: ψ(Y) = f{r, F(x)} Pigou, 1941, p. 58	$r = MEK = \Sigma Q_t d_t$ Keynes, 1936, p. 137 $I = \phi_2(\omega,r)$ Rymes, 1989, p. 125	2. $I = I(r)$ 191 2a. $I = I(r,Y)$ Hicks, 1937, p. 196 general case	2. $I = I(r,Y)$
$S = S(r,v,q,)$ Pigou, 1941, p. 113	Psychological law (MPS = 1-MPC) S = (Y) and Y = f(I) Keynes, 1936, p. 184	3. $S = S(Y)$ Hicks, 1937, p. 191 3a. $S = S(r,Y)$ Hicks, 1937, p. 196 general case	3. $S = S(r,Y)$
MV = $p_1F(x)+p_2\psi(y)$) Pigou, 1941, p. 68	$Y = C + I; Y = C + S; S = I$ Keynes, 1936, p. 63 $Y = \phi_1(\omega,Y) + \phi_2(\omega,r)$ Rymes, 1989, p. 125	4. $S = I$	4. $S = I$ 4a. $X = C + I, I = X - C = S$ Modigliani, 2005, p. 346 4b. $kPX = M^s$ Modigliani, 2005, p. 331
$x + y = \phi(x)$ Keynes, 1936, p. 274	$\Delta Y_w = k\Delta_w$ Rymes, 1989, p. 115		5. $Y = PX$
3.Elasticity of demand of consumption: η_1			
4. Elasticity of demand of Investment: η_2			

5. Demand for labor	$D = f(N)$ Keynes, 1936, p. 25		
6. Supply of Labor. SS = f[(W/P) = g{x}]. Thus, $n = \chi(x)$ Keynes, 1936, p. 274	$Z = \phi(N)$ Keynes, 1936, p. 25		6. $X = X(N)$ 7. $W = X'(N)P$
1.Output of Consmption goods: F(x)	$C_w = \chi(Y_w)$ Keynes, 1936, p. 90 $C = \phi_1(\omega, Y)$ Rymes, 1989, p. 125		8. $C \equiv Y - I$
Special Labor SS	Wage Ridigity		9. $W = \alpha W_0 + \beta F^{-1}(N)P$ 10. $\alpha = 1, \beta = 0$ *for* $N \leq N_0$ $\alpha = 0, \beta = 1$ *for* $N > N_0$ 11. $\alpha \equiv 1, \beta \equiv 0$

Notes

Equations are arranged to correspond to Modigliani's numbering.

1. Hicks uses I for income and i for interest. We substitute Y for income and r for interest.
2. Pigou listed 7 equations. In Pigou's equations p_1 and p_2 are prices for consumption and investment goods, respectively. Pigou used x for employment in wage-goods and y for employment in consumption goods industries. His saving function S = f(...) can be positive or negative (Samuelson, 1941, 549), q is rate of time preference, v is a correction factor.
3. Hicks uses Ix for investment, we use I.
4. Keynes uses Q_r r = 1,2, 3. ... n for the prospective yield of an investment over time, and dr for the respective present values. We substituted t for r to represent the time subscript.
5. Pigou is from (Pigou, 1941); Keynes from (Keynes, 1936); Hicks is (Hicks, 1937 in 1984); Modigliani is from (Modigliani, 1944)
6. In C and I functions, Keynes used W as state of the news: $I = \Phi_2(W, \rho)$; $C = \Phi_1(W, Y)$ Rymes, 1989, p. 125. The news refers to information and expectation is conditioned on information in a Beyesian sense. We replaced $r = \rho$ and $\omega = W$. Dimand (1988, 162) called attention to another possibility, $C = f(Y,A)$, where A is "the excess of actual sales proceeds of goods selling in period plus the change in the value of capital."
7. Modigliani's final form is from his Gospel article in (Modigliani, 2005). A "0" subscript is the value the variable takes when wages are fixed.

We pick up Hicks' review on the striking note which he has advanced that S = I is a necessary condition. Hicks demonstrates this equality along the lines of simple demand and supply curves. First, Hicks lumps expectations or anticipations with the givens or part one of Keynes' summary. Second, the givens will determine demand and supply. Third, demand and supply will determine prices. To state the schema for equality differently, assume disequilibria market conditions prevail. Let the market condition be that supply has exceeded demand that day. The first adjustment that comes to mind is that prices will fall to clear the market. But suppose the sellers do not want to sell at a lower price. Then the sellers will have some "unsold stocks." How should we classify this "unsold stock?" One way to classify it is to claim that it belongs to the "current supply." A better way to classify it is to claim that it belongs to the "future supply." If we claim that the "unsold stock" belongs to the "future supply," then current supply is equal to current demand. This appears simple so far, until we point out that the equality cannot be attained without bringing into the picture the concept of expectations. As people stock up goods for the future, any unsold stocks must "depend upon their expectations of the future."[42]

Expectations are not only central to the S = I concept, but to Keynes' theory of employment as well. To demonstrate this, let us follow Hicks' review again. Let us define the short-term to be a period in which expectations do not change. It is tied to the price that producers expect at the time they commit to produce something. Long-term expectations have to do with expected returns. If the producer purchases or manufactures finished output, then somehow that act will cause changes in the capital stock. To bring out the influence of expectations on employment, we reason that short-term expectations relate to consumption goods, C, and long-term expectations relate to investment goods, I. Assume also that there is unemployment and that wages are fixed. We are required to demonstrate that employment will increase in the C-goods industry. Pretend that there is an increase for C-goods from demand abroad that cannot be matched by an increase in imports. How would foreigners pay for the increased imports from the U.S? We can lend them the money to buy our exports, but the traditional consequence of that is for the rate of interest, r, to rise. As the modern textbooks have it, $C = a + bY - dr$, so C will fall as r increases.

How then does Keynes prevent the rate of interest from adjusting in the goods market? He has done this in an ingenious way. Keynes "believe[s] that the explanation is to be found in an increased production of consumption goods, which so improve the position of these people that they are able to consume more than before, and yet have an increased surplus to satisfy the needs of the investment industry."[43] Hicks thought this was a plausible argument and that it would lead to increased employment. But he continues in a different direction by arguing that the increased exports should come from stock of C-goods, that is, it will require time to make more C-goods via increased investment. Keynes seems to have accepted Hicks' point to the extent that "increased investment is not foreseen."[44]

With those arguments, Keynes then restated the classical position. The argument we have just discussed supports this view that an increase in I will cause a decrease in C. Keynes' view by contrast was that C will increase (not decrease) in that situation. He stated, "I am not sure that the following is not the best definition of full employment in my sense: 'There is less than full employment if, the propensity to consume being assumed unchanged, an increase in investment will cause an increase in consumption.'"[45]

Hicks' review then turned on the determination of the interest rate in Keynes' system. Hicks considered the monetary way of determining interest as dispensable, "interest arises out of the exchange of present money for future money."[46] Since liquidity preference is a choice between holding money versus lending money, r enters as a balance between demand for and supply of money. Now some if-then statements enter into the argument that sound a "Walrasian bell" by Walras' law – if excess demand is zero in the markets for goods, factors and loans, then it will hold automatically in the market for money as well.[47] Similarly, if excess demand is zero in the markets for goods, factors, and money, then the loan market becomes dispensable, making savings and investment automatically equal. Keynes prefers this latter if-then argument.

Hicks was wedded to the Walrasian approach. It first appeared in his (1939) *Value and Capital*, and in his (1937) "Mr. Keynes and the Classics." Hicks tried to "construct a typical 'classical' theory, built on an earlier and cruder model than Professor Pigou's,"[48] and clearly demonstrated the notion of reducing a 3-dimensional model to a 2-dimensional plane, using the Walrasian numeraire system.[49] Apparently, he had written that chapter before the publication of his interpretation of Keynes' *General Theory*. In his cruder-than-Pigou system approach, he reduced three elements of the Keynesian system – marginal efficiency of capital (bond market), consumption (goods market), and liquidity preference (money market) to two. The model's two variables are income, Y, in terms of wage units, and the interest rate, r. In Keynes' investment function, I(r), and savings function, S(Y), Y responds to r to make S = I, yielding the famous I-S curve. Similarly, the demand for money function, M(r,Y) traces out the L-M curve, given the supply of money in terms of wage units.[50]

Keynes commented that Hicks' 1937 model implies that "the quantity of money is capable of increasing employment."[51] For Keynes, this can happen only under special circumstances. For instance, if the money wage rate is fixed, then prices will also be fixed. In this situation, the quantity of money will have an effect on employment and output.[52] Instead of toeing that line of thought, Hicks proposed at least six ways in which price and the rate of interest can be determined. For example, effective demand and supply for goods and services determine prices; demand for money determines interest rate, S and I should be equal for equilibrium.[53] Keynes was not happy with that outcome because one possibility was for interest to be determined by S and I, a "no no" for Keynes.[54]

Keynes wrote, "if I were writing again, I should indeed feel disposed to define full employment as being reached at the same moment at which the supply of output in general becomes inelastic."[55] Along with the IS-LM diagram, an inelastic supply of output curve made the standard textbook Keynesian paradigm for many years. Hicks also expressed an early dissatisfaction with Keynes on how the liquidity preference schedule determines the interest rate. He wrote to Keynes: "What you do is to determine the rate of interest by the demand-for-money equation – and this means that you have to pack an unconscionable lot into the demand for money."[56] In one of his replies, Keynes stated that the classics think that the rate of interest is a "non-monetary" phenomenon.[57]

Modigliani's model

The early 1944 model that Modigliani built is labeled "1–9" in Table 2.2. To examine his work, we give his equations a sub-label to indicate his last thoughts on the matter, which are found in the 2003 *Gospel* article. As a guide, therefore, 1a, 1b, 4a, and 4b indicate that the equations are taken from the *Gospel* article.

Modigliani started from a point of agreement with Hicks, with the view to build on a common knowledge foundation. He wrote: "In reconsidering the Keynesian system we shall essentially follow the lines suggested by J. R. Hicks in his fundamental paper, 'Mr. Keynes and the "Classics."' Our main task is to clarify and develop his arguments, taking into account later theoretical developments."[58] The words "essential," "clarify," and "develop" are critical for our purpose. We shall show that while they agree in essence, they differ on particulars, and this illustrates Modigliani's originality.

Modigliani and the classics

In his 1944 model, Modigliani listed a set of equations that represent Keynesian thought, and a set that represents classical thought. Indeed, Modigliani was charged with an attempt to revive classical economics.[59] This charge sparked off many research ideas. We explore below several research ideas leading to controversy in Modigliani's work.

General vs. specific

Keynes was the first to raise the thought that the classical model is a special case of a more general model.[60] We have seen glimpses of what Keynes meant by "general." From the tabulation in Table 2.2, the inclusion or exclusion of a variable such as the interest rate in an equation gives a sense as to which model is more general. But that in-or-out of a variable operation must be related to the necessary and sufficient conditions for full employment. As noted above, Keynes explained his difference from the classics by stating that the shape of the consumption function leads to a knowledge of full-employment. According to Adolph Lowe, one of Modigliani's teachers, "the consumption function which, coupled with the psychological and intuitional blocks to steady investment, forms the cornerstone of Keynes' 'special' theory."[61] As we emphasize below, Modigliani seized on a special shape of the supply of labor curve to build his model on Keynes' method.

Dichotomy, Say's Law, Walras' Law and Homogeneity

Dichotomy

The mercantilists equate money with wealth. For Adam Smith, money emerges as an instrument of commerce. Theories for barter and monetary economies could take separate discussions. We can write down a system of equations on the one hand that are solved for relative prices, and a quantity equation on the other hand that is solved for absolute prices. The challenge we face is whether absolute prices influence the real sector. If money is "neutral" or a "veil," then we obtain no influence. In 1963 Modigliani included the bond market with the money market.[62] But in 1944 Modigliani had a unique way of dividing money and real sectors. His novel dichotomy invited some criticism that he addressed in a subsequent revision. This section provides the background information for those criticisms and revisions, Say's and Walras' laws, and the homogeneity postulate which support such dichotomized analysis.

Modigliani's linking of the two sectors: Y = PX

We start with the equations of Table 2.2. All the schools show at least one equation each for the real and monetary sectors. Our focus turns to Modigliani's equation 5, $Y = PX$. This equation is a result of a two-step procedure. One step is to find a solution for the equation of the two sides, Y, and PX, and the other step is to bring the two solutions together to find the general price level. The mechanics involved in solving the equation appear in the solution section. Now, we address the salient nature of the solutions.

To solve the equations on the real and monetary sides, Modigliani used the old fashioned method of counting equations, unaware that Leon Walras had popularized it. From the point of view of counting equations, we have n-equations representing n-commodities. The n-equations are split into n-1 equations for the real sector, and one equation for the monetary sector. To solve these n-equations for unknown prices and quantities, Modigliani had a choice of using three tools: the homogeneity postulate, Walras' Law, or Say's Law.

Homogeneity postulate

The homogeneity postulate holds that if prices and income are changed by the same proportion, then the quantity demanded will not change. The example often used to illustrate this postulate is the consumer maximization problem. Given two commodities, x_1 and x_2, their prices, p_1 and p_2, and consumer income, w, the budget set (p_1, p_2, w) yields the same demand as the set (kp_1, kp_2, kw), where k is a proportional constant.[63] Homogeneity of zero degrees implies that $(kp_1, kp_2, kw) = k^0(p_1, p_2, w) = (p_1, p_2, w)$. The degree is that to which the constant "k" appears. First, is to write $p = \{p_1, p_2 \cdots \cdots p_n\}$ for all prices. Two further specifications may be helpful. The consumer budget set can be written as B(p,w). This way we can apply additions and subtractions to income in a compact way. For instance, we can let money be defined as the value of a consumer initial endowment, e. Then $w = pe$ is the consumer's initial money. Second, we can introduce the role of money as a unit of account, store of value, or medium of exchange in a convenient way. For instance, when a consumer buys a bond, a debt, d, is incurred. The consumer's budget set can now be written as $w = pe - d$.[64]

To Modigliani, the homogeneity postulate appears to be doing the work of Say's Law. To flesh this out, we must distinguish between Say's identity, and Say's equality. The identity looks at the real side of the dichotomy. Money, as we know it, need not apply. Relative prices, and not absolute monetary prices, are relevant on the real side. To attain relative prices, we can elevate one of the $n-1$ commodities we have to act as a standard reference for the values of all the other commodities. This procedure is so common as to have its own name. Walras calls it a numeraire. Keynes spoke of a "labor-unit" as a real measure and "wage unit" as a monetary measure of employment.[65] Modigliani used the "wage rate" as his arbitrary choice of a numeraire.[66]

Say's law

Say's Law has been a main pillar of the classical school. Suppose we claim that supply is demand. In the English language, it is known as a metaphor. In logic, we look at it as a true and false statement. If, when supply is true and demand is true, and when supply is false demand is false, then we have an identity. The identity sense is what we call the law. It refers mainly to the real sector. Although the law omits the monetary sector, we can still discuss price in the real sector without money. Whenever we discuss price without money, we express the price of one good in terms of another – a numeraire. This use of price is referred to as "inside money," because it is internal to the private sector. If some authority outside of the private sector, such as the government, were to issue money, then we would use the label "outside money." These two new adjectives for money are important for the definition of "neutrality" of money, which means that outside money does not influence the real sector.

Say's equality conjures up an adjustment process. We learn from the classics that a change in the supply of money affects prices, because velocity and transaction are constants, or can change only by exogenous factors. With Keynes', Hicks', and Modigliani's equations from Table 2.2, the transmission mechanism pivots on the interest rate variable in the demand for money equation. This idea of a transmission mechanism is critical for the acceptance of Modigliani's model. One way to look at the process is through the real-balance argument. To illustrate, when the supply of money exceeds the demand to hold money, money holders spend more. The increase in spending will cause more money to circulate, creating higher prices. Prices will then rise to balance the money market again.

Modigliani states that the "homogeneity of the supply and demand equation does not depend on Say's law; it depends on the assumption of rationality and the homogeneity of the expectation functions." We may interpret the word "rationality" to mean that the consumer does not suffer from "money illusion," that is, the consumer would not mistake a price rise for a real increase and accordingly increase demand for commodities. This statement was in conflict Walras' Law, which we discuss in the next section.

Patinkin's and Hahn's objections

Don Patinkin sensed a contradiction in the classical model. By noticing two dichotomies in the classical system – a real and monetary sector, and relative and absolute prices.[67] He sourced the inconsistency to behavioral relationships that are in the real sector, but not found in the monetary sector. For instance, the quantity theory equation has behavioral assumptions governing the velocity of money that are not in the real side of the dichotomy. Patinkin's proposition was that the real sector depended on relative prices, B(p, pe) by the above budget equation. The monetary sector, through the quantity theory of money, gives absolute prices. By the dichotomy, the two sectors do not interact. Outside money is neutral. Prices are accounting prices because inside-money only provides the function of a unit of account. Patinkin proposed to make the classical theory consistent by introducing a real balance effect. The demand and supply of commodities would now vary with relative prices and real cash balances.[68] If we bridge the system with real balances, we would not have a dichotomy. This Patinkin did in a way that maintains the neutrality between the real and monetary sectors.

Say's law and Walras' law

In building his model with the real balance effect, Patinkin concluded that "Modigliani's discussion of the relationship between Say's law and homogeneity (as well as Lange's concession to him on that point) is incorrect."[69] The objection to Modigliani surfaced in his dropping of Say's law. We follow Baumol in stating that Say's identity or law applies only to the goods market.[70] Central to Say's law is the notion that the supply of goods and money must be equal to the demand for goods and money. Suppose we think that people need money only to buy goods and services, then Say's law is applicable solely to the market for goods and services, and by Walras' law the money market will be balanced. Hahn stated the problem succinctly by formulating Walras' law as PXg + Xm ≡ 0, where "X" refers to excess demand, and the subscripts "g" and "m" refer to the goods and money markets, respectively.[71] If excess demand is in the goods sector, then Say's identity (law) is violated. Prices will adjust in the money market, but they will have no influence on the goods sector. The simultaneous balance in the money market and the imbalance in the goods market contradict Walras' law in that the demand for the goods and money will not equal the sum of the supply of goods and money. In other words, the first term in the equation will be positive; the second term, zero, and they cannot sum to zero, as Walras' law requires. Hahn suggested that the contradiction occurs because Modigliani did not assume Say's identity (law), which would have made the goods market balance.

Modigliani's response to criticisms of his 1944 model

Initially, Modigliani ignored the criticism of his 1944 model. He thought such criticisms were "barren endeavor[s]."[72] However, he appended a response to a 1960 reprint of the 1944 article. The postscript started to expand the n-equations by adding a bond market to yield n+1 equations. Apparently, bonds were important because as Patinkin put it, "though the commodity excess-demand equation is independent of the price level, the bond excess-demand equation is not."[73] Modigliani responded, "that the bond market is, at times, not given explicit treatment, is accounted for by the fact that through the so-called Walras law, one of the markets is necessarily cleared when the remaining ones are cleared, and hence need not be explicitly exhibited."[74] So, the criticism revolved around the neutrality of money argument.

Modigliani's 1960 postscript to his 1944 article showed how neutrality can be repaired for the dichotomy of the goods and monetary equation. This procedure is to make all money a kind of "bank money." Two conditions are required: "(a) the given money supply consists entirely of bank money which is offset by the debt of the private sector to the banking system and (b) all existing bonds represent claims on, or liabilities to the private sector (including banks), then aggregate private real wealth will be invariant under a proportional change of all prices (no Pigou effect exists)."[75] In his 1963 model, Modigliani offered a more elaborate response, updating the 1944 model in several directions. We will summarize the substance of the 1944 model below, and discuss the 1963 revision of it later on in this chapter.

Explication of Modigliani's objection to his 1944 model

Our visit to the 1944 model can be summarized as follows. Considering the price of money as unity, we need to determine only n-1 prices from the supply of and the demand for the n-1 commodities. These supply and demand conditions form excess demand, by subtracting supply from demand. By Walras' Law, only (n-1) −1 = (n-2) excess demand equations need be investigated. Similarly, by using a price ratio, expressing all the prices in terms of one price – a numeraire, we have only n-2 price ratios. So, we have (n-2) equations to solve for (n-2) prices, a determinate system as far as counting equations and unknowns go. The actual prices are constructed from the n-2 price ratios through the demand for money equation.[76] In light of Pigou's and Patinkin's "real balance" effects, we saw arguments rejecting Modigliani's interpretation of the classics excluding Say's law. Patinkin argued that "Modigliani's discussion of the relationship between Say's law and homogeneity ... is incorrect."[77] In this vein, Hahn also argued that Modigliani's model and conclusions are incorrect.[78] Modigliani added a postscript in 1960 to address these criticisms. He redefined money to be a kind of "bank note" and in 1963 he revised the model to include, among other things, the bond market.

Partial vs. general equilibrium

A third difference between Modigliani and the classics revolves around partial versus general equilibrium. By attempting to form a static model from a dynamic IS-LM procedure, Modigliani's method was criticized for "the lack of an adequate method to deal with general equilibrium."[79] An issue here was whether Modigliani's approach is Marshallian, dealing with a single market, or whether it is more general, including the markets for goods and money.[80]

One argument is that Modigliani did not adopt a full Walrasian system. Modigliani was accused in particular of not using "the budget constraint and the tantonnement methods."[81] The charge went even deeper: "The program derived from Modigliani aimed to extend the scope of IS-LM (open economy, Phillips curve, macro econometric applications) and to deepen the understanding of its components (the consumption function, the investment function, etc.) while keeping them insulated from each other. The emphasis was put on the pragmatic applications of IS-LM."[82]

One cannot deny that Modigliani was pragmatic. If partial or specific means that a model must have statistical specification, then Modigliani is guilty of being partial, because his model laid the foundation for the specification of the MIT-PENN-FRB econometric model. One also cannot deny that Modigliani held the view that the Walrasian system was more complete. He offered his 1944 model as a "choice between rigor and convenience; the only rigorous procedure is to set up a complete 'Walrasian' system ... but the system is cumbersome ... The alternative is to work with a reduced system, but we shall check our conclusions with a more general system whenever necessary."[83]

Although Modigliani followed Hicks in many directions, he appeared more Walrasian than Hicksian in some instances. Morishima proclaimed that Modigliani's model "is a model from which supply and demand for bonds have already been eliminated. In Walras' own model too, no explicit attention is given to the bond market. They are contrasted, in this respect, with Hicks."[84] Hicks' early model had bond, money, and goods equations, but dropped the investment and savings equations, which are parts of the goods equation. The criticism that Modigliani's model is not general enough is also an old one. Morishima brought another sense in which "specific" and "general" are distinguishable terms for Modigliani and the classics.

Hicks and Modigliani

Earlier in this chapter, we mentioned Hicks' role in the development of Keynesian economics. Modigliani built on that foundation. Here we delineate their models more precisely.

Similarities and differences in their models

Table 2.2 shows that the similarity between Hicks' and Modigliani's formulations are exact with respect to the first four equations. By "sameness" we mean that we can find similar equations expressing the relationships among the variables. Those equations take on their general form for the corresponding first four entries in the Keynesian columns. If we follow Hawtrey's review and let $M_2 = 0$, we obtain a special case of the monetary equation. But as Pigou's contribution indicates, setting the speculative demand to zero does not mean that the rate of interest is overlooked. Pigou made the case that M depends on r. He also argued that velocity changes in the positive direction with p and r.[85] As Modigliani suggested, the relationship between k and r is a decreasing function, and between V and R is an increasing function.[86]

Both Modigliani and Hicks agreed that Keynes' treatment of liquidity preference set him apart from the classics. But they differed in their interpretation of its use. Hicks noted that for Keynes: "It is the liquidity preference doctrine which is vital."[87] On the other hand, Modigliani advanced three propositions restricting the importance of liquidity preference:

> The liquidity-preference theory is not necessary to explain under employment equilibrium ... is neither necessary nor sufficient to explain the dependence of the rate of interest on the quantity of money ... The results of the liquidity preference theory is that the quantity of active money depends not only on the total quantity of money but also on the rate of interest and therefore also on the forms and position of the propensity to save and invest.[88]

Modigliani drew inferences from these three propositions. With flexible prices, r, MPS, and MEK determine prices and with rigid prices, r, MPS, and MEK deter employment and output, which may appear as a foreshadow of the new-Keynesian paradigm. Both Hicks' and Modigliani's solutions focused on the explanation of employment, but they proposed different ways to improve it. From Hicks' point of view, the existence of fixed money wage and a liquidity trap will prevent monetary expansion from improving employment. From Modigliani's point of view, the existence of a conditioned supply of labor function, and the possibility of a liquidity trap will not prevent monetary expansion from improving employment.

Equation 9 in Table 2.2 also shows Modigliani's special contribution in the labor market. The disagreement between Hawtrey and Keynes on the labor supply curve had reached an area of agreement when Pigou supplied the kinked supply of labor curve. Both Hicks and Modigliani made continued appraisals on the matter throughout their lifetime research. The divergence of views comes to light when they linked wage rigidity with employment and output.

During his lifetime research, Modigliani remained tit-for-tat with Hicks on many new evolving issues. The comparisons thus far have proceeded on the basis of Modigliani's 1944, and Hicks' 1937 articles. The time is now right to show our protagonist's solution to his 1944 model, and its subsequent expansion and articulation.

Birth, solution, explanation and prediction of Modigliani's model

We have alluded that after his 1944 dissertation, Modigliani built on that model both theoretically and empirically. The next section shows how to approach the model with the intention of keeping track of subsequent developments.

Description of the 1944 model

The last column of Table 2.2 presents Modigliani's first interpretation of Keynes. We first note the classification of his variables. Most variables take on values only when we solve the equations. They are called *endogenous* variables: income, X, consumption, C, investment, I, savings, S, aggregate demand, X^d, employment, N, labor supply, N^s, and money income, Y. Then we can make a list of the price variables. They are the price of output, P; the price of labor, W; and the interest rate, r. Some variables are given to the system. They are called *exogenous* variables: fixed wages, W, and the money supply, M.

Modigliani had the reader's interest in mind when he embarked on his first model. He did not want to build a "Walrasian" system to link these variables because it would require too many equations and variables to determine prices and quantities for each commodity in the system. He chose a smaller number of relationships. His first three equations were therefore very compact: M, I, and S were made dependent on r and Y. If we assume equilibrium, then S = I, which serves as a fourth equation. Money income, Y, is just a product of PX, a fifth equation. So far with the first five equations, we have similarities with Hicks' model. We can therefore say that the IS-LM model is an integral part of Modigliani's system. If it is accepted that Hicks' model is a fair representation of Keynes and the classics, then we have the greatest agreement we can hope for in the first part.

A sixth equation appears when we consider how X is produced. We must let X depend on some inputs, N in this case, yielding X = X(N). Keynes speaks of labor as "the sole factor of production, operating in a given environment of technique, natural resources, capital equipment and effective demand."[89] In considering Keynes' place in the history of economics, some writers would not give him dominion over the production function. Keynes worked in the short period, and was not concerned about long-run growth where the production function is the drive of growth. However, except for his special treatment of effective demand, Modigliani's characterization of the production function would be in line with Keynes' statement.

Now, we look to the labor market for a seventh equation. We have choices. We can deal with the relationship of N on W or the inverse, W on N. Say we write N = F(W/P), then the inverse would be $W = F^{-1}(N)P$. According to equation six, output, X, is also related to N, allowing us to write W = X′(N)P or W/P = X′(N) as our seventh equation. It means that wage is determined by the marginal product of labor. We note that C is equivalent to money income, Y, less investment, I, which we call equation eight, even though it is an identity.

We have enumerated seven equations, but have eight variables: M, I, S, r, Y, X, N, W. The search for another equation takes place in the labor market. In the classical system, W and P will determine the maximum number of workers, N. But Keynes thought that the supply of labor, N, may be perfectly elastic, meaning it is a horizontal curve fixed on the wage axis. At that fixed point, we find an additional ninth equation to close our system.

Equation 9 relating wages to either its minimum or employment, has been a subject for study and dissection in the literature. The general feeling is that it is sometimes rigid, and sometimes flexible. The problem is then, how to reduce those two situations to one equation, or one category of thought. The versatility of algebra allows Modigliani to write an equation with some conditions. The conditions modify the equation depending on whether the system is in equilibrium or not. If we let N_0 represent "full employment," then the two conditions are either $N \leq N_0$, or $N > N_0$. In the former condition, the equation can take the form $W = \alpha w_0 + \beta F^{-1}(N)P$, where $\alpha = 1$ and $\beta = 0$, and then when $N > N_0$, $\alpha = 0$ and $\beta = 1$. The eight equations and one identity make up Modigliani's 1944 version of Keynesian economics.

Solutions to Modigliani's 1944 model

One way to appraise Modigliani's contribution to post-Keynesian economics is to show his novel solutions to macroeconomic equilibrium side-by-side with the solutions of the other models in Table 2.2. In his review of Pigou's book from which we listed the equations in Table 2.2, Samuelson offered the idea underlining a classical solution of full employment in terms of Say's Law.[90] Let M be exogenously fixed by authorities, and V be constant in $MV = g(r)$. A fall in consumption, F(x), is reflected in investment since $I = \psi(y) = f\{r, F(x)\}$. Often, Say's approach is considered too abstract, involving counting equations and unknowns for a set of homogeneous equations.[91] The discussions that follow look at the concrete aspects of the model. In view of the classical dichotomy, we examine a set of equations for money, and a set for real quantities, and afterwards indicate how the two sets come together.

Solution to the first part of Modigliani's 1944 model

For Modigliani, the first part refers to equations 1 through 4, which yield a solution to the "monetary equilibrium."[92] For equation 1, we notice that Keynes splits it into transaction demand $M_1 = L_1(Y)$, and speculative demand $M_2 = L_2(r)$, Both Hicks and Modigliani considered the case of asset demand where r and Y enter jointly into the demand for money function. We consider their approaches further.

Modern popular introductory textbooks of macroeconomics standardize a solution feature called, "the Keynesian Cross" diagram. The diagram explains that if consumers are told what different sets of prices (P, r) and income (Y) would be, then they are able to state the amount of goods and services they "desire." If consumers desire less than their income can buy, then they would want to store some of that income away. Such a choice to save a part of their income would increase their "cash balance." Similarly, if they desire to spend more than their income, then they would want to draw down on their "cash balance." Because "cash balance" is an important part of the story, most models of Keynesian economics would have an equation to describe how it works. Modigliani used the first equation, $M = L(r, Y)$, discussed above, to account for cash balances.

Modigliani considered his equation first in terms of the individual, and then in terms of the firm. Assets are physical in nature and include money and securities. They vary according to their liquidity and risk[93] (information is not considered). To pose the problem, if all the prices and incomes are known, then what amount of goods and services will individuals and firms desire? Individuals may desire goods and services up to what their income will allow at the known prices. Similarly, investors would demand investments within their income constraints for given prices. Prices include the prices of commodities and services, and the interest rate.

Modigliani made the individual's decision dependent on the interest rate, $D_a = D_a(r)$, and the firm's decision dependent on the money income, $D_T = D_T(Y)$, He stated the individual problem as follows: "(a) he must decide what part of income he will spend on consumption and what part he will save, (b) he must determine how to dispose of his assets."[94] He stated the firm's problem as follows: "*money needed to carry out transactions planned for the coming income period is not an asset,*"[95] [Italics original]. In the end, the demand function for money resulted in the LL curve in Hicks' terminology, is what is known as the liquidity and money curve in modern textbooks. Having determined the form of equation 1, we are now ready to complete part one by subsuming equations 2 and 3 into equation 4. This provides the relationship for the IS curve.[96]

Modigliani discussed his solution for both the short (the income period) and long-term (price and quantity do not change).[97] Solutions for the money market are short-term because period-by-period decisions are carried out immediately for given levels of the interest rate. Decisions for investment and savings are long-term in the sense that they are plans, *ex ante* concepts, that do not equate instantaneously, but may require a lag period to materialize.[98] The lag is the period between when income is earned and income is spent. Since I, and S, are done only from disposable income (not money income, Y), Modigliani introduced a new variable for disposable income, $Y_{d.t} = C_t + S_t$. All the variables are now time subscripted, except M, and $Y_t = C_t + I_t$. The solution path for the variables can now be traced. We know that stability requires that the variables in time tend to their equilibrium values. He therefore expressed his results hypothetically in terms of "if the system is stable, each variable approaches some definite value it will maintain in time," or again: "If the stability conditions are satisfied, the variables approach their equilibrium values."[99]

In the first part, equations 1–4 yield a solution for r and Y. We notice a difference from Pigou's system in that the latter has prices included in his equilibrium condition. This represents the so-called "real balance" effect, which marks a major difference between Pigou and Keynes. Modigliani introduced price in equation 5, which serves as a bridge between the solution of the first part, determining money income, Y, and the second part to be discussed below, which determines real output, X.

Solution to the Second part of Modigliani's 1944 model

Having studied monetary equilibrium where r and Y are determined, Modigliani turned to the determination of the real side where physical output (X), employment (N), and real wage (W/P) rates are determined. His equation 7 borrows from the idea that employment will expand up to where fixed money wages is just equal to the marginal revenue product of labor (MPL), yielding $W_0 = X'(N)P$ from marginal productivity. We can substitute for $P = Y/X$ in equation 5 to yield $W_0 = X'(N)(Y/X)$, keeping in mind that Y is determined in the monetary part. This reduced form of equation 5 and 7 can now be merged with equation 6 to determine X and N.

The equation $Y = PX$ plays a pivotal role in Modigliani's system. It links the monetary and the real side. When solving for price, $P = Y/X$, we find that prices vary only with real output X, since Y is determined in the monetary part. To show how it works, let prices, P, be given, and let $W_0 < \text{MPL}$. Perfect competition dictates an increase in employment (N), which in turn will increase output, X. Prices will then fall. Why? From the relationship P = Y/X, we can reason that the ratio of money income to output falls. But we can also reason that since MPC <1, all income generated from increased employment is not spent, creating excess supply, causing prices to fall. Whatever the cause, variations in the price level do not mark an end to the story. Pigou argued on behalf of the classics that lower prices have real balance effects. For instance, wealth holders do not need to hold on to the same level of assets when the price level is low. They will liquidate some assets and provide the consumption needed to keep prices from falling. However, the Pigou effect did not have as much empirical support at that time as it has today.

A critical point in the analysis is now attained as to whether the employment and output generated are at the full employment level, N_0. Modigliani insisted that it represented involuntary unemployment, "due entirely to the assumption of 'rigid wages' and not to the Keynesian liquidity preference."[100] The argument started from the determination of money income, Y. If liquidity preference is not important, we can back away from M = f(r,Y), and write just that M = kY. This may not be consistent with Keynes' idea as expressed in Chapter 19 of the *General Theory*, where Keynes denies that his conclusion depends on rigid money wages.

Modigliani's 1963 model

Modigliani's 1963 model[101] was designed to address problems with his 1944 model, and new developments from the mid-1950s. The revision provided more general equilibrium checks, created a bond market, improved some functions, adjusted some functions for the homogeneity postulate, and expanded on the rigid wage concept. We discuss the main points of his efforts in these directions.

According to Fischer, the 1963 model is "more sophisticated than the 1944 version in its handling of the banking system and the distinction between inside and outside money, the consumption and investment functions, and the explicit inclusion of a government budget constraint potentially linking monetary and fiscal policies."[102] Fischer surmised that the 1963 model is also a response to Patinkin's criticisms, and Gurley-Shaw's inside-outside money development.[103]

Modigliani essentially maintained his 1944 paradigm in the 1963 update. Output and its price, P; labor and its price, W; and the future price of a dollar, 1/(1+r) are now made to stand out in his discussion. Uncertainty, no money illusion, and unity price expectation elasticity are still assumed. Modigliani discussed five differences of the 1963 model from the 1944 version. A noticeable difference is that the 1963 model projects a more general equilibrium outlook, incorporating supply and demand equations for each commodity. The model now has 12 equations – 9 real equations, and 3 monetary equations. The wage equation is respecified to express the maximum supply of labor.

Among the significant differences, Modigliani corrected for the first degree homogeneity assumption for consumption, and investment and money functions in the 1944 model. In particular Y = PX, PS, PI, and r were made to change when M changed in the 1944 model. While the 1944 model led to correct inferences without the 1963 adjustments, the changes made the model a more reliable tool.

The consumption function now shows wealth effects. This allows for analysis under wage-price flexibility, and addresses real balance effects raised by Pigou and Patinkin. Modigliani argued that money is neutral, i.e., X, C, I, N, S, p/w and r are independent of M. We still have a dichotomy between the real and money sectors, and money remains neutral. However, Modigliani now insisted that we do not need to study behavioral relations of velocity on the real side, as Patinkin thought.

Implications of the 1963 model

Many possible starting points compete for our attention in this section. One is whether Modigliani's contribution sided with partial or general equilibrium analysis. If we follow general equilibrium, we can then pose the problem this way: Given excess supply of labor in the labor market, can we still have an equilibrium? The answer is not clear-cut. In his 1944 model, Modigliani separated money, the nth commodity, from the n-1 goods. Some may argue that true general equilibrium that follows Walras' Law requires no such separation. Money is just like any other commodity.[104]

Rubin argued that Modigliani's 1963 update was an attempt to steer his model in line with Patinkin. As stated above, Modigliani's 1963 article included an explicit bond market, correction for problems with the homogeneity postulate, and a new formulation of wage rigidity.[105] However, we find that others are willing to drop the bond market, and even consider Patinkin's interpretation with regard to Keynes' model as misconceived.[106] Also, the ultimate model of general equilibrium, the one Walras conceived, did not explicitly have a bond market, and can express value in terms of another commodity that acts as money.[107]

Another point that competes for our discussion is whether concerns in other markets dominate wage rigidity in explaining involuntary unemployment. For instance, Leijonhufvud discussed Keynes in terms of "spot prices: wages vs. asset prices."[108] He reasoned that an increase in asset prices implies high demand for consumption and investment. Therefore, it is not high wages, but high asset prices, that are out of equilibrium. Besides, Keynes argued that money wages are volatile, and therefore cannot be relied upon to have an equilibrium price.

In response, we recognize that Leijonhufvud presented a different paradigm from Modigliani's 1944 Model-T version. The Model-T version has the support of "James Meade, Roy Harrod, John Hicks, Brian Reddaway, A. P. Lerner, Oskar Lange, Paul Samuelson, A. C. Pigou, and Joan Robinson," that according to Samuelson rely on the core of the *General Theory*.[109] In contrast, Leijonhufvud was more influenced by Keynes' earlier book, *Treatise on Money*, where Keynes emphasized expectations and uncertainty over rigid wages.

We refer the reader to the original 1944 article for a solution to the 1963 updated model. Because the literature still tries to fit money into the classical framework, such a procedure does not appear fruitful. Also, there is the devastating argument advanced by Hahn that this cannot be done. A recent survey by D. Gale summarizes the literature, and shows yet another attempt. Perhaps because of a lack of a proper solution, Modigliani lets reality dictate the course of further developments. In 1977, Modigliani ushered the paradigm in a more practical direction, toward stabilization policies. We will discuss that topic in the next chapter.

Conclusion

Modigliani invested a lifetime of research into Keynesian apparatuses. With Hans Neisser, Modigliani helped to build one of the most respected Keynesian models for the U. S. economy. He continued to advocate the Keynesian perspectives, despite the challenges and responded to criticisms by further revising and refining his models.

Early in the 1940s, Modigliani developed the Model-T Keynesian model that survived the post-war era. To accommodate new developments in the mid-1950s, he updated the 1944 model while keeping its core intact. He also addressed criticisms from other Keynesian model builders. Modigliani indicated that his intention to put Keynesian thought on classical grounds is consistent with his original idea about Walras' and Say's laws, and homogeneity. In his 1963 update, he showed how the criticisms can be accommodated in his 1944 model, by including a bond equation among other things. But he maintained that by following the Walras' law, he could have still omitted the bond market, and relied only on the new definition of bank money to answer his critics. With the Keynesian framework now in place, Modigliani began to articulate it from a policy point of view, where money is not neutral but is an important variable that influences economic activities. Modigliani advocated a discretionary view of monetary policy as opposed to a fixed rule. The next chapter discusses the framework's ability to stabilize the macro economy.

3

The Gospel of Keynesian Reality, Development and Application of Modigliani's Model, 1944–2003, The Realm of Stabilization Policies

Introduction

Prior to the Great Depression, John Maynard Keynes embraced the cyclical mechanisms that are the bedrock of full employment analysis in his monetary studies. Around 1923, Keynes recognized that "the problem of stabilization has several sides."[1] Inflation and deflation attracted paramount attention, relating to the problem of devaluation of exchange rates, and restoration of the Gold Standard.

The U.S. established the Federal Reserve System on 23 December, 1913 to cope with business cycles and to hopefully enhance stability. Through its discount window and open market operations, it could increase discount rates and sell government securities to control a speculative economy. During the 1920s, the Fed followed an easy credit policy, which resulted in inflation. To use a pun, President Coolidge did not cool the economy. He thought that prosperity was sound and stock prices were cheap. President Hoover inherited a heated economy when he took office in 1929, approximately seven months before the stock market crash on 29 October, 1929. At that time, President Hoover wrote, "Professor Irving Fisher of Yale said that stocks had not even reached their full values."[2] He continued, "Our overpriced stocks and real estate were bound to come down; and the degree of down is influenced by the degree of up."[3] His statement implies a famous stabilization policy pronouncement which economists find funny to make: what goes up must come down. Keynes was to change that.

During what Keynes called the Great Slump of 1930, nearly 10 million people were idle in the U.S., U.K. and Germany for lack of demand. As the cost of production exceeded income, producers of consumption goods were selling their goods below cost. Either people should spend more, or producers should produce more capital goods (not consumption) to restore stability, but producers were not investing. Keynes said that the cause of the slump was "the lack of new enterprise due to an unsatisfactory market for capital investment."[4]

The Great Slump quickly turned into the Great Depression. Keynes announced that the economic problem was international in nature. Unemployment was high, and the focus was on how to create jobs. The spirit of Keynes' policy was captured in his statement concerning his wish to raze "the whole of south London from Westminster to Greenwich, and make a good job of it,"[5] in building more and better houses, parks, and in general public infrastructure. The economy was sick, and the patients should be kept working. He saw that "Government borrowing of one kind or another is nature's remedy."[6]

Keynes demonstrated that the shortage of cash was an early problem of the Great Depression. On its eve, Keynes argued that a fall in money value affected the wealth holder adversely. Frequently, people borrow money to buy real assets such as "buildings, stocks of commodities, goods in course of manufacture and of transport, and so forth."[7] The loans are made through banks which obtain their funds from depositors and extend loans to debtors. As the monetary value of assets collapsed, banks became less willing to make loans. Keynes saw the problem as "the choice between finding some way to increase money values towards their firm figure, or seeing widespread insolvencies and defaults and the collapse of a large part of the financial structure."[8]

The statement that Keynes provided " ... little in the way of concrete policy recommendation"[9], might not strictly be true. The Keynesian model acted as an analytic background for the policies Keynes advocated during the 1920s and 1930s. Samuelson's neoclassical synthesis formed the basis of Keynesian macroeconomic policies in the post- WWII period. It targeted real as against nominal goals, and advocated active demand management, fiscal and monetary policy mix, and wage-price policies.[10]

Modigliani based his interpretation of Keynes' theory on three propositions: wage rigidity, liquidity preference, and aggregate demand for output, although Keynes would drop the rigid money wage proposition. He found that "a quantity of money insufficient to finance a full employment output results in an unemployment equilibrium."[11] In what follows, we describe how Modigliani's stabilization model expanded Keynes' work and deviated from other Keynesians. His innovations in the areas of consumption, investment, and model specification to include lags, clarified the relationship between liquidity preference, rigid prices and aggregate demand on the one hand, and income-money relations on the other.[12]

Theory of Stabilization for the Great Depression

Keynes is for stabilization policy. But Keynes had many themes of business cycles running on parallel tracts. On the one hand we observe liquidity traps, interest inelasticity, and wage rigidity. On the other hand, we observe states of disequilibria. In the previous chapter, we found Modigliani following Hicks' model that was in the spirit of Walras' general equilibrium. We also know that Patinkin chose disequilibrium as his starting point.[13] Modigliani considered all of these views.

From the disequilibrium position, monetary and fiscal policies were not effective in tackling the problems characterized by the 1930s. The country witnessed abnormal bank failures, bankruptcies, and delinquent mortgages during this period. As a result, monetary policy was ineffective in avoiding liquidity traps, interest rates that reached minimum levels, a fiscal policy revealing interest inelastic responses of investment demand, and income policies that were ineffective in confronting the cycle of falling wages and deflation.[14]

In such a scenario, fiscal policy through the initiation of public expenditures and investments could help. Such efforts could put the unemployed back to work. If it is demonstrated that "the autonomous decisions of the micro-units are unlikely by themselves to achieve the same effect,"[15] the aggregate demand in the disequilibria state must be increased. This requires a control mechanism, such as the government. If government expenditures were forthcoming, employment and income would rise and would have secondary rounds through the Keynesian multiplier. Dishoarding would also take place, increasing the circulation of money. This stabilization process would then move towards full employment and full production. When that goal is reached, the stabilization process would not need more initial spending.

A contrasting method would be the monetarist quantity theory approach. During the Great Depression, the money supply was currency and bank deposits, M and M', and their respective velocities were V and V'. But banks were reluctant to lend and credit-worthy borrowers did not wish to borrow, so that money and velocity were acting as countercyclical variables.[16] Under these circumstances, it was impossible to increase M+M'.

The Fed could have acted to increase M′ by lowering reserve requirements. But it is questionable whether there were enough credit-worthy individuals to borrow more from the banks if the reserves were to fall. An alternative would be for banks to buy government bonds with the reserves. In that case, interest rates would tend to fall, thereby lowering the velocity.[17]

The above discussions indicate how difficult it was to increase the money supply during the Great Depression. Recently, Stiglitz and Greenwald reiterated the reason for this. The liquidity trap made the monetary side look like "pushing on a string."[18] In other words, monetary authorities found it difficult to reduce the interest rate because it had reached a minimum low level, and conversely, the price of long-term bonds had reached such high levels, that investors expected it to fall. As a result, monetary policy was rendered impotent.

Stabilization theory after the Great Depression

Deflation was observed during the recessions of 1948–1949 and 1953–1954. But an anomaly surfaced during the 1957–1958 recession when inflation increased in the face of a steep drop in the unemployment rate. According to Tobin, "the Eisenhower Administration, 1953–61, was unfriendly to the whole idea of a government-guided and stabilized economy."[19] This resulted in three recessions.

Samuelson and Solow tried to distinguish whether the causes of the post-war inflation were demand-pull or cost-push.[20] In their model, they introduced a modified Phillips Curve that dominated stabilization theories for a long while. Movements on the curve were due to demand factors, while shifts of the curve were sourced to those on the supply side. The introduction of the Phillips Curve was taken as a choice between inflation and unemployment for monetary policies in the U.S. Over the years, the monetarists who developed the Phillips Curve pushed it in the direction of the natural rate hypothesis, which the rational expectationists have used to validate forecasts when misperception prevents the economy's return to its equilibrium level. Modigliani stands as a precursor to the use of the Phillips Curve, which explains the NAIRU, the non-accelerating inflation rate of unemployment.

Modigliani's stabilization gospel

Modigliani wrote, "I regard as the fundamental practical message of the *General Theory*, that a market economy is subject to fluctuations in aggregate output, unemployment and prices, which *need* to be corrected, *can* be corrected, and *should* be corrected. Monetarists on the other hand hold that there is no real need to stabilize the economy as long as the growth of money supply follows a simple predictable rule,"[21] [Italics original]. The triumvirate of output, unemployment, and prices according to Modigliani's gospel of stabilization could be observed from both the theoretical and practical points of view. Both sides have problem areas, which we explore in this section.

In the Keynesian world, "macroeconomics began as the study of large-scale economic pathologies; prolonged depression, mass unemployment, persistent inflation, etc."[22] Keynes stood by active monetary and fiscal policies with feedback. In theory, feedback is like filling a glass with water. We put the glass under the faucet and turn the water on with our hand. As the glass fills, we adjust the level. The monetarists advocated rules without such feedback. According to Milton Friedman, the money supply should be set at a fixed percentage growth rate. John Taylor states that

> a policy rule is not necessarily a fixed setting for the policy instruments, such as a constant-growth rate rule for the money supply. Feedback rules, in which the money supply responds to changes in unemployment or inflation, are also policy rules. ... Research on the design of policy rules frequently finds that feedback rules dominate rules with fixed settings for the instruments.[23]

Today, policy makers operate models with various instruments to attain certain goals. Policy makers may want to use, for example, the instruments of monetary and fiscal policies to attain a low 2 per cent rate of inflation, and a 4 per cent growth in GDP. As an example, contemporary students study the influence of money on output where the money multiplier can be determined by probabilities and therefore the target output is uncertain. Alternatively, students can study cases where the money multiplier is known for certain, resulting in policies reaching their targeted output. A simple approach would express GDP or nominal income as a function of the money supply. When Modigliani found that nominal income was lower than a target level, he took another look through his NIRU or NIRO concepts (that we shall define later in this chapter) in order to explore the options for policy makers. Others have taken alternative paths, such as a loss function that could incorporate information about the multiplier, whether it is deterministic or probabilistic.[24] Therefore, in the realm of stabilization, Modigliani kept abreast of the topical issues of the time, giving us many policy determinations for individual problems.

Modigliani's policies for stabilization models

This chapter is a walk through some of these efforts, starting with his 1944 contribution. We will discuss his ideas of fiscal and monetary policies as they evolved in reaction to changes in the economy. We point out the novelties of his contributions as we go along.

Policies following the 1944 model

Modigliani often interpreted his model for policy implications. In his dissertation, Modigliani developed two policy cases for the relief of unemployment.[25]

One case is dubbed "normal," referring to when the rate of interest for full employment is higher than the minimum interest rate determined by institutions. The other case is dubbed "Keynesian," referring to when the minimum institutional rate exceeds the full employment rate.

In the normal case, Modigliani proposed an increase in the money supply as the main policy tool for stabilization. He explained that public investment should be in the form of increasing money, not through borrowing money from the public or increases in taxes. The government should not borrow money because that would push up the interest rate and cause investment to fall. Instead, the government should create money which would also avoid interest on debt to be paid. The Keynesian case of monetary policy was found impotent, which we now know was due to the liquidity trap argument. Therefore, Modigliani suggested that the authorities should resort to fiscal policies to attain full employment.[26]

Policies following the 1963 model

In his 1963 update, Modigliani considered two cases where the monetary authority would fail to attain full employment. One case imitates the pronouncement of the 1944 model. It holds that when full employment interest is low, "even with flexible wages, there would be no set of prices and interest rates capable of simultaneously clearing all markets." The system will find equilibrium only at a low level of employment and output. Improvement in the economy can be achieved by resorting to fiscal policy. Monetary policy will also be impotent with wage rigidity. Output will reach a "ceiling" below the full employment level, and "any attempt to expand employment beyond that ceiling, through expansion of the money supply (or fiscal policy) will only succeed in increasing prices and wages without increasing output and employment."[27]

But we find some expansion of stabilization policies as well. In his 1963 update, Modigliani also adjusted for market imperfections and wealth effects. Imperfection can enter when prices are a markup on wages, $P = (1+m)(WN/X)$. "The main implication is that monetary expansion and money wage cuts need not have a symmetrical effect on output and the other real variables, since the equilibrium value of these variables, while still a function of M and W, no longer depends merely on their ratio."[28]

Some other expansions of the 1963 update include explicit accommodation of government monetary and fiscal operations. We find a tax receipts equation, and a government budget identity equation. What is referred to as the "government model" did not need the bond market to study its implications. Policy measures evolved in two pure policy directions: "One is pure monetary policy which would consist in expanding the money supply or enforcing a lower interest rate or both. Pure fiscal policy on the other hand would consist in manipulating taxes or expenditure or both."[29] Many mixed and "if ... then" conclusions are now permitted. We must weigh the merits of private versus public consumption, the yield of private versus government capital formation, consumption versus capital formation, as well as the extent to which lower taxes and debt financing would shift the burden to future generations. We should also consider the "reliability of the tools" we are using, the role of a "built-in stabilizer," and counter cyclical changes in expenditures and tax rates.[30] Finally, in his 1963 update Modigliani anchored Keynesian stability concerns of liquidity preference and wage rigidity,

> Because of liquidity preference, a change in aggregate demand ... will produce a corresponding change in real demand for money or velocity of circulation, and hence in the real stock of money needed at full employment ... wage rigidity prevents the necessary increase in the real money supply and the concomitant required fall in interest rates.[31]

Policies in 1977, 1985 and 2003 models

This section draws on research from several of Modigliani's writings. Some related materials for stabilization policies are in Volumes I, III, IV, and V of Modigliani's collected works. Part II of Volume III is called

"Stabilization Policies," and Part III covers international monetary systems, focusing on Special Drawing Rights (SDRs). To stabilize SDRs, Modigliani proposed to use price indexes for globally traded commodities. The title of Volume IV of his collected works is *Monetary Theory and Stabilization Policies*. Part I of Volume V addresses "the effectiveness of simpleminded rules versus discretion to stabilize the economy."[32] The works that stand out on this matter are Modigliani's 1977 opening article in Volume I, the whole of Volume IV, and his lectures and articles from 1986.[33] The latter includes an essay delivered in 1977 at Luigi Bocconi University under the auspices of the Raffaele Mattioli Foundation. The old paradigm of rigid-wages and liquidity preference is greeted with the requirement of an active dose of stabilization policy, much as one would take doses of vitamin C to counter a common cold.

Stabilization in the 1970s

The 1970s was a topsy-turvy world for policy makers. OPEC supply shocks put the policy makers to task. In 1974, policy makers targeted an approximate 6 per cent growth of M1 money and wanted to prevent interest rates from falling. Modigliani thought that the targeted money growth rate was pessimistic. Because of "significant deviation of the growth of monetary aggregates from its initial targets," the federal fund rate increased to 13.5 per cent.[34] The economy sagged; demand for money and the interest rate began to drop. Modigliani wisely disagreed with the use of monetary policy for monetary targets. "Instead, monetary targets should be set, and adjusted, in the light of explicitly stated goals of real output and employment and money-income targets consistent with them."[35]

Modigliani observed that the fall in the demand for money created a positive demand shock. It was due to the increase in money circulation and the increase in output relative to the money supply. In turn, if the propensity to invest or consume fell, then the interest rate would likely fall, also. At this point, through the liquidity preference, the demand for money could increase or velocity could decrease, resulting in an increase in output relative to money supply, in turn, causing a negative demand shock. In general, "liquidity preference translates real disturbances into changes in velocity or demand shocks."[36]

The consequences of demand shocks work through wages and prices. If wages and prices were flexible, Modigliani suggested that they would create changes in the real money supply, Ms/P, bringing it in line with the NIRU and NIRO levels of inflation and output. Staying in the domain of price flexibility, it might be difficult to predict the course of prices. One reason is that when contracts are set, price forecasts would be needed. If prices were unstable they would be more difficult to forecast correctly. This would result in a disruption in the system. Therefore, a need for stabilization policies seems warranted within the price flexibility assumption.

Leaving price flexibility, we detect a more devastating consequence arising from rigid wages and prices. Given a negative demand shock, prices will not fall in order to bring an increase in the real money supply, Ms/p, in line with the NIRU level of output. The actual output will fall. The money supply must be increased, but we have no way to make that happen. The consequence is a state of "permanent" unemployment.

Overall, the degree of the consequences differs for "real" and "money" demand shocks. On the real demand shock side, (1) a high multiplier creates more instability; (2) a higher elasticity of aggregate demand to interest rate, (dX/dr)(X/r), will result in smaller income responses to demand shocks because the initial shock from a fall in the interest rate will be largely offset; and (3) an inelastic demand for money, (dMd/dr)/(Md/r), will be stabilizing as a fall in the velocity is followed by a large change in interest rate, thus increasing demand and neutralizing the disturbance.

On the money demand shock side, a low elasticity in the demand for money, the third scenario in the previous paragraph, will be destabilizing because a large increase in r would be required to counter a declining velocity. In regard to the second scenario, high elasticity of demand is also destabilizing because a change in interest rate, dr, required by the demand for money will be larger than a change in output, dY.[37]

Modigliani complemented his position of the 1970s with parameter estimates from the MIT-Penn-Social Science Research Council model (MPS). The short-run MPC in this model, which was below 0.5, was lower than the estimated long-run, and the elasticity of the demand for money with respect to the short-term interest rate was between one-half and one-third. The result was that "an expansion of the money supply tends to have a significant direct expansionary impact on consumption."[38]

Phillips Curve, NIRU and NIRO

Modigliani also looked at the predictions emanating from the Phillips Curve. Essentially, stabilization polices are captured by the Curve, which shows a trade-off between inflation and unemployment. The thesis is that some growth in the money supply is inflationary, and the way to control inflation is to lower the money supply. The following propositional presentation follows the development of his work, as illustrated in the fourth volume of *The Collected Papers of Franco Modigliani*.

Proposition I[39] *(Monetary Mechanism): The focus of M1 as a determinant of nominal income is a special case of the monetary mechanism.* Modigliani argued that the monetarist and Hicksian models fall under this proposition. He diverges from them to the extent that those models tend to ignore the financial structure of the economy and the stability of behavioral relationships. To elaborate, besides money and interest rates, monetary authorities can control the money supply through bank credit and bank liabilities. In those scenarios, the control mechanism is how bank credit affects investment. In contrast, an interest rate policy would depend on how financial markets compete, which are constrained by credit rationing and ceilings. Modigliani's first preliminary conclusion asserts that when investment and money demand functions are stable, the bank credit target, M2, is more preferable than the monetary target, M1. This conclusion should be generalized to cases where deposit rates are unresponsive to market rates and price flexibility is assumed, as well as the presence of government and the foreign sector. We look at some generalizations following the discussion of the propositions.

Proposition II[40] *(Tax Effect): If the financial structure is to include six financial instruments and markets, taxes, and inflation, then an increase in money and inflation will have cross effects. Its effect on leverage and the debt-capital ratio will cause an upward pressure on after tax real rate. Its effect on nominal tax gains and reserves will put a downward pressure on the after tax real rate.* The results incorporate, to a certain extent, the idea of price flexibility with some limiting cases of price rigidity, assuming rational and static expectations. If we begin with supply shocks, Modigliani maintained that a narrow M1 will stabilize output more than M, but prices will be unstable. If we begin with demand shocks, Modigliani argued that the target differs according to the source of uncertainty. If the stock market, money markets, and investment markets are the sources of instability, then the M2 target will be more effective for stabilization. If saving behavior, firm financing policies, and bank behavior are the sources of instability, then the M8 target should dominate.

Proposition III[41] *(Policy Rule): A policy rule should serve as a check on discretion, and discretion should serve as a check on policy rule.* Reviewing the state of monetary policy during the early 1980s, Modigliani concluded that a number of monetarists defected from a rigid monetarist policy rule, seeking instead a policy rule that would take into account variation in the velocity of money.[42] Modigliani simulated the economy for the 1980–1986 period, using a simple rule that planned money supply depends on previous velocity. For the period, he found significant deviation from actual and simulated output and money supply. The actual mean value of output growth was 7.5 per cent, compared with the simulated mean of 2.9 per cent growth. The actual mean value of money supply growth was 9.1, compared with the simulated mean value of 4.5 per cent growth. In both cases, the simulated values were significantly lower than the actual values.[43] Using the range of the deviated values as a measure of variation, the income path indicates that the velocity of money is unstable.

Proposition IV[44] *(Optimal Demand Policy): Optimal demand response to a large inflationary shock creates unbearable social burden.*

Modigliani created a model to fit the U.S. data for the inflation rates from 1953 to 1977. The model regressed the inflation rate on current unemployment, lagged inflation rates and three exogenous variables – terms of trade between non-food imports and non-food domestic prices, terms of trade between farm and non-food prices, and labor productivity adjusted for trends. For the purpose of deviation analysis, optimal inflation was set at 2 per cent; optimal unemployment at 4.8 per cent, and the optimal exogenous variables are their mean values over the sample period.

In his inflation specification, the errors of forecasts depend on specifying the independent variables. Modigliani assumed that the variables were estimated with perfect foresight. Also, he measured welfare cost on the assumption that unemployment had twice the social cost than inflation. The results from 1971 to 1975 indicated that "actual policy produced costs 34 per cent higher than the optimal policy (9.72 versus 7.28) for the five years."[45] Other assumptions could be made, too. For example, it could be shown that when imperfect foresight is assumed, the result "is not very different from the perfect foresight path."[46]

In the above discussion, the role of the Phillips Curve was central. Of course, this approach attempted to invalidate the classical version of the IS-LM curves. Modigliani considered the Phillips Curve paradigm because the empirical data were showing that the LM curve appears more inelastic, while the IS curve is more elastic. Introducing the Phillips Curve has, at minimum, created a micro-revolution in Modigliani's post-Keynesian paradigm, as wage rigidity now shifted from "extreme downward rigidity" to "new empirical evidence ... suggesting that nominal wages did, after all, respond to excess demand as measured by the rate of unemployment."[47]

Modigliani's contribution has the novelty that it is tied to his NIRU concept, the idea that the inflation rate is expected to fall as long as the actual unemployment rate does not fall below a critical level.[48] Corresponding to that level of inflation is a level of output and employment. Elsewhere, Modigliani coined the term non-inflationary rate of output (NIRO).[49] The NIRU and NIRO concepts are endowed with optimal and expectation implications. Set expected price, p^* to equal the price in the last period, p_{t-1}. We can then make the difference between actual price and expected price, $p-p_{t-1}$ dependent on the unemployment rate. A NIRU is a solution to that function.[50] A possible path to the solution can be an efficient turnpike as when the economy moves straight down on a vertical line anchored on the natural rate of unemployment for an inflation rate above its critical level. Another turnpike path can occur when the economy diverges to a short-run Phillips Curve before achieving its critical level.

Modigliani maintained that the introduction of the new Phillips Curve tool "did not appreciably weaken the case for active stabilization policies."[51] It became an explanatory tool to complement the IS-LM apparatus regarding inflation. The Curve can be used to get to full employment, but active policy can reduce the waiting for the adjustment to take place. We observe that the ideas of full employment and equilibrium unemployment were abandoned. "The policy makers could now choose their preferred rate of 'permanent' unemployment out of a selection represented by all points on the Phillips Curve provided, of course, they were also prepared to accept the associated permanent rate of inflation."[52]

Precursor to Macro Rational Expectations Hypothesis (MRE[53] or MREH[54])

Further development of Modigliani's stabilization policies revolve around technical specifications of models. In reviewing Modigliani's AEA presidential address, Bennett T. McCallum wrote, "support for ... Modigliani's argument is provided by the most drastic propositions of the 'rational expectations' branch of the monetarist school. This proposition, which Modigliani termed the MREH, asserts that – in his words – 'any attempts to stabilize the economy by means of stated monetary or fiscal rules are bound to be totally ineffective.'"[55] Modigliani positioned the MREH as an anticipation of the Lucas RE hypothesis. The essence of the arguments in this section are also closely tied to practical results obtained from the MIT-Penn SSRC model and are presented from a non-technical standpoint.

Self-referent models

Modigliani's philosophy about MREH began with his observation that some types of expectations are self-fulfilling. This is a kind of self-referent, or reflective, philosophy. Modigliani is proud to say that "I have contributed an important concept which is, I think, at the essence of rational expectations, namely, the existence of expectations that map into themselves."[56]

A forecast is self-referent if it can alter someone's behavior so that the forecast can come true. Modigliani advanced a proof that self-fulfilling forecasts exist. The proof is based on the mathematics of a fixed-point that was developed by L. E. Brouwer. The usual way to explain this concept is to start with a box with its off-diagonal drawn in. Here is how Samuelson explained it:

> Draw a square and pencil in the 45-degree diagonal connecting its southwest and northeast corners. Is there any way to draw a curve that goes from the square's east side to its west side without taking pencil off the paper, such that the curve and the diagonal have no single point in common? Brouwer's fixed-point theorem in one dimension proves that there is indeed no possible way.[57]

Modigliani's argument that the expectation of the future is self-fulfilling rests on some assumptions. One assumption is that the behavior has to vary with the forecast. Grunberg and Modigliani relate the actual price in the next period, p(t+1), to the predicted price, P, to get the relationship that p(t+1) = R.[58] This is a reaction function showing how agents behave in relation to the predicted prices. The other assumption is that the graph of the reaction function should be a continuous curve, meaning that if we were to draw it with a pencil, we should not lift the pencil up before the curve is completed. Now, if we plot the relationship between actual and predicted price in a bounded box, the reaction function will cross the diagonal line at least once, marking the equality between the actual and predicted prices. If we can find such a point, then it will represent the point where the actual and expected forecasts are the same, proving that a true forecast exists.

Relation of self-referent models to rational expectations

The rational expectations analysis is part of the solution to Modigliani's self-referent model. With the above arguments concerning a reaction function that is continuous and of bounded continuity, Kenneth J. Arrow said, "it would appear that the possibility of rational expectation cannot be denied."[59]

The school of MREH developed a reduced form macro econometric model of the form that "the inflation rate depends on the rate of monetary growth and random (unexplained) shocks while output is basically independent of the variables under the control of the macroeconomic policy."[60] In some instances, Modigliani doubted the validity of the MRE hypothesis. One of his arguments shows that the ineffectiveness of monetary and fiscal policy predicted by the MRE hypothesis is based on the assumption of perfect competition. He wrote that "the most glaring flaw of MREH is its inconsistency with the evidence: if it were valid, deviations of unemployment from the natural rate would be small and transitory – in which case *The General Theory* would not have been written."[61] Modigliani anchored criticism of the MREH based on Keynes' concept of imperfection in the labor market.[62] There are many ways to approach this imperfection in the labor market. Hahn and Solow (1995) adopted the method of monopolistic competition in their modern investigation of the labor market. Modigliani used an oligopoly pricing specification for the wage-price sector in the M.I.T.-Penn-Social Science Research Council (MPS) model. However, the use of the market imperfection model in the MRE hypothesis is not without question. McCallum, for instance, argued that "observing that many industries are highly concentrated will not ... discredit the contention of the rational expectations school: that systematic monetary and fiscal stabilization policies will be systematically ineffective."[63]

In his AEA presidential address, Modigliani delineated other problems of MREH besides the above inconsistency problem with Keynes. One has to do with the correlations of the errors of prediction. The reason why actual employment output, y, deviates from full employment output, y_p, is due to random shocks in the error term to the money supply, ϵ_t. Modigliani's argument was that the value of a current error, ϵ_t, should not affect the value of a future error, ϵ_{t+1}. In statistical parlance, the expected value of the future period error should be zero, in which case it would not affect the deviation of actual from full employment output. However, in reality the error terms are serially correlated, $E(\epsilon_t, \epsilon_{t+1}) \neq 0$, meaning that past errors find their way into future errors. As Steven Sheffrin explains, "If the economy is in a boom this period, most likely it will continue next period and conversely, for recessions. In other words, movements of output, employment and unemployment all tend to persist."[64] Subsequent researchers have looked for other explanations as to why unemployment may persist. One argument for the persistence of unemployment is that the individuals may not know what their mistakes are, and therefore cannot correct their errors. Another argument is that the potential output can vary if and when the shock affects inventories or capital. A third way for persistence in unemployment output to occur is if the firms suffer adjustment costs when they change their stock of labor.[65]

Modigliani made two other points. The first is the anticipation to stabilize REH. The second is that the government cannot pursue policies to stabilize errors. If the private sector is taking care of shocks, the government can help only if its information is better than that of the private sector.

FMP model and stabilization

During the early 1970s, the Board of Governors of the Federal Reserve System was using an econometric model that Modigliani pioneered. Modigliani called it the Federal Reserve-MIT-Penn Model (FMP) and used it to illustrate how bank reserves, money supply, and short-term interest rates could be used for stabilization purposes. He emphasized that "consumption is one of the most important, if not the most important, single channel through which the above tools affect directly and indirectly the level of aggregate real and money demand and thus, the level of output, employment and prices."[66] We will discuss the FMP model and the consumption function later in this book. In this section, we will only look at the possibility of stabilization through them.

To show how consumption stabilizes full employment output, Modigliani started with the simple Keynesian model, $Y = C + E$, and $C = Co + c(Y - T)$, where Y is income, C is consumption, E is exogenous expenditure, and T is tax revenues. He then added a wealth variable, W, that changes with time, t, and is a result of savings, S.[67] We now have that "aggregate consumption in any year t could be expressed as a linear function of aggregate income, say YL, and of aggregate private wealth, A."[68] In current textbooks, this model is carried as the life-cycle hypothesis, where consumption depends on annual labor income, YL, and the average propensity to consume is the ratio: annual income times working life, WL, over number of years of life, NL. In other words, $C = \frac{WL}{NL}YL$.[69] Modigliani discussed both fiscal and monetary impact of consumption on full employment output. We discuss these impacts below.

Fiscal stabilization policies

Modigliani developed fiscal policies from the Keynesian point of view. What Keynes meant by fiscal policy is captured in the expression, "A simple prescription for the Government to lower tax rates and increase spending actually did make good sense in the early 1930s when grass grew on main street and one bank failure led to another."[70] Modigliani followed that Keynesian vision in working out the fiscal implications for stabilization policies when changes in autonomous expenditures, dE, and taxes, dT affect income, Y. Modigliani defined taxes as a proportion of income, $T = \theta Y$. The resulting simple Keynesian income multiplier now shows a leakage for the tax rate. Instead of dE's influence of just $\frac{1}{1-c}$ on Y, without taxes, the influence becomes $\frac{1}{1-c(1-\theta)}$, with taxes.

Modigliani elevated the consumption function by adding another important variable, wealth, to capture the "wealth effect" on stabilization policies. As mentioned above, he identified wealth with savings. His precise definition is:

$$W(t) - W(t-1) = S(t-1) = Y(t-1) - T(t-1) - C(t-1).$$[71]

Simply put, previous period saving is the excess of personal income over taxes and consumption for the same period. That excess is the increment of wealth. One modern interpretation of Modigliani's definition is the inclusion of "liquid wealth – money, bank accounts and other very liquid assets – plus other assets such as equities, long-term bonds and homes."[72] Another modern interpretation is that it includes "human capital, real capital and financial wealth."[73] This broad definition provides ample room to indicate how changes in wealth can lead to stabilization of full employment income.

The addition to the wealth variable changes the income multiplier effect on income. Modigliani wrote: "the multiplier effect of an autonomous increase in expenditure is indefinitely large if the marginal tax rate is zero."[74] He has shown that the income multiplier will approach $\frac{1}{\theta}$, an expression that is independent of the consumption function. To explain the process, we need to follow a change in autonomous expenditures in two phases. In the first phase:

> The increase in the exogenous expenditure dE can be looked at as an increase in 'offset to saving' which causes savings in every period to increase by the same amount dE. But the increase in savings in turn increases wealth which again increases consumption and income, forever.[75]

In the second phase, the analysis that leads up to income approaching $\frac{1}{\theta}$ can be explained thus:

> As consumption and income rise under the impact of the original change in dE and the induced increase in saving and wealth, tax

> revenue also rises and this reduces disposable income and savings, and hence accumulation. The process comes to an end when the increase in income has become large enough so that the increase in tax take, ... is just enough to offset the increase in dE.[76]

Modigliani singled out two elements in the autonomous expenditure variable, E, for their special fiscal effects. One is the budget deficit, a situation where $G > T$. The other is the international sector, which is captured through the balance of payments.

Budget deficit

On the budget deficit, Modigliani addressed several questions. The questions were built around the impact a deficit would have on current and future generations. One question is whether an increase in national debt favors the present generation. Another question is whether it would transfer a burden to future generations. A third question is whether the influence would be symmetric if the national debt is decreased rather than increased. Finally, we want to know whether the interest charge on debt could be a measure of its influence, and the difference it might make if G enhances the real income of future generations.[77]

The budget deficit argument can be also be explored from the points of view of "transfer and burden" arguments. One position is that if G is financed by debt, savers would voluntarily buy government bonds instead of other assets, so that no burden is placed on the current generation. This is different from financing G through taxes, which would create a burden on current taxpayers. However, the argument continues, the debt would have to be repaid in the future, so that debt financing is seen as shifting the burden to future generations. Modigliani remarked, "This argument does not imply that a debt-financed expenditure will necessarily affect future generations unfavorably ... the net outcome might even be positive if the expenditure undertaken produced greater benefits than the private capital formation which it replaces."[78]

Modigliani argued that the Keynesian budget deficit argument is consistent with the classical "transfer and burden" approach. Starting with full employment levels of G, T, and interest r, the Keynesian model holds that consumption would respond to T and not to r. If we hold T constant, but increase G, then the deficit, D, would increase by $dD = dG$. To maintain full employment without inflation, $dD + dC + dI = 0$, would yield $dD = dG = -dI$, as taxes and change in consumption is zero.

Modigliani gave an explanation of this outcome to assess the burden of debt vs. tax financing of G. Starting from a position of no government deficit, he increased government expenditures by reducing private capital formation, $dG = S - (D = G - T)$. We observe that savings are decreased by the amount of the deficit expenditure, D, which represents a decrease in private capital formation, or a decrease in investment, where investment is $I = \Delta K = S - D$. This is a different issue to argue that a later generation would have to pay more taxes to cover the interest charges on debt. It is different because Modigliani argued that the burden is the loss of income from capital. Modigliani entertained the idea of interest as a measure of burden coming in from a different angle. Interest can come in if we want to approximate the loss of output from the decrease in investment by $r^*(dD)$, where r^* is the marginal productivity of capital. The question then turns to how good a measure of r^* we have. If we assume that the government will borrow money to finance the deficit, then the long-term interest rate can be an approximate measure of the marginal productivity of capital. Notice that there is no other way to recoup the decrease in I besides repaying the loan.

Modigliani contended that the long-term interest rate may not be a good measure for other reasons. If the government debt is large, the government may significantly drive up the interest rate when it attempts to borrow, then the interest rate may overstate the burden. Also, the government may be able to borrow at favorable rates such as during war time when banks and financial institutions can be forced to hold below market interest rate bonds.

Thus far, Modigliani's analysis of the debt can be summarized in the following quote:

> The debt-financed expenditure must be accompanied by an equal reduction in capital formation (with the help of the appropriate monetary policy) ... this expenditure puts no burden on the "current" members of the community. Their (real) disposable income is unchanged by the expenditure, and consequently so is their consumption, as well as the net current addition to their personal wealth or private net worth ... the deficit-financed expenditure will leave in the wake an overall burden on the economy in the form of a reduced flow of income from the reduced stock of private capital.[79]

Furthermore, Modigliani's position is that the burden for reducing private net worth comes from "*loss of income from capita*l and *not in the taxes levied on later members to pay the interest charge,*" [Italics original].[80]

In analyzing the deficit of the 1970s, Modigliani maintained that interest was not a good measure of debt, and that inflation was the cause of the deficit. In a later presentation he distinguished between a naïve and a sophisticated no-burden view. The naïve no-burden of deficit view was ruled out on the grounds that "it is impossible for this generation to eat the wheat of future generations. We can only eat the wheat we produce. Thus, we cannot shift the burden from the present to the future generation."[81]

Modigliani then redressed the interest burden argument in terms of a bequest view. This view argues that we can affect the future level of output by the amount of capital we bequeath. Deficit is financed from current savings, thereby reducing current investment that could have produced future output. Modigliani looked at whether this future loss to output was permanent by viewing it through the life-cycle hypothesis that uses permanent income and wealth. In this model, wealth is not transferred through bequest. Wealth is transferred rather through "humped savings." The bottom line is that wealth is generated partly by bequest and partly through life-cycle savings. Government debt then "occupies a portion of the wealth that people would wish to hold, and thereby reduce the portion of wealth available to finance capital. … The government deficit crowds out capital because the desire for wealth is satisfied by the government debts instead of being satisfied by productive physical capital."[82]

This new way of looking at the sophisticated burden reinforces the view that the interest is not a good measure of the burden. If the government debt was $1 trillion, then capital will be crowded-out by that amount. A 5 per cent interest rate would measure the burden as $50 billion. If the marginal productivity of capital was 10 per cent, then a 50 per cent business tax rate would yield an after tax return to business of 5 per cent, equal to the interest rate. But it is clear that the use of the interest charge alone would not measure the burden because it would not account for the losses in an estimated $50 billion in tax revenues. This is also not the end of the calculations; the government may use the debt amount to finance public capital, yielding a social return. The economy may also be in a slack period, in which case the government's use of the private capital might be investment-enhancing. The latter may depend on whether the slack was needed to rein in inflation, or what other mixed-policy measures including monetary policy were in effect at the time.

Modigliani also turned his attention to a "super-sophisticate no-burden argument"[83] relating to the theorem of Robert Barro.[84] The foundation of this view is the work of David Ricardo. The argument aims to show that tax and debt financing have the same effect, because the burden comes out of how the resources are used, not in how the debt is financed. Modigliani explained that T = D if people's lives are infinite. We can raise $100 for deficit financing by either taxing the current generation on that amount, or pay, say, $5 annually on a bond forever for that amount.

Modigliani discussed Barro's hypothesis in terms of how parents are concerned about the future resources of their children. The government would raise $100 in deficit, leaving the interest to be paid by the next generation in the future. So as not to change the original plans parents have for their offspring's future, they would look at the problem the following way: The government did not tax the parent, the bond financing is like a tax subsidy to the parent, and the parent can therefore buy the government bond with the $100 tax they should have paid, and pay the $5 earning each year to the tax collector. The situation would leave the original plans for their offspring unchanged, and would make T and D equivalent. Modigliani summed up this argument as follows:

> The initial allocation is still available since the fiscal reshuffling does not change the budget constraint. In fact, that allocation can be easily secured by not consuming the rebate and using it to buy the debt. This incremental investment in government securities is first used to pay the new tax ... and then left as a bequest to be used by the heirs to pay their new taxes, without changing consumption.[85]

Modigliani then addressed theoretical and empirical arguments against Barro's hypothesis. Modigliani wrote that, "The most obvious objection to the Barro model is that life is finite, and that this circumstance is sufficient to establish the intergenerational effects of deficits."[86] People are not neutral regarding T and D. A family without children would prefer a tax on a family with children, and a family with children would rather have the tax paid now. Modigliani also pointed out an asymmetry in the intergenerational argument, namely the impossibility of negative bequest. A situation may require that the offspring should transfer the bequest to parents. Such a situation presents itself when a parent decides to consume more and children should then consume less than their lifetime income. The problem is that bequest can be zero, but not negative.

On the empirical side, one hypothesis is to test whether the government borrowing leads people to accumulate more to offset the burden of the debt on their children. The hypothesis advanced is that people intend to give their children a greater chunk of wealth to pay for the future debt. Using data from 1900 to 1958, Modigliani correlated wealth/income with debt/income ratios. The result was −0.4. For 1900 to 1980, the correlation was the same, indicating again a negative correlation.[87] For Barro's hypothesis to hold, the coefficient should be perfect, or equal to 1. Modigliani performed other tests and reached the same conclusion. On the issue of deficits and inflation, Modigliani held that stagflation causes deficits. Inflation implies high interest rates, or large interest payments. Higher government deficit is likely through debt financing, unless the policy is to reduce the deficit by taxes.[88] The next section will examine Modigliani's approach to international trade.

International sector

Modigliani was interested in the international sector early in his career. In 1944, Modigliani collaborated with his teacher, Neisser, on a project which culminated in the publication of a book, *International Incomes and International Trade*. Modigliani made an important contribution in reformulating the model of international trade.[89] His international concerns straddled the U.S., European economies, and developing countries. Following Keynes, Modigliani's 1944 model was essentially closed. By the time of his 1963 update, activities in the open economy did not require significant change in the 1944 model. The problem was "the real exchange rate in an open economy version of the 1963 model would have been constant and the current account a simple function of the level of income."[90] However, regarding major changes in the open economy since the early 1970s, including flexible exchange rates, supply shocks, and capital mobility, Modigliani decided to accommodate changes in his model to study the open economy's influence on domestic output and interest rate.[91] Some of the additions would show how exchange rates affect the goods and monetary sectors. Fischer suggested that the amendments to Modigliani's model should follow the basic schema of the Mundell-Flemming model.[92]

In an early account, Modigliani commented on Mundell's model. He wrote, "it has been shown, notable through the works of Mundell (1963), that, once we allow for movement of capital, in response to interest rate differentials, balance of payment (BP) equilibrium and domestic stability goals can be reconciled."[93] At that time, he advocated the use of the saving function to attain a target output and interest rate to keep the foreign sector in equilibrium. He wrote the saving function as $S(T,\hat{Y}) = E - T + K(\hat{r}) + \hat{B}$, where S is savings, T is taxes, K is domestic investment, Y is output, B is current account, and the carets indicate targets.[94] Subsequently, Modigliani brought in the current account as well: $S = I + NX$, where NX is exports minus imports.[95]

Modigliani claimed that the open economy system through which E and T can stabilize savings has a flaw. B determines how much capital should be moved. The reverse should have happened, namely, B should have been determined by the flow of capital.[96] While the Mundell model would require three targets for stabilization policies – full employment, balance of payments equilibrium, and the distribution of domestic resources between the government and private sectors – it would be difficult to achieve a target level of saving. Saving has to match up with domestic investment that depends on the world rate of interest plus the given level of the current account. Matching S and I requires that we change consumption through taxes, and balance savings with government deficits. What should happen is that the flow of capital between countries should equilibrate saving and investment, and not require policy makers to force them into equality.[97]

Modigliani preferred an open system where adjustments take place gradually. When he accepted the suggestion to amend his model for the open economy, he stated that he preferred the "assumption that the adjustment in capital markets is instantaneous a formulation allowing for a gradual response of capital movements to the gap between domestic and foreign rate."[98] In describing how the U.S. should adjust to the OPEC crises in the 1970s, he advocated a transient system of crawling parities. The "rational solution is not that of competitive devaluation. What was called for instead is a transient remedy, which can only consist, fundamentally, in the acquiescence on the part of the industrial countries to a deficit, initially of large proportions, but rapidly shrinking in time."[99] He went on to enunciate that this policy would require the participating countries to set off a crawling parity system where they would manage their currency in terms of the U.S. dollar. That would affect their exchange rate with the dollar, and therefore affect the U.S. balance of payments, without the U.S. having to convert dollar reserves at institutions such as the IMF. In effect, Modigliani was advocating reforming the international financial institution.

In Modigliani's Raffaele Mattioli lectures, Paolo Baffi, then governor of the Bank of Italy, asked some general questions concerning stabilization policies. One question was whether money should be expanded at a constant rate, as advocated by Milton Friedman.[100] Modigliani responded that a constant rate of money supply was not compatible with a fixed exchange rate, "Friedman's Supreme God, to which everything else – including fixed exchange rates – had to be sacrificed was the rule that money growth should be constant."[101] In an interview in 2000, Modigliani remarked that "I've been moving toward open-economy macroeconomics and especially international finance ... it's an area where wage rigidity is very important. ... With nominal wage rigidity, you will want floating exchange rate. With real rigidity, there's nothing you can do about unemployment."[102] He also expressed this opinion in his last published work on the open economy.[103] The comments may not hold, of course, if the assumption of diminishing returns to labor is dropped.

Monetary stabilization policies

In this section, we review the essentials of Modigliani's monetary policies. He wrote in his 2003 article:

> my view, which I believe would be broadly acceptable to those who understand the fundamental Keynesian message, is that employment stabilization should be primarily the responsibility of monetary policies, except for automatic fiscal anti-cyclical stabilizers, while the main effect of non-cyclical budget deficits should be recognized as that of redistributing resources between generations.[104]

In the Raffaele lectures, Professor Franco Bruni criticized Modigliani for providing a "negative answer to the questions posed in his 1976 American Economic Association address, namely 'Should We Forsake Stabilization Policies?'"[105] Bruni's question was whether there should be discretionary policy or a fixed rule. If the former, he was concerned whether the discretion should be undertaken independently by the Central Bank or whether the government should have controlling influence.[106] Modigliani was for Central Bank independence, so it could use any tools it wants, and should be held accountable for the consequences. The government's role is to set the target. The Central Bank participates in target setting, and accommodates the government's chosen fiscal means. It should also use intermediate targets, which means some monetary aggregates "had to be flexible and should be changed in line with changing circumstances."[107]

Classical and Keynesian monetary stabilization views

Modigliani's 2003 analysis of the two schools started with their basic points of agreement. The two schools agree that "the demand for money depends on the value of transactions ... assumed proportional to the value of Gross National Product expressed in terms of money, at an 'annual rate (Y).'"[108] The supply of money is determined by the Central Bank, exogenous from the market system. However, the classical school assumed wage and price flexibility; the Keynesian school assumed wage and price rigidity. "Keynes instead elaborates a mechanism that is valid regardless of the degree of rigidity of wages. It is the formulation of this mechanism that constitutes his crowning achievement."[109]

A little bit of history will put this into perspective. Jean Bodin proposed that high prices resulted from an abundance of gold and silver, and not much from currency debasement, scarcity, or the extravagance of kings and lords. Gerard Malynes, a mercantilist, stated that an abundance of money in an economy makes goods more expensive and vice versa. The best statement in the seventeenth century about the quantity theory is by John Locke, who wrote about the velocity of circulation of money and the total number of transactions.[110] Also, Sir Roy Harrod noted that the first attempt to put monetary theory in symbolic form was by Irving Fisher.[111]

The symbolic history of the money equation has many simple forms. In the tradition of Fisher, it may be written as $MV = \Sigma pq$, or $MV = PT$, or $MV + M'V' = PT$, where V is circulation of money, T is volume of trade, M' is bank money, p is price of commodities, and q is quantity of commodities. To see how the equation works, we need to place restrictions on some variables. The following three restrictions[112] and their implications are:

a. Given V and q, then a change in price with respect to a change in money will be q/V
b. Given M and T, then a change in price with respect to a change in velocity will be M/T, and
c. Given M and V, a change of price with respect to transactions will be negative $1/T^2(MV)$.

In the hands of Alfred Marshall, money is notes and coins. Bank deposits are excluded, but can easily be accommodated. The famous statement that inflation is a monetary phenomenon, meaning that an increase in the money supply will cause an increase in prices, comes out clearly in Marshall's version. The process is as follows: "In the bullion market, an increase in the quantity of gold will cause temporary decline in the rate of interest. This in turn will induce speculation causing price levels to rise thus increasing the demand for money. Finally, the rate of interest will rise to its previous level."[113]

In his *Tract on Monetary Reform*, Keynes[114] compressed the quantity equation into n = kp, where "n" is currency notes and cash held by the public, "p" is an index number of cost of living, and "k" is the percentage of income people desire in the form of money balances. If the constant, k, is just people's cash holdings, then we have to add the proportion that banks hold in cash, r, of their checking deposits. Now we have n = p(k+rk'). Keynes noted that he was following Marshall and Pigou in drawing the essential direct relationship between (n = M) and P. This is the version of the equation M = kY in Modigliani's 1944 paper.

In the Hicksian framework, if actual employment is less than full employment, the banking system can use monetary policies to steer the economy back to a full-employment level. The mechanism is for an increase in money to decrease the interest rate, and then increase investment and income. In a grave situation such as the presence of a liquidity-trap where the public would want to hold all the increase in money, say for precautionary motives, the mechanism will likely fail.

Modigliani's schema focused on wage and price rigidity. He defined the demand for money as proportional to price times output, $M_d = kPX$, and took the supply of money, M, as given. In the classical case, $M_d = M$, when prices adjust because they are flexible. In the Keynesian case, $M_d = M$, where output adjusts because prices are rigid. In other words, adjustments take place when unemployment changes.

> The great contribution of Keynes was to explain the mechanism by which an excess demand for money leads to a contraction of output, and there you need liquidity preference and the multiplier. Then you can see that unemployment is not a disequilibrium mechanism but an equilibrating mechanism for clearing the money market.[115]

Monetary policy in Modigliani's model

Monetary policy became more important when inflation started in the late 1950s. In the post-war recessions of 1948 to 1949 and 1953 to 1954, the U.S. economy experienced deflation. But during the 1957 to 1958 recession, inflation resurfaced. The Phillips Curve was popular then because it was seen as a trade-off between inflation and unemployment through the wage rate. Policy makers can get lower inflation by accepting some unemployment. However, stabilization policy was poised for a change. The new paradigm was a vertical Phillips curve. Modigliani stated that "a very important first step had already been made by Richard Lipsey who introduced a lag on the rate of inflation. Because after all what is the Friedman statement, it is that the coefficient of the lag is 1."[116]

Using the new Phillips Curve paradigm, the monetarists defined "a natural unemployment rate, independent of the steady state rate of inflation. More dramatically, the natural rate hypothesis implies that the long-run Phillips curve is vertical."[117] We get that kind of result only in the long-run when expected inflation is realized. Modigliani later called it the NIRU and NIRO, relating inflation to unemployment and output, which was prior to the NAIRU hypothesis. On the practical side, it means that monetary policy could not influence output. This is the hard-core position of the monetarists. The search then became significant to find out the conditions under which the slope of the long-run Phillips Curve is vertical. The Federal Reserve Board (FRB) took the lead in this matter.

From 1965 to 1970 the FRB was developing a model with the assistance of Modigliani and others. Modigliani stated that the purpose of the model was to sustain stabilization policies. He wrote: "My support was proved by the fact that I agreed to build the model for the Federal Reserve, the so-called FMP model. It was built in the 1960s, about 1966, and it was to be used for stabilization purposes ... I have built four such models, one for the United States, one for Italy, one for Spain and one for Sweden."[118]

The model had a monetary effect through the consumption-wealth model, through the foreign sector, and through credit rationing. In Modigliani's life-cycle hypothesis, the price of stocks acts as a wealth variable. When increase in the supply of money leads to an increase in stock prices, then financial wealth, consumption, output, and employment are also increased.[119] However, the whole wealth effect is considered transitory. Modigliani felt that he had done away with Pigou's wealth effect. The wealth effect, as we know it, is driven by falling prices. Modigliani reasoned that even a *"continuous fall or deflation,"*[120] [Italics original] would not make consumption the engine to drive full-employment because real interest rates would rise, reducing investment, and through the multiplier, reduce output and employment.

Although the idea of rational expectations was known at the time the FMP model was being formed, it was not yet practical. The researchers at the FRB used instead the adaptive model. They knew that "an adaptive expectations Phillips Curve would explode if the lag coefficient was one ... [the] Phillips Curves became very, very steep at low unemployment rates, implying that inflation would become uncontrollable at low unemployment rates."[121] The outlook of the long-run Phillips Curve was an unstable system in that "for the same rate of unemployment you would get more and more inflation."[122]

But REH was an attractive model that found a home even in the FMP model. In the 1970s, three overlapping ideas were integrated. Econometric models captured the decision rules that people reached about their consumption, investment, and portfolio behavior; large deficits and supply of money, and many supply shocks. The REH transformed all three problems by building on the expectation hypothesis of Modigliani and Brumberg. Robert Lucas was able to create a practical REH framework to integrate these problems. However, the basis of REH is policy ineffectiveness, ruling out fiscal and monetary policies for stabilization of employment. REH is also a market force mechanism, in opposition to Keynes. At one time the "casual acceptance of competitive assumptions got Keynes into trouble right away, by leading him to assert that real wages should behave counter cyclically, falling in upswings and rising in downswings. When it was pointed out, as early as 1937, that the facts were otherwise, Keynes was quite happy to recant."[123]

Modigliani stayed within the Keynesian paradigm on matters of stabilization, leaning towards imperfect competition. He pointed out four reasons for not being convinced on REH and its market assumptions. An article by Benjamin M. Friedman, based on learning theories, argued for the defense of adaptive expectation hypothesis and learning models.[124] Another one by Stanley Fischer argued that wage rigidity stems from workers and management setting long-term contracts. But his main objection was that the REH does not explain reality because of imperfect competition.[125]

According to Modigliani, "stabilization policy should be designed to achieve explicitly stated employment, real income and money income targets, which should of course be deemed attainable and mutually consistent."[126] Market imperfections prevent the attainment of these goals for several reasons. Although suppliers may find that their losses are small if they do not increase their prices, the so-called menu-cost arguments, if a large number of them act that way, then the sum of the effect would be significant in the aggregate. Also, sellers with market influences should base their decisions on reaction of their competitors and the state of the economy. Modigliani therefore considered including oligopoly-like elements to represent Keynesian concerns in his model.

This is evident in his specification of the Federal Reserve Board econometric model called the MPS model, where he used oligopoly-like pricing to argue against the REH hypothesis.[127] We have more to say on the MPS model in a later chapter.

Modigliani extended and applied Keynesian thoughts to European economies as his heart was attached to Italy and other European countries. His autobiography reflected this interest in that two of its three chapters were dedicated to the European scene, and the other to the United States. Earlier, we have alluded to Paul Samuelson's comment that Franco Modigliani's contribution formed a Model-T version of Keynesian economics. Milton Friedman, a leader of the monetarist school, also noted that Modigliani was a leader in defending the tenets of Keynesian economics in the controversy that "came to be referred to as the battle of the radio stations" – FM (for money) and AM (against money).[128] Friedman had in mind Modigliani's contribution in the areas of stabilization policies, and not to the Permanent Income and the Life Cycle hypotheses, respectively, a legacy they both shared. As we have already discussed Modigliani's legacy in the hard core Keynesian areas of consumption in the form of the LCH hypothesis, investment in the form of the M&M model, and stabilization polices, we next examine his less well-known contributions to macroeconomics revolving around European concerns.

Extending the Keynesian apparatus to European countries: The theoretical and empirical sides

In this section, we demonstrate how Modigliani modified the Keynesian paradigm to solve problems within the European economies. On the theoretical side, he tailored the model to suit the economic problems at hand. On the empirical side, he emphasized that the problem of unemployment is a failure to adopt the Keynesian demand side policies.

Modigliani extended Keynes' tools to the Italian economy during the 1961–1965 periods. From 1961 to 1963, the Italian economy experienced rapid growth in money wages and prices, balance of payment deficits, and restrictive monetary policies. By 1964, the Italian economy went into a recession, from which it recovered during the first half of 1966. Modigliani's contribution centered on critiquing the Bank of Italy for following an accommodating monetary policy rather than a Keynesian solution. He wrote: "In the Bank's model, there are partially conflicting statements on the determinants of the level of prices, but, by and large, one can say that, in that model, prices directly depend on the supply of money. Our view is different. We hold that an increase in money wages, larger than productivity, will affect prices even if the quantity of money is unchanged."[129] Reflecting on that explanation, Modigliani later wrote that "the monetary rigor and loss of jobs could have been avoided if an income policy had been implemented."[130]

Modigliani's Keynesian interpretation of the Italian economy holds that once aggregate demand is given, real wages are determined and prices are set to make money wages correspond to the real wages.[131] A relationship in which wages and prices correlate, he held, is also predicted by an oligopolistic model with mark-up price determination. Change in aggregate demand will then, in turn, affect the distribution of money wage rate, and the price level, given productivity per head. In this model, "the distribution of income is determined by aggregate demand; in the Bank's model distribution of income determines aggregate demand."[132] To link up his Keynesian views with the trade deficit, Modigliani postulated that the MPC for imports should be larger for consumption than for investment goods. He doubted this could be achieved. Therefore, he attributed the deficit to cost and price inflation due to a wage-price spiral mechanism.[133]

Another theoretical application of Modigliani's Keynesian view was demonstrated for the Belgian economy. During the 1970 to 1976 period, real wages in the Belgian economy had risen by 50 per cent, compared with only a 30 per cent increase in the EEC countries. At that time, the Phillips curve was integral to policy analysis from both the monetarist and Keynesian camps. Modigliani developed an explanation from the Keynesian view that abided by short-term phenomena and his versions (NIRO, NIRU) of what is now known as the NAIRU concept. His view was that the Phillips curve would not reach a vertical shape. In other words, the path he envisioned the economy would take from a high level of inflation to a lower level is not by traveling along the long-run Phillips curve, but to veer off quickly to the short-run Phillips, and then to invoke policies that would trade off unemployment for inflation. In the case of high wages for the Belgian economy, he asserted that the trade-off of unemployment for wage-push inflation should occur in the face of a binding balance of payments constraint.[134]

As for Modigliani's empirical side, there was a communication of his Medium of International Transaction (MIT) reserve currency plan to reform the international monetary system. He positioned the MIT plan as a program in the spirit of Keynes' Bancor proposal during the Bretton Woods days. As with Keynes, Modigliani's concept was rejected by the

IMF in favor of a gold and dollar standard. He justified his proposal, however, by arguing that during the 1960s, European countries were accumulating gold reserves through the IMF system. In particular, France was converting nearly $5 billion reserves into gold. France was not sympathetic to the U.S. running a balance of payments deficit and purchasing financial assets with loans from European countries.

Modigliani explained how the MIT currency system would have worked: "Each of the players of the game fixed a currency reserve target. This target took account of its foreign trade and of variability in the balance of payments. At the start of the game, a new MIT-bank would take the place of the International Monetary Fund and credit each country with a current account equivalent to its own reserve target (guaranteed by an equal amount of national currency)."[135] In this plan, the accumulation of reserves by European countries would reflect the balance of payments deficit that the U.S. created. Modigliani's solution was to urge the European nations to spend their excess reserves in order to stimulate demand and increase investment in their own countries, rather than to convert the excess reserves into gold. His advice, however, fell on deaf ears: France continued to convert its reserves into gold with some malice that he expressed thus: "De Gaulle's aim is to create serious embarrassment for the dollar and achieve a revaluation of the price of gold ... there has been a gaullist-inspired fashion in Europe to viewing American investments as part of a sinister American economic-imperialist plot."[136]

When Modigliani's MIT currency reserve plan was rejected, he proposed an alternative one. This required that the U.S. either pay interest on the dollars being held as reserves by the European nations, or guarantee against exchange rate risks. European countries would thus receive interest payments rather than gold for the reserves they accumulate. The U.S. could then also devalue its currency in relation to gold and special drawing rights, which would have decreased its imports and increased its exports to resolve its deficit. Rather, in August 1971, the U.S. imposed a 10 per cent surcharge on imports, which only reduced imports and did nothing to increase exports, thereby leading to a decrease in the volume of world trade. On 12 February, 1973, in reaction to speculation on the German mark, the U.S. did devalue the dollar by 10 per cent against gold and special drawing rights, but according to Modigliani, the timing was too late to avert a collapse of the Bretton Woods gold standard system. The U.S. then opted for a floating exchange rate system within limits.

During the 1980s, Modigliani traced the economic problems of European countries to their reactions to the world economy and scrutinized the history of the European countries' misguided policies in the 1970s in relation to the supply shocks caused by OPEC. In the early 1980s, when the United States had recovered from stagflation, in contrast to the rest of the world, Modigliani saw that " ... the root of this situation can be traced to an inconsistency between the fiscal monetary mix of the United States and that of Europe and the rest of the industrial countries."[137] The United States ran large deficits, which absorbed private savings, increased its interest rates, attracted foreign capital, and created a current account deficit of approximately $150 billion. On the other hand, European countries such as Germany, the U.K., Italy, and France that were running budget deficits in the mid-1970s pursued fiscal policies that raised taxes and reduced government expenditures to balance their deficits. While savings for investment became available during the process of budget adjustments, the demand for these funds resulted in high interest rates that were supposed to halt the flight of European capital to the United States.

Modigliani's most updated concerns for the European economy were comprehensively expressed in the European Manifesto.[138] As expected, his Keynesian perspective made him focus mainly on unemployment and the demand side policies. From 1981 to 1990, the average unemployment rate in the EUR 11 and EUR 12 countries was approximately 9 per cent, or 2 per cent above the U.S. rate of 7.1 per cent. From 1991 to 1992, the average unemployment rates increased to 10.4 per cent, or approximately double the U.S. rate of 5.6 per cent.[139] In 1998, the average unemployment rate was about 11 per cent (reflected in 19 million unemployed workers), compared with below 3 per cent rate in the 60s and early 70s in the European economies. The consequence was a waste of resources, through loss of output and saving-investment potential.[140]

Modigliani traced the high unemployment rate in the EMU to the Maastricht Treaty of 7 February, 1992. This treaty tied the hands of policy makers in the EMU by being restrictive in the areas of debts, deficits, monetary, and exchange rate policies to manage employment and growth. The EU started by publishing several criteria regarding fiscal deficit and debt, and by June 1998, the European Central Bank (ECB) took control of monetary policies. A single currency was launched on 1 January, 1999. From the start of the union to the adoption of a single currency, countries followed an Exchange-Rate Mechanism (ERM). The revised mechanism (ERM II) allowed the currencies of countries that did not join the union on 1 January, 1999, to fluctuate from the EURO by 15 per cent. The policy mixes established for managing the EMU called for the European Central Bank (ECB) to control monetary policy and for each member country to control its fiscal policy. This separation of policies required cooperation of a gaming nature between the member countries and ECB. In this game, fiscal policy discretion tended to become expansionary, as each country had an incentive to use the instrument in order to expand its economy. Discretionary monetary policies, on the other hand, tended to be on the tight side, as the ECB's goal was to control inflation. One problem with this approach was that fiscal policy offset the monetary moves. An argument against this suggested that by combining the policies, the levels of output and inflation tend to be more excessive than if the member countries had control of both fiscal and monetary policies.

Modigliani's position was that the consequence of restrictive monetary policies and the separation of fiscal and monetary instruments drove European unemployment higher. An outline of his argument was that unemployment lowered government revenues that decreased government spending on infrastructure. Further, as countries maintained a narrow band on their exchange rates, monetary policies became tight, increasing the interest rate, lowering investment, and, therefore, decreasing employment. Other labor market rigidities that increased unemployment included adoption of minimum wages, and job security measures that discouraged hiring. Modigliani's Keynesian solution was to increase jobs through investment by lowering interest rates.

Modigliani also studied the aggregate unemployment problem of his mother country, Italy. He had performed two empirical tests on the Italian economy, one from 1951 to 1968,[141] and the second from 1960 to 1983.[142] In the post-war period study, 1951–1968, Modigliani viewed Italy as a developing country and tailored the Phillips curve analysis for such a country. The new approach led him to "separate the labour market into three micromarkets. The first related to the employed ... The second included the trained unemployed ... The third included the untrained unemployed."[143] Modigliani modeled a short-term Phillips with the compositions of the unemployed, and for the price variable, he found that "in the Italian economy, the institutional and legal practice is to tie wages explicitly to prices through escalator clauses."[144] He showed that a standard Phillips curve model would underestimate the Italian unemployment rate in 1963 by approximately 20 per cent and reasoned that the curve did not predict well for a country that is in the process of development because, as the trained labor force grows relative to the total labor force, the relationship between the growth of wages and the unemployment rate is not unique. Therefore, a family of Phillips curves is more relevant to a developing country where the shallow pool of trained labor acts as a barrier to development.

In the mid-1970s, the unemployment rate in Italy exceeded that of other OECD countries, and it experienced a balance of payments deficit. The two problems of high unemployment and deficit during the mid-1970s he sourced to high wages that were rising faster than productivity, and that were inconsistent with full employment and the balance of payments constraints. The deficit problem he attributed to the decline in world demand.

Modigliani looked at the possibility of reflation of world demand for Italy's output through some coordinated effort. His idea was that "world economies are not growing fast enough to absorb the growth in the labor force. Most countries still have a labor force that is growing though some are approaching the end of the process."[145] The question as to how to get world demand to increase was left vague. As Modigliani stated, "The paramount problem in the world economy is somehow to get demand moving. Basically, it is the old story that we have learned from Keynes in the '30s."[146] Modigliani found that the export multiplier for the Italian unemployment rate was too small. With a 5 years' lag, it would be around 1.75 per cent, which would require not a 10 per cent but a 50 per cent reflation of world demand for Italy's output to solve their unemployment problems. Simulation results for the Italian economy for the 1980–1983 period suggested that a combination of reflation of world demand and wage cuts would be feasible. The task would still remain formidable for a 15 per cent reflation of world demand for Italy's output, since it would require a 25 per cent cut in real wages.[147]

Modigliani attempted to assess the performance of the Belgian economy as well for the period 1970 to 1976. His methodology for this endeavor is noteworthy. He collected some empirical estimates from various econometric models, and combined them with estimates for the international sector of the Belgian Planning Office's SERENA model. The findings were somewhat disappointing: imprecise estimates, low elasticity between real wages and employment (−0.2) in the short-run and somewhat larger in the long-run (−2), with the implication that exchange rate adjustments would not make much difference for the unemployment picture.

Conclusion

In this chapter, we have explored Modigliani's model in order to investigate stabilization policies. We have seen that he made novel contributions in both the fiscal and monetary policies areas. Both fiscal and monetary policies are vindicated through the need for stabilization policies to adjust for market imperfections. Modigliani stayed within the Keynesian paradigm in his defense of stabilization policies, even when he seemed to be moving to more neutral grounds by admitting in the 1970s that "we are all monetarists now." His steadfast belief in the Keynesian paradigm is maintained on the premise he started with in his 1944 contribution that wage rigidity prevails in the real world, but which Keynes explicitly denied.

Although Modigliani shifted emphasis in his policy arguments, he was not daunted by the rapid evolution of new tools for macroeconomic policies. He adopted the Phillips Curve when it became a major policy tool in the 1960s, and amended it for his own insights on non-inflationary unemployment rate and output levels. Although he is seen as a precursor to the development of the rational expectations hypothesis, he did not embrace it – mainly because it defended policy ineffectiveness. Modigliani saw an important role for stabilization policies because real economies are imperfect. Modern research in the direction of market imperfection is still ongoing, although it is not restricted to the area of oligopoly that Modigliani sanctioned and implemented in the MPS model.

4
The Life Cycle Hypothesis

Introduction

Keynes' consumption function, the absolute income hypothesis, revolutionized economics by shifting macroeconomic analysis from the supply side to the demand side. Total demand includes four major components relating to the household, business, government, and foreign sectors – the areas that have attracted varying degrees of scientific research since the post-WWII period. Modigliani's life cycle hypothesis (LCH) contribution to macroeconomics fits in the domain of household consumption, the only component for which Keynes had advanced a psychological law that "men are disposed, as a rule and on the average to increase their consumption as their income increases, but not by as much as the increase in their income."[1]

Besides income, Keynes made household consumption dependent on other objective and subjective factors. The objective factors are changes in the wage unit, windfall changes in capital values, the rate of interest, taxes, and expectations. Subjective factors include, among other things, unforeseen circumstances, and a future connection between income and the needs of the individual, such as in old age.

During the late 1930s, economists placed a premium value on the scientific research of the consumption function. Researchers explored various forms of the function to ascertain the influences of their estimates. Some found confirmation of Keynes' consumption function, and others found that income has a lagged effect. As with Keynes, Jan Tinbergen[2] found that the influence of the interest rate on consumption was insignificant.

Modigliani's investigation started at the juncture of the prediction of savings, and ended with the development of the life cycle hypothesis (LCH). Modigliani's LCH elevated the importance of income, wealth, and age distribution to explain the discrepancy between short-term and long-term household behavior. In the modern literature, the LCH of savings is a "hypothesis that seems to throw more light on the cross-sectional and historical facts of capital formation than any other single explanation."[3] We aim to investigate such claims in this chapter.

Problems with the absolute income hypothesis

The Keynesian consumption model, despite its revolutionary contribution to the literature, had both theoretical and empirical problems. Over the years, many new specifications of it have emerged. Modigliani's unique extension and articulation of Keynes' original specification is the subject of this section. First, we distinguish between the forms in which the model is confronted with data. Second, we consider the problems of empirical observation on consumption behavior. Finally, we turn to Modigliani's contribution.

Theoretical problems with the estimates of the consumption function

In its simple version, household consumption depends linearly on income, with income measured net of taxes, or disposable income. Keynes wrote, "For whilst the other factors are capable of varying ... the aggregate income measured in terms of the wage-unit is, as a rule, the principal variable upon which the consumption-constituent of the aggregate demand function will depend."[4] Technically speaking, if we approximate the relationship between C for consumption and Y for income, and drop the non-linear terms, the result is $C = a + bY$ where a is autonomous consumption, that is consumption that will take place when income is zero, and b is the marginal propensity to consume (MPC), that is the increase in consumption that results from an increase in one additional dollar of income on the average. In other words, the linear consumption function captures two important ideas – autonomous consumption or consumption not dependent on income which is measured by the intercept of the line, and induced consumption or consumption dependent on income which is measured by the slope of the line.

The advantage of having the consumption hypothesis in linear form is the ease with which we can confront it with data. Keynes intended his model to be testable. He wrote:

> It should not be difficult to compile a chart of the marginal propensity to consume at each stage of a trade cycle. ... The best for the purpose, of which I am aware, are Mr. Kuznets' figures for the United States ... if single years are taken in isolation. The multiplier seems to have been less than 3 and probably fairly stable in the neighborhood of 2.5. This suggests a marginal propensity to consume not exceeding 60 to 70 per cent.[5]

However, research suggested different estimates and other problems, puzzles, and anomalies to solve.

Specifying the consumption function as a line does not imply that a "single equation estimate" would yield the best results. In fact it's well known that such estimates are biased in a statistical sense. Modigliani recognized this. He explained that the bias of a single equation estimate comes from several sources. One source of bias is that "The observed values of the variables that enter into the relevant relation are not determined exclusively by the given equation, but by some or all other equations of the system as well."[6] Bias can also be introduced through omitted information. For instance, Modigliani wanted to study both personal and corporate savings. He decided that corporate savings could not be treated as a predetermined variable. So he accounted for it by defining income to include corporate savings as well. In the end, Modigliani was able to get around the single equation bias estimate by using a two-equation system for savings and income.

Empirical problems with the consumption function

Data made available for the first time by Simon Kuznets,[7] in the form of 13 decile estimates from 1869 to 1938, showed little variation in the ratios. The variation was from 0.84 to 0.89. The implication was that the C/Y, and S/Y ratios are stable. However, other researchers such as A. Smithies[8] found an upward drift of the consumption function over time for several reasons:

1. The migration from farms to cities increased the spending of migrants;
2. Income became more evenly distributed across age groups; and

3. Improvements in the standard of living allowed people to spend a larger proportion of their income on the consumption of high ticket items such as refrigerators and cars.

Smithies thought that the Keynesian model needed a time trend variable to capture the additional variations in consumption he had identified. He made consumption depend on income and time that captures an upward drift in consumption observed in the post- WWII data. According to Modigliani,[9] Smithies' time adjusted consumption function required income per capita to grow approximately $8.8 a year to justify a *C/Y* ratio of 0.89. Since Kuznets' data showed that the average growth of per capita income was $8.5 for his time series sample period, Smithies' time trend variable was used to reconcile the upward drift in the consumption function.

Modigliani then proceeded to show where Smithies' model failed. It failed in its prediction of the *S/Y* ratio from 1940 to 1950. Smithies' formula predicted that real income would increase approximately $40 annually from 1940 to 1950. This implied that the *S/Y* ratio should increase by 20 to 30 per cent more than Kuznets' data indicated. Applying Smithies' formula to the last decade of its sample period, Modigliani found that the model predicted a $16 annual increase in per capita, almost twice the $8.8 rise for the full sample. The corresponding *S/Y* ratio increase for that sub-period was 26 per cent higher than the actual increase. Also, revised data from the Department of Commerce indicated that Smithies' time trend coefficient was much lower – 0.83 instead of the original 1.15. Modigliani concluded that "if we accept Smithies' hypothesis ... we must accept also the hypothesis that the apparent long-run stability of saving-income ratio is essentially due to chance, that is, to the coincidence of the time trend of income with the 'independent' time trend of consumption."[10] He therefore proceeded to advance a counter-hypothesis.

Modigliani's novel contribution to the consumption function

Modigliani's contribution to the consumption function can be viewed from two major stages. In the first stage, he looked for ways to explain and forecast the savings ratio,[11] which he extended in later papers.[12] In the second stage, he developed the LCH, which was one of his contributions that earned him the Nobel Prize in 1985. We examine these contributions in turn.

Predicting the savings ratio

Analyzing the 1930s, Modigliani noted that "the portion of income people choose to save bears a definite and slowly changing relation to this income; therefore, for each level of aggregate income there must be a corresponding level of aggregate saving."[13] From income we determine saving. To realize that saving, investment must generate the income. Pondering these relationships, Modigliani gave us the following hypothesis and its converse about the relationship between income and savings: "If we can estimate the relation between saving and income for every level of income, we will also know what level of investment is required to produce any given level of income. Conversely, if we have a knowledge of the saving income relation and of forthcoming investment, we can then estimate forthcoming income and employment."[14]

In this first stage, Modigliani made clear that the objective of a savings theory was to explain full employment. Examining Jacob Mosak's[15] and Arthur Smithies'[16] forecasts of full employment for 1950, Modigliani found that approximately $30 billion potential savings will be required to generate their forecasts of national income at $195 billion. He was pessimistic about that forecast because investment in 1946 was at its peak level. Catching up from the war it was only about $18 billion, not enough to generate that level of income. Modigliani, therefore, predicted substantial unemployment.[17]

Modigliani thought that his predecessors (Mosak's and Smithies') independent forecasts were off track because they used an old template. He thought that their forecasts were based on the old behavioral patterns of the 1920s and 1930s, with no regard for business cycles. His objective was to layer the explanation of savings with cycle and income distribution theory. In this quest, he foreshadowed the concept of relative income that was being independently formulated by James Duesenberry. Here is Modigliani's version of the relative income effect on savings:

> The proportion of income saved by individuals depends not on the absolute level of their income but rather on their relative position in the income distribution. While it is true that rich people save a large proportion of their income and poor people save little or even dissave, the notion of rich and poor is a relative one; income receivers whose income is well below the average "feel" poor and save little or even dissave, regardless of the absolute income received. As aggregate and average income increase gradually, people rise to higher income brackets. In each bracket; they save less than the previous

> "inhabitants" of a given bracket; they still feel poorer than the people to whose income level they aspired and therefore try to keep up with the latter in spending. Thus the proportion of aggregate income saved tends to remain unchanged.[18]

In addition to relative income, Modigliani added cyclical influences besides absolute income to explain low savings. In a recession, for example, consumption by households is maintained at the cost of savings. The reasons for that are the other components of relative income, (Y_{t-1}/Y_2), dissaving of the unemployed and changes in the income distribution.

Also, in recession, business income tends to be in greater proportion to other incomes, thus leading to a greater fall in personal savings because businesses also save, making the proportion of personal to total savings smaller. Corporate savings behavior is similar to personal savings behavior, as dividend policies tend to regulate business savings in a similar manner as habits regulate personal behavior. In prosperous times, corporations increase dividend payments gradually; in downturns dividend payments come out of accumulated reserves. This way dividend policies are stabilizing factors.

Modigliani has added two independent variables, secular and cyclical movement of income, alongside absolute income to explain variation in the savings ratio. "By the secular movement of income we mean a movement that carries real income per capita above the highest level reached in any preceding year; by cyclical movement we mean any movement, whether upward or downward that leaves real income per capita below the highest previous peak."[19] Both of these effects can be captured by a variable showing the "highest previous level of income."[20]

In symbolic form, Modigliani defined a cyclical income index as $(Y_t - Y_t^0)/Y_t$, where Y_t is real income per capita in current time, and Y_t^0 is the past peak level of such income. If the consumption or savings ratios are regressed on this cyclical index, with a constant term, then the cyclical and secular effect would be captured, respectively. Modigliani's "single equation estimate" for the secular effect was approximately 0.1 per cent, and for the cyclical was approximately 0.125 per cent. Modigliani's "simultaneous equations" estimate yielded a saving-income ratio of 11.5 per cent, and slightly higher, 11.7 per cent, when the 1936–1938 period is omitted. This depended on the growth rate of income. Modigliani concluded that "as the two estimates are within the range of earlier forecasts, we have no reason to modify our conclusion."[21]

How good a model did Modigliani present at the time? Examining the residual of his estimates, Wassily Leontief[22] commented that systematic, rather than random, patterns are inherent in the residual plots. He hypothesized that peak income alone is not an adequate specification for Modigliani's model, and recommended trying lagged income, or a moving average of 5-year lengths. Modigliani responded that such analysis of the existing data at that time did not yield satisfactory results, partly because of the greatly reduced sample size after lags were introduced. Recently, Klein and Ozmucur[23] revisited Modigliani's specification with a much larger sample size and were able to reaffirm the robustness of his model and its findings.

Birth/emergence of the Life Cycle Hypothesis (LCH)

Reflecting on the development of the LCH, Modigliani listed half a dozen propositions about consumption models during the mid-1950s. Some of these propositions overlap with Smithies' three propositions already addressed. Modigliani discussed each and ear-marked two in particular as foundations for the LCH model:[24]

1. *S/Y* is higher in rich countries than poor countries;
2. S is higher for farm families than urban families;
3. Lower status urban families save less than other urban families;
4. If a higher future income is expected, more of current income will be consumed now;
5. In countries with rising income that is expected to continue to increase, the *S/Y* will be smaller;
6. Property income that mostly accrues to the rich is largely saved, whereas wages that are mostly earned by the poor are largely spent.

Underlying these propositions is the idea that the LCH is a conservation concept, meaning that a consumer's lifetime consumption and savings preferences are constrained by their income, bequests, or gifts. Several simplifying assumptions are made. One is that bequests are neither ignored nor expected, making consumption for a particular age cohort proportional to lifetime resources. Modigliani called this the "Elementary LCH"[25] that can be written as $C = \alpha Y$. After the consumption pattern is set, savings is the excess of receipts for a period over an appropriately chosen lifetime consumption path, given the agent's lifetime resources. People do not get direct utility from savings. It is "only the means through which resources are carried back and forth to enforce the chosen consumption path."[26] As he expressed it in his Nobel Laureate award speech, "save it when you need it least; have it when you need it most." The consumption path is based on classical economic theory on how consumers make choices.

In the LCH model, the concept of relative income that Modigliani pursued in his early framework is maintained. Income is high or low relative to a person's lifetime income. Current income can be higher or lower than lifetime income. People fall sick, are sometimes unemployed, work overtime, accumulating human capital through schooling and on-the-job training, and their income on average falls when they are retired.

Income in the LCH is characterized more as a lifetime resource, which can take on a temporary dimension. Modigliani explained that the concept of permanent income in the literature approximates his definition of lifetime income if the time span, such as life, is of a finite duration. People save when they are working, spend when they are old, and make bequests to their children.

Modigliani acknowledged that other theories were constrained by the above-mentioned six points. For instance, he mentioned that points 2, 3, and 4 are also explained by Milton Friedman's permanent income hypothesis.[27] Studying the implication of these propositions against the evidence, Modigliani found that propositions 2 and 4 seem to hold up, and all the others are falsified. For proposition 4, if you expect higher income in the future, you would consider your current income low or below average. Accordingly, you may want to save less than a person who expects future income to be the same as their present income. The evidence that supports proposition 2 is that urban dwellers spend based on the psychological propensity to keep up with their neighbors, while country dwellers are traditionally thriftier.

Modigliani and others have articulated the LCH in many other directions that generated other propositions. In the following section, we consider two broad approaches in the development of his model over time. One approach deals with a stationary situation, the other with growth. While in the early model, empirical evidence was lacking, later as data became available, Modigliani and others confronted the LCH with the evidence. For instance, Modigliani's estimates and models were tested with better statistical techniques of the day and an expanded sample size up to 2004. The result is that "the specification for the 'workhorse' equation has held up well."[28] We turn now to these further developments.

Classical foundation of the LCH

In 1954, Modigliani and Brumberg[29] published a "general analytical framework" to unite an abundance of facts and reconcile theories of the consumption function. They took a classical approach, one that used utility as the objective to maximize, and income, wealth, age, and other broadly defined variables to act as constraints.

According to the LCH, consumers would want to get the most out of their consumption expenditures over a lifetime. They have a rate of time preference, δ, between present and future consumption. If they prefer to consume more at present, then their rate of time preference would be high. The consumer has an incentive to spend less at present because what is not consumed now will grow at a rate of interest in the future. So, both the rate of time preference and the rate of interest are behind the LCH model. They are behind a utility function that the consumer wishes to maximize. Such a function can be stated symbolically as:

$$U = U(c_t, c_{t+1}, \cdots c_L, a_{L+1}) \tag{4.1}$$

where U is utility, c is consumption, t is time, and L is lifetime.

For any person, lifetime resources will naturally limit lifetime consumption. All lifetime resources for every person will have to be discounted to the present and aggregated for the economy in order to understand their lifetime constraint. For instance, if a person expects to earn \$1 next year, and the interest rate is 10 per cent, then the income from that investment at the present time is \$1 = \$10/(1+r). To apply that little knowledge to the consumer's expected future earnings and consumption, we assume that all consumers spend the same way, regardless of their age or income distribution, then we can sum over their income to aggregate consumption for the whole economy. The aggregate consumption constraint will be expressed as: Initial wealth + Expected future earnings = End of period wealth + Consumption.
Or, symbolically:

$$a_t + \sum_{\tau=t}^{N} \frac{y_t}{(1+r)^{\tau+1-t}} = \frac{a_{L+1}}{(1+r)^{L+1-t}} + \sum_{\tau=1}^{L} \frac{c_\tau}{(1+r)^{\tau+1-t}} \text{[30]} \tag{4.2}$$

where c is consumption, y is income, a is asset, r is interest, L is lifespan, t is time, and τ refers to periods of time marking expected income and planned consumption.

Maximizing equation 4.1 subject to equation 4.2 solves the consumer maximization problem for the LCH. Just as a person eating a burger meal tries to maximize utility of the meal by eating it in a unique way – taking a bite of the burger then a sip of the soda and eating a few fries, so too the consumer would want to allocate his/her consumption over time in a unique way in order to maximize utility. What we wish to get out of the solution is an expression that shows the consumer obtaining the same marginal utility from consumption over its lifetime. Symbolically:

$$E[MU(c_{t+1})] = \left(\frac{1+\delta}{1+r}\right) MU(c_t) \tag{4.3}$$[31]

The expression explains that we expect, E, the individual will equate his/her marginal utility, MU, over different time periods, t, given their rate of time preference, δ, and the rate of interest, r. Two inequalities may prevail that would start the adjustment of marginal utility equalization. They are:

$$y_t + ra_t \neq c_t \tag{4.4}$$

$$y_\tau + ra_\tau \neq \overline{c}_\tau \tag{4.5}$$

In the first inequality, ra_t is the return on assets, and the individual will save or dissave as consumption exceeds or falls short of resources. In the second inequality, the individual will be *planning* to save or dissave. The motives for saving specify what direction the inequalities will take. Modigliani listed four motives. One is that saving is done to "benefit one's heirs." The other is that preferred consumption will not be supported by current and expected income. A third motive is precautionary savings, and the fourth is uncertainty. When a consumer owns an asset such as a house, it can satisfy several of the motives for savings. A house may be transferred to an heir, it can provide future income for retirement, or it can be a source of funds for emergency. In order to study some of these motives, we need to have an equation for empirical testing. Simply put, consumption depends on both income and wealth. But Modigliani had many other ways to express this simple relationship.

Specification of the LCH for empirical analysis

For the first time in 1966, Modigliani gave a "humpback" diagrammatic view of his hypothesis.[32] Savings will accumulate in the shape of a camel's back, peaking at the date the person retires, and drawn down gradually until the person is dead, i.e., mortality rate is one. In that scenario, consumption is uniform, a fixed line as a function of time, expressed as:

$$C(T) = \frac{N}{L}\overline{Y} \tag{4.6}$$

As equation 6 is pivotal for the LCH, an explanation of the variables Modigliani used, the meaning of the apparatus, and some essential implications follow:

1. Figure 4.1 shows that L and N are measured on horizontal or age axis, T. The letter L is the number of years the representative individual lives; $N < L$ is the number of years the individual earns labor income. Upon retirement, an individual will stop earning labor income.
2. Income, Y, is measured on the vertical axis along with consumption, C, and assets, A. Average income, $\overline{Y}$, is represented by a flat line, $Y(T)$ up to N, which falls to zero after N, when the individual retires. Since income is earned for N periods, lifetime income is NY.
3. Savings is defined as the excess of $Y(T)$ over $C(T)$. It is positive up to N, because income falls to zero after that point. $C(T)$ is below the income line, and it continues after N to L, or in the interval $M = L - N$, when no income is earned and dissaving takes place. A major assumption about consumption is that it is done uniformly over a person's lifetime. The advantage of this is that the person will be able to minimize the diminishing return from consumption in a period of plenty by transferring some consumption to a period of little consumption.

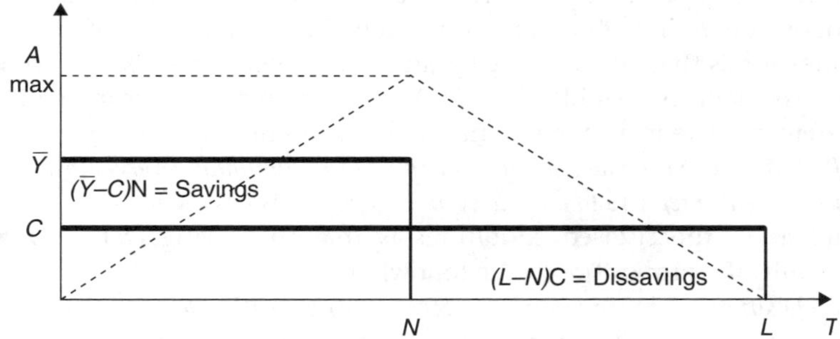

Figure 4.1 Modigliani's Life Cycle Hypothesis

4. Because consumption levels will be uniform over time, CL will represent lifetime consumption. Since lifetime consumption must equal lifetime income, assuming no bequest, then $CL = NY$, or $C = (N/L)Y$, which for each time period gives the equation $C(T) = (N/L)\bar{Y}$ above.
5. By assumption, the only source of dissaving is saving. Therefore, saving = dissaving, which can be seen by equating the expressions for the two areas. From $(\bar{Y} - C)N = (L - N)C$, we obtain $N\bar{Y} = CL$, and since the area CN is common to the two areas, then savings and dissavings are equal.

A further development of the LCH is to add wealth to it. In the description thus far, we may assume that a dollar saved is a dollar of wealth that is accumulated. In other words, saving is dollar-for-dollar, the creation of wealth. To further simplify the model, we assume that wealth does not earn interest, which makes it possible to avoid calculating compound interest at this point. The area of dissaving, $(L-N)C$, represents the total consumption that will take place from accumulated savings. It is also the maximum amount of wealth, i.e., Max(A) = $(L-N)C$, which is marked on the vertical axis. Modigliani preferred to substitute the value of $C = (N/L)\bar{Y}$, and then calculate the area of the wealth triangle using half of the base times height. For that, it follows that the wealth to income ratio is: $A/Y = (L-N)/2 = M/2$.

We can now examine some of Modigliani's propositions under four stylized assumptions: 1. Income is constant up to retirement, and zero after that, 2. Interest rate is zero, 3. Consumption is constant over lifetime, and 4. No bequest. Some major implications of the model then follow:

Proposition (Wealth to Income): The main parameters that control the wealth-income ratio and the saving rate for given growth is the prevailing length of retirement.[33] The wealth-income proposition leads to another proposition under stationary conditions. The implication of the last expression is that given average years in retirement, the wealth income ratio is half of that. Goldsmith's findings concerning a 10-year length of retirement were incorporated into Modigliani's proposition.

Proposition (No Bequest): An economy can accumulate a very substantial stock of wealth relative to income even if no wealth is passed on by bequests.[34] Implicit in the stylized conditions is that the savings rate is zero. Formally, the proposition is the following:

Proposition (Zero Saving): Between countries with identical individual behavior the aggregate savings rate will be higher, the higher the long-run growth rate of the economy. It will be zero for zero growth.[35]

The zero savings proposition follows from the fact that what is saved during the labor income earning age is spent during retirement. As the wealth-income ratio is $A/Y = (L-N)/2 = M/2$, wealth cannot get beyond $A = MY/2$, except through a shock that would push wealth upwards. Like any shock, a wealth shock will not be permanent, but will converge back to its equilibrium level over time.

Modigliani then considered his model under stationary and growth situations. Some other propositions can be established under a growing economy. Working with Modigliani's several representations of variables,[36] the savings-income ratio can be made to grow from the following definition:

$$s \equiv \frac{S}{Y} = \frac{\Delta A A}{A\ Y} = p\frac{A}{Y} \equiv pa \tag{4.7}$$

Equation 4.7 merges several notations of Modigliani's. The growth of the economy is measured as p, which is taken to be the growth of wealth in a stationary economy. The wealth-income ratio, a, is dependent on the LCH.

From stationary conditions, the value of p in equation 4.7 will be zero, implying that the savings-income ratio will be zero as well. However, Modigliani proceeded with the wealth-income approach because "it is most conducive to an understanding of the complex channels through which social security and (average) retirement age can affect saving and wealth."[37] We can show this representation as follows. To indicate the effect of social security benefits, we have:

$$Y = N(e - t) + SST = Ne + \lambda Mc \tag{4.8}$$

where e is the accrual of income at a constant rate, t is the social security tax rate, c is the constant level of consumption, M is the years of retirement, and λ is a proportional constant. From equation 4.8, savings up to the point a person retires will proceed at a constant rate, $e - t - c$, that is, a savings rate that reflects an adjustment to income accrual, represented by social security taxes and consumption. After retirement and until a person dies, savings will be drawn down at a constant rate as well. That rate will be the average social security benefits that are received less that fraction of social security income that is consumed, $SST/M - \lambda c$.

Simulating the LCH

A simulation model requires elaborate set up considerations. What Modigliani was interested in was mainly a validation of the LCH. With his simulation, Modigliani reflected that the LCH was "much later to be dubbed 'overlapping generation.'"[38] He proceeded to demonstrate this with his five-period simulation model. The simulations are done for a stationary and a growing economy. Stationary is defined as a situation whereby each generation's expected income in the future is equal to the income it received in the past, say 20 units per decade. A growing economy means that while each generation gets the same income, the income doubles each decade.[39]

Econometric results of the LCH

The econometric version requires us to add a wealth variable. A proposition about the behavior of wealth as savings is that it peaks in the period of the person's working age when income is highest, with the corollary that consumption is made uniform from the saving and dissaving of wealth.

In reality, wealth is not all from savings. Some people inherit wealth. Let the initial stock of 11wealth be A0. A person at some point in life, τ, will make the following consumption expenditure:

$$(L - \tau)C = A + (N - \tau)Y \tag{4.9}$$

Solving for consumption gives an expression of $C = (\alpha_1 + \alpha_2)Y + \alpha_3 A$.[40] A model of consumption dependent on income and assets becomes here the basis of scientific testing for the LCH model.

Testing and predicting the early LCH

The testing of the LCH model evolved particularly in line with the accumulation of data. In the past, income and assets data were crude in form. Brumberg[41] broached the empirical test in terms of saving depending on income, expected income, and assets. We are aware through a priori knowledge that the coefficients must be positive, but the levels of the coefficients are uncertain. A short-run coefficient for the sum of current and expected income should be in the 70 per cent range, with the understanding that lifetime income is much larger. The asset variable would have an intercept effect, lifting the consumption function upward during a boom, and lowering it during a recession. Data problems abound in terms of how to measure assets and expected income. A first measure of assets is past period savings plus capital gain. An index of stock prices could be a surrogate for capital gains, as the latter are not easily available. The idea of rational expectations had not been born at the time Modigliani made his definition of expected income. The fall back was to look at the change in income as a guide. These data problems were overwhelming, thus resulting in weak results. Perhaps the weakest part was that the income coefficients were of the wrong signs. The premature death of Brumberg one year later in 1954 put further research of the LCH model on the shoulders of Modigliani.

The work by Ando and Modigliani[42] marked the next major milestone in testing the LCH. Among the novelties of their test is a modified definition of expected income, and the addition of the unemployment variable. Their first hypothesis makes expected income approximately equal to current income adjusted by a scale factor equal to the inverse of employment. This definition has several implications for the unemployed; the most important is that their expected income will be equal to those who are employed. After several trials, the new test involved fitting consumption on current income, the ratio of the labor force to employment times current income, and previous period assets.[43]

Ando and Modigliani experimented with several specifications of the LCH. In taking a first step away from the Keynesian absolute income approach, they had separated income into labor income and non-labor or property income. This result did not give a significant coefficient for the property income variable. However, it reinforced their use of a net worth variable as a measure of the wealth effect because they could now proceed with defining assets as net worth, and not worry that it was a measure of property income. Property income could, therefore, be thought of as having a transitory effect.

The major finding of Ando and Modigliani was that consumption depends on current labor income and total assets. Income changes have permanent effects on consumption, while asset changes have temporary effects – permanent reflects all future income, and temporary represents a one-time capital gain such as from the stock market. Applying this model to post-WWII data yields the following results:[44]

$$\begin{array}{l} C = .766Y + .073A \\ \quad\quad (.134) \quad (.020) \\ R^2 = .995 \quad\quad DW = 1.63 \end{array} \tag{4.10}$$

The result of this specification is that the relation between consumption and income in a period can be separated because a person's planned consumption is for the balance of the person's life, while a person's income for that period is only one element influencing such a plan.

In 1963, Ando and Modigliani advanced the development of the LCH model a further step. They explained the need to "generate the type of hypothesis that can be easily tested against time series data."[45] It is worth noting that the earlier Modigliani and Brumberg version was concerned more with cross-section data, whereas this latter version that used time series data presented new problems and challenges.

In 1966, Modigliani attached some dynamic components to the LCH. One dynamic effect is the rate of population change, p.[46] If the size of the age cohorts grows at the rate p, then population and income will grow at the same rate. Younger households who accumulate will increase relative to older households who dissave, increasing the net savings. As a result, savings and wealth will grow at the rate p. Given $S = sY$; $A = aY$, the savings-income will grow at the rate p. However, the relative increase of the younger age group is expected to make the asset-income ratio negatively associated with p. Regarding the saving-asset ratio, since S/A grows at the rate, p, then $S = pA$.; $S/Y = pA/Y = s = pa$. Taking the total derivative, and considering that assets change negatively with population growth, then s should rise with p.

Another dynamic aspect of the model is discerned by holding population stationary and allowing productivity to increase. The model predicts a positive savings rate and increases in wealth. Successive cohorts will get larger income from which they will spend more. Their target level of consumption for retirement will be higher than the preceding generation, implying a higher level of saving. A further boost to saving will occur as the tendency to dissave will be less than the tendency to save.

Modigliani was able to reach some generalizations about the saving-income and the wealth-income ratios, consequent to the rate of growth of population, p, and productivity, y. He concluded that "the saving ratio and the rate of growth is quite similar whether the growth is due to population only, productivity only, or, consequently, some mixture of the two."[47]

Modigliani demolished the idea that the wealth-income ratio is just a surrogate for the capital-output ratio. Starting with the naïve accelerator which postulates that the capital-output ratio is constant, he wanted to tell

> whether this stability reflected the accumulation and wealth holding pattern resulting from the life cycle mechanism leading in turn to the

> choice of technologies having the appropriate capital intensity; or whether, instead, it reflected rigid technological requirements leading, through some other mechanism, to the accumulation and holding of the appropriate amount of wealth.[48]

He concluded that the long-run stability of the wealth-income ratio is not explained by the naïve accelerator, but by the forces of the LCH. Rather, the constancy of the capital-output ratio is partly explained by the LCH based on stable long run growth trends.[49]

Another dynamic implication of the LCH is in regard to the national debt. When people hold the national debt, *G*, their net worth, *A*, is expected to be reduced by that amount. Modigliani proposed to test the hypothesis of the influence of *G* on *A*, when income varies around a stable growth trend. His conclusion was that "the national debt has tended to displace private tangible wealth roughly on a dollar per dollar basis."[50] However, the impact need not be one-to-one if other tangibles, acting as a wedge, pick up some of the influence *G*. Modigliani estimated that other tangibles could attenuate the effect of *G* by as much as 30 per cent.[51]

Modigliani also looked for evidence from the international scene. In 1970, he amassed a cross section of 36 countries to perform various tests on the LCH.[52] Modigliani borrowed Houthakker's[53] methodology to account for variations in savings across countries. Modigliani first tested a counterfactual to his LCH, namely that the proportion of income saved is dependent on per capita income, but found no evidence for it. Rather, the age structure defined in terms of the ratios of the retired to the labor force, and the minors to the labor force were significant in explaining the savings-income ratio. In summary, age structure and income growth were the most significant explanatory variables of the LCH at the international level.

As the model developed, four assumptions became discernible.[54] First, the homogeneous assumption indicates that an additional dollar is allocated to consumption by the same proportion of previous dollars. Second, the individual does not expect to receive or give any inheritance. Third, consumption is evenly spread over a person's remaining lifetime. Fourth, the rate of return on assets is constant over time. The result is a model of age-dependent-consumption responding to resources and the rate of return on capital. Its influence reverberated in macroeconomics in the areas of growth theory, policy analysis, pension and social security, inter and overlapping generation theories.

The novelty claims include the stunning statement that "*the proportion of income saved is essentially independent of income,*"[55] [Italics original]. We at once see its breakaway from the Keynesian psychological law of savings. The separation of savings from income occurred because of observed systematic deviation of *S/Y* from a normal level. Such unsteady relation appears because savings are done either to cushion variation in income or for precautionary and retirement motives.[56]

Reconciling long and short-term consumption

An observation that struck the consumption theorist in the mid 1950s was that the savings-ratio and income were not correlated in the long-run. Studying the savings behavior of the U. S., Richard Goldsmith made this remarkable discovery:

> The main enduring characteristic and chief structural changes of savings in the United States during the past half century (disregarding distortions during wars) may be restated with the utmost brevity and not without unavoidable over implication as follows: (a) Long-term stability of aggregate personal savings at approximately one-eight of income, and or national savings at approximately one-seventh.[57]

The long-term measure for the MPC was closer to 1. A big effort in the Keynesian literature ensued to reconcile the two estimates, and in 1985, Modigliani's idea of the LCH became a Nobel Prize answer to that puzzle. Early attempts were made to justify Keynes' psychological law of consumption. A budget study of regressed average consumption on average income for 1929 found that the MPC in the U.S. ranges from 0.50 to 0.69 for non-farm, farm, total, and unattached individuals.[58]

One simple arithmetic way of viewing the reconciliation is to use the finding of the wealth to income ratio equal to $(L-N)/2$. As Modigliani wrote, "for an earning span of, say, forty years, and a life span of fifty years (from the date of entering the labor force), aggregate wealth in our stationary society would come to five times annual income."[59] We can use equation 4.8 to illustrate this arithmetic. We keep in mind that we wish to reconcile the short run MPC that takes on values between 70–80 per cent, and the long-run MPC that takes on values close to 100 per cent. If we assume that labor income is approximately 80 per cent of personal disposable income, and assets are approximately 5 times income, then by substitution into equation 4.8 above we get a long-run MPC of approximately $0.98 = 0.8(.766Y) + 5(.073Y)$.

The essential reconciling attribute of the LCH is that change in the assets component shifts upwards the consumption function. Equations 4.7 and 4.8 can explain the increase in the consumption function in the post-WWII period when the accumulation of wartime savings led to the accumulation of assets. Also, the drop in the stock market in 1973, which led to a drop in the market value of assets, can explain the slowdown in consumption. The presence of the wealth variable also helps to explain the effect of the 1987 stock market crash on consumption. This is an important point, in that some economists ask for the justification of wealth in the consumption function. The stock market lost approximately $500 billion in value on 19 October, 1987. If the estimated coefficient of wealth is 0.073 in equation 4.8, then the model predicts that consumption should decrease by approximately $36.5 billion (500*.073). However, consumption actually declined by nearly twice that amount by approximately $66 billion, since people saved more, perhaps because of the uncertainty about future events. Thus, the presence of the assets component in the consumption function was more than justified. The signs of the parameters of the model are correct, but its levels are low because some variables are omitted. To enhance its prediction, and perhaps to be able to predict more complex phenomena, such as the bubble during the Clinton-Gore 1995–96 period, we need to look at newer developments in the LCH.

New directions of research on LCH

Uncertainty

The area of uncertainty, such as during the 1987 stock market crash, has plagued many models. According to equation 4.3, the LCH model equates marginal utilities for age cohorts over time, which requires knowledge of future marginal utilities. But neither future marginal utilities nor future consumptions are known for certain. The model of REH has some suggestions on how to deal with uncertainty.

Modigliani's contribution to the consumption function continues as a live research program in the current literature. A 2003 Nobel Laureate in economics had this to say on the testing of Robert Hall's theory of consumption in terms of the life cycle and other income hypotheses: "The theory was like manna from heaven to macro-econometricians. It was easily stated and understood, and appears to be easy to test."[60] Central to this model is the fact that consumption follows a random walk model where the expected next period consumption should be equal to current consumption. In practical parlance, consumers will tend to adjust their individual consumption so that it will not differ from an expected level. This fact reinforces the underlying principle that consumers tend to smooth out spending over time, and that this practice relates to some uncertainty about income. If consumers have a quadratic utility function, then they will want to consume at the level where their future income will equal its mean value.[61]

The major breakthrough in applying expectations to LCH has been the contributions of Robert Hall, who is said to have the best approach to uncertainty in consumption. The essence of Hall's model is that whatever level of consumption one expects in the future can turn out wrong only by some surprising events. This is a breakthrough because we expect surprise to be random, and consequently to take on the properties of a random error very much like the properties we attribute to the error term in regression analysis. Hall expressed it this way:

> [Modigliani] formulated a simple empirical test of the idea that consumers maximize the expected value of lifetime utility subject to an unchanging real interest rate. The basic idea is to look at the Euler equation describing the optimal behavior of such a consumer. The Euler equation characterizes the equality of the marginal rate of substitution between consumption this year and consumption next year to the relative price of the two. That relative price is simply the present discounted cost of a unit of future consumption.[62]

The Euler equation has the form of equation 4.3, which is a solution to the consumer maximizing problem. Hall tested the Euler equation directly in the form of $C_{t+1} = \lambda C_t + error_t$. The information to test future consumption is inherent in the consumption data itself. The name for such a model is random walk. Flavin,[63] a student of Hall, had studied the implications of this model for the LCH. One finding is that future consumption is sensitive to the previous level of consumption and can show a strong variation. However, another finding is that the surprise element does not cause much variation in future consumption. Campbell and Mankiw[64] had the great idea of combining these two elements in a convex way. This means that a proportion of the variation will be captured. Following Hall's model, the surprise element varies by a certain proportion and thus income will explain the less than proportional expected consumption. A combination of Hall's model with the LCH consumption such as equation 4.6 above is possible. The end result is a simple test of a change in consumption based on a change in disposable income.

Liquidity

Among the factors that threaten the LCH, liquidity is frequently cited. Central to the LCH is the assumption that consumers will smooth consumption over a lifetime. The liquidity constraint threatens this assumption. It holds that consumers may not be able to smooth their consumption because they have few assets, the assets may be illiquid, or they may have credit problems that prevent them from borrowing. In general, the liquidity constraint will prevail when the credit market is imperfect. Hall and Mishkin[65] found that up to approximately 20 per cent of consumption expenditures may be so constrained. Subsequent tests have given credence to that estimate. Mariger,[66] and Jappelli[67] established that it is approximately 19.4 and 19 per cent, respectively.

Modigliani was concerned that "significant liquidity constraints could affect quantitatively certain specific conclusions, e.g. with respect to temporary tax changes."[68]A recent example of such temporary tax changes was President George W. Bush's *Economic Growth and Tax Relief Reconciliation* Act of 2001 (EGTRRA). It was designed to end in 2010. However, there is a strong drive to make its provisions permanent before its 10-year expiration date. Modigliani and Steindel[69] argued from the LCH point of view that to stimulate the economy through transitory income taxes or rebates would have a small effect on consumption. They reasoned that consumption depends on lifetime resources that are not significantly affected through temporary tax changes. Basically, their evidence came from examining predictions made by the LCH in the specification used by the MIT-Penn-Social Science Research Council-MPS econometric model. In that model, consumption equations were fitted for both durable and nondurable goods. The finding was that "through 1975 the response is consistently about half as large as the predicted one, a result reminiscent of the 1968–69 experiment."[70] Again, studying the 1964 and 1968 tax changes, "from the second half of 1968 to the end of 1969, the reduction in consumption was roughly half as large as it would have been had the tax been permanent."[71] In the case of President George W. Bush's tax cuts, Modigliani was one among 10 Nobel laureates, and over 400 economists, who signed a statement opposing the Bush tax cut.[72]

Myopia

In order to smooth out consumption over a lifetime, consumers need to possess a strong measure of foresight and understanding. However, they may be short-sighted rather than forward-looking; able to deal only with current and not lifetime income. This myopic view would run counter to the LCH because planning for a lifetime is required. Modigliani argued that as the assets held at the peak of the life cycle are approximately five times average income, the evidence that consumers are myopic is not empirically valid. He declared that "such a multiple appears broadly consistent with the maintenance of consumption after retirement."[73]

Bequest

Perhaps through love, or through miscalculation, the elderly have been leaving savings to their younger generations. Therefore, dissaving seems modest in retirement age and the wealth-saving ratio seems to appreciate. Modigliani estimated that approximately 20 per cent of wealth is inherited.[74]

Bequests present a problem for economic models because it seems inconsistent with the idea that people consume in order to gain utility. The plan to leave an inheritance implies a marginal utility equal to zero. Also, we assume the individual is planning consumption over one's own lifetime, and not the joint lifetime of himself/herself and the heirs. However, Modigliani hypothesized that life savings, LS, tend to increase with income, Y, and decrease with the bequest received, BR. This implies that the humped saving diagram must show an increase in the wealth path to account for BR. With positive growth, we could see higher savings, higher wealth-income and saving-income ratios.[75]

Modigliani did not think that the bequest motive was significant. He reviewed evidence that mainly the "highest economic classes" are likely to leave an estate behind. Bequest is not a precautionary motive because it seems to rise with wealth. He wrote that "because overall share of inherited wealth can be placed below 1/5, we seem safe in concluding that the overwhelming proportion of wealth existing at a given time is the result of the life cycle accumulation."[76]

To further clarify the role of bequest in LCH, Modigliani distinguished between private and annuity wealth.[77] Private wealth is subject to bequest, while annuity at best can be passed on to a survivor. If the elderly do not draw down their inherited wealth during their retirement, then we can say that they have a bequest motive. However, in the case of Italy, Modigliani found that private wealth, too, is subject to being trimmed down during retirement, which led him to fall back on the earlier explanation for bequest, namely that it is the rich that practice inheritance.

LCH vs. Permanent Income Hypothesis (PIH)

Many modern studies tend to use the LCH as synonymous with the permanent income hypothesis (PIH), without drawing a distinction. Milton Friedman, the originator of the PIH defined "transitory income" as the difference between current and lifetime income. He delineated the following model:

$$C_p = k(i,w,u)Y_p$$

$$Y = Y_p + Y_t$$

$$C = C_p + C_t \tag{4.11}$$

Where p is permanent income, t is transitory income, i is interest rate, and u is taste and preference. One implication of these PIH equations is that consumption based on permanent income will be constant if the bracket items are constant over time.

Equation 4.11 takes on an infinite income horizon. Permanent income is a measure of past income. How far back in the past should we go? It could be one period, or way back to negative infinity. In estimating consumption, Friedman actually suggested a 17th degree distributed lag in income. The lag in income is therefore a distinguishing feature of the PIH. We need only to note that Modigliani dealt with a finite horizon, whereas Friedman dealt with an infinite horizon.

Although we have permanent and transitory phenomena, we expect consumption to be smooth over time. Temporary effects are not easy to figure out. If you get paid for overtime, or a once in a while Christmas bonus, you may consider that income temporary. The tax cut in 1964 by President John F. Kennedy was permanent. The one year tax surcharge passed by President Johnson in 1968, and the ERTRRA tax cut in 2001 by President George W. Bush are clearer examples of transitory phenomena. Because transitory income is consumed over many years, its effect on consumption may not be felt. One way to distinguish temporary from permanent in reality is to plot the percentage change of per capita income and consumption over time. One notices that while the change in income has many sharp spikes, the change in consumption does not react to those spikes, and is rather uniform over time. Therefore, we can assert that transitory income has a negligible effect on consumption.

According to Modigliani, Friedman assumed that the life of the individual is infinite, and that the representative consumer expects to get a constant flow of income over that infinite duration, which he called permanent income. The consumer intends to consume from permanent income at a uniform rate. The excess of lifetime income over current income is transitory income. Saving depends on this transitory income in the short-run, but is independent of the permanent income. "A fundamental implication of both models is the hypothesis that the share of permanent income consumed – and therefore the proportion saved – is independent of all sizes of permanent income: Families with a high level of permanent or lifetime income save, on average, a fraction of this income similar to that saved by permanently poor families."[78]

To get around the dilemma of permanent versus temporary income, we need a pragmatic approach. The literature suggests that we should estimate permanent income as a measure of past income plus a change in income from the past to the current period. This solves two problems: the last period income persists in the future, and the consumer will not likely treat the increase in income as being permanent. Having defined permanent income, we can now make consumption a function of it. If we do not tack on the unique features of the LCH, we can understand what is meant by merging the two to get LCH-PIH. The most unique variable of the LCH is the inclusion of the wealth variable. Therefore, past income, change in income, and wealth would be a minimum requirement for both the LCH and PIH.

Some aspects of the LCH will remain at variance with the PIH. The LCH gives much emphasis on the savings factor as opposed to the PIH. According to Modigliani, "from the life-cycle hypothesis, you have a rich set of consequences. At the *micro* level, you have all the consequences of "permanent income," including the fact that consumption depends upon (is proportional to) permanent income, while savings depends basically on transitory income: The high savers are not the rich, but the temporary rich (i.e., rich relative to their own normal income),"[79] [Italics original]. In essence, the PIH, by postulating an infinite life horizon, ignores the life-cycle effect of savings, varying over youth, middle age, retirement, and through death, bequest.

Another difference between LCH and PIH is in relation to growth. In PIH, growth leads to a decrease in saving because it sets up the expectation that future income will exceed current income, allowing people to spend more currently. But it is the hallmark of LCH that it does not depend on current income, but on life cycle income. Since the lifetime is finite in LCH, people calculate that they would dissave when they retire and so they save when income grows, the opposite of what is predicted by the PIH.

LCH vs. the Relative Income Hypothesis

We must also give credit to another development of parallel research on the consumption function. Modigliani[80] stated that while he was developing his version in the 1940s, reconciling the cyclical variation of the saving rate with the stability indicated from long- term data, James Duesenberry was also working on a similar model, the relative income hypothesis that relates consumption to both current and previous peak income. Central to this hypothesis is that "the propensity to save of an individual can be regarded as a rising function of his percentile position in the income distribution."[81] In other words, an individual's propensity to save depends on relative income, or past consumption behavior has an influence on present consumption. These arguments amount to two basic propositions: The consumption of a family is related to the consumption pattern of another family, and consumption patterns are irreversible over time – the past influences the future.

To illustrate Duesenberry's argument, consider the effect of a change of income on consumption. If income falls, then, by the first proposition, the family will try to maintain the current level of consumption either through borrowing or dissaving. In the second proposition, the family is influenced by its previous peak disposable income, and it acts to maintain and eventually rise above the peak income.

Duesenberry's work was done independently of Modigliani's LCH and Friedman's PIH, yet they all solve a common problem. As with the LCH and PIH, Duesenberry's relative income hypothesis reconciled short- and long-term observations on the MPC. Duesenberry[82] gave the saving-income ratio as relating to current-initial income ratio by an intercept of negative 0.196, and a slope of 0.25. From this it follows that if income grows at a rate of 0.03 per cent, then consumption will be 1.196–0.25(1.03), making the long-run MPC equal to about 0.94.

Similarly, Modigliani provided the saving-income ratio as relating to the cyclical income ratio by an intercept of 0.098, and a slope of 0.125. His consumption function was $C_t = 0.902Y_t - 0.125(Y_t - Y_0)$. If income grows secularly, then the intercept will approximate zero, and the MPC will be 0.902 in the long run. Without growth, there will be no deviation in the second term, leaving the initial level of income constant. The consumption function will therefore be: $C_t = 0.777Y_t - 0.125Y_0$. The short-run MPC of 0.777 is therefore less than the long-term MPC of 0.902, reconciling the discrepancy between cyclical variation in the savings rate with long-term data.

Because of their similarities, the early form of Modigliani's consumption function, and Duesenberry's version were referred to as the

Duesenberry-Modigliani hypothesis. While Duesenberry was content to base his hypothesis on the psychological justification that people in a downswing will maintain a high consumption in order to keep up appearances, Modigliani went on to give his model a more classical foundation.

Policy implications of LCH

Modigliani listed some major areas of policy where LCH is involved. In the short-run, LCH is an economic model to be used for stabilization policy. On the monetary side, aggregate demand is affected through the market value of assets and consumption. On the fiscal side, transitory tax cuts will have only a small effect on consumption.

In the long-run, a tax on consumption rather than income would be more equitable. Consumption is made out of permanent income. Taxing consumption may have some effect on savings, but it approximates permanent income better then current income. Modigliani also mentioned deficit financing in the short and longrun. If government expenditures are financed by taxes, the current generation pays, and if it is financed by deficit, then the future will pay. According to Modigliani, "government debt displaces capital in the portfolio of households and hence in the economy."[83] Assuming that gross saving is equal to gross investment allowing for depreciation but no net savings, in such a stationary situation, if government expenditures take away from the savings that would replace capital, then debt financing will reduce the capital and income of the future generation. However, it will not reduce the net wealth of the individuals because a part of their wealth will now be held in the form of government debt.[84] A tax on government financing on the other hand will decrease consumption, savings, and private capital and its burden will be borne by the generation being taxed.

Modigliani refined the above arguments in several ways. He held that the argument for the stationary state also applies to a growing economy.[85] However, rival theories such as the Ricardian equivalence, have led to some unsettling debates on the empirical front of the LCH. We have noted that with deficit financing, net wealth is not affected. With government deficit financing, the public may hold a government bond. The Ricardian equivalence theory asks whether government bonds are net wealth. The answer is in the negative because a government bond is not considered net wealth, since it has to be paid back later by increases in taxes. Barro[86] has advanced the Ricardian theory from the point of view of bequest and the absence of liquidity constraints. It holds that when deficit financing takes place, the private sector will then save more to offset the effect it might have on future generations. The implication is that the current generation is particularly concerned about its heirs. Modigliani took the position that "Barro's theorem, despite its elegance, has no substance."[87] Modigliani tested this theorem for data during the Reagan tax cut from 1981 to 1992. The federal debt had increased by 3.25 per cent, and income by 117 per cent. Net wealth also should have expanded by that amount, but the LCH predicted that it expanded by 94 per cent. In actual fact, net wealth expanded by 88 per cent, which approximates 94 per cent. Modigliani concluded that the difference (117−94 = 23%) was due to crowding out, but the Barro model does not consider this.

Finally, research has made it evident that most assets are in the "locked-up" form, such as retirement programs, mortgages, life insurance, and social security. " ... (A)s long as families can make full use of locked-up accounts, their actual behavior will be almost the same as predicted by the life-cycle model."[88]

Conclusion

In this chapter, we traced Modigliani's research on the consumption function over time. While each stage had its comparable rival research, such as the relative income hypothesis, the permanent income hypothesis, and adaptations for rational expectations analysis, Modigliani's hypothesis stands out for its unique features. Even the secular and cyclical features of his earliest 1944 model are still validated in its predictive ability in a recent update by Klein and Ozmucur.

By adding the classical aspects to the LCH model, Modigliani gave it a firm foundation for future research. Its novel contribution is the inclusion of wealth along with current income in the consumption function. The model took a long time to be accepted because the data were slow in evolving. Research is ongoing, based on the model's prediction for social security, bequest, liquidity constraints, myopia, and intergenerational phenomena. The model remains distinct for its explanation of saving behavior over a life cycle and has advantages over the PIH. It also foreshadows research in intergenerational analysis that is widespread in the current literature.

The LCH added many other novelties to the original Keynesian absolute income hypothesis. Because people's spending depends on expected income over a lifetime, and not just current income, we can explain how they react to expectations. If they have favorable expectations of lifetime income, they would consume more at present. Their spending is also determined by age, wealth, and states of the economy – boom, bust, stationary, and growth conditions. The model predicts that small effects result from temporary income such as were effected during the 1970s, 1980s, and recently by the ERTRRA 2001 temporary tax relief. Modigliani used the Reagan tax policies, in particular, to validate the LCH prediction compared to more modern models such as the Ricardian Equivalence theory.

5
Modigliani and Miller's (M&M) Hypothesis

Introduction

Integral to the Keynesian paradigm in economic theory is the study of how investment affects the economy. The Keynesian investment demand schedule relates an aggregate investment to a riskless rate of interest. Modigliani felt that the Keynesian model of investment was inadequate, since it did not deal with uncertainty, and it focused mainly on debt. Financial and managerial economists were more interested in the cost of capital vs. risk. They wanted to extrapolate the idea of uncertainty to the maximization of profit and the value of the firm.[1]

Modigliani realized that under uncertainty, profit maximization lacks operational meaning. The concept cannot be well defined. Models of uncertainty under profit maximization yield multiple solutions rather than one unique one and are based on subject probabilities. In such a milieu, when a firm raises capital through debt issues rather than equity, the consequence may be an increase in expected returns, but at the expense of an increase in the variability of outcomes.

Early attempts at improving the Keynesian investment demand function for practical application focused on an expectations hypothesis. The object was to maximize the expected profits. But some well-known paradoxes plagued that approach. It does not explain why most people will choose a certain payoff of approximately $20, which is found in experiments vs. an infinite dollar sum from an expected payoff. Attempts were made to salvage this expected model via a utility function, leading to utility rather than profit maximization.

Modigliani therefore looked at the maximization of value approach to supply the missing operational structure for the cost of capital and investment. He found that this approach eschewed the concern of subjective value. The main test for cost of capital and investment should be whether " ... the project, as financed, raise[s] the market value of the firm's share ... If so, it is worth undertaking; if not, its return is less than the marginal cost of capital to the firm. ... Such a test is entirely independent of the tastes of the current owners since market prices will reflect not only their preferences but those of all potential owners as well."[2] The purpose of this chapter is to lay bare the market valuation approach to cost of capital and investment, as advanced by Modigliani and Miller. Merton Miller's scholarly collaboration with Modigliani started when he visited his seminar at MIT. As Modigliani recollected later, "I unveiled my proof in a class in which Miller happened to be an auditor. He was convinced instantly and decided to join me in the crusade to bring the truth to the Heathens."[3]

Prior theory of market valuation

The theory of market valuation can be traced through the classical and Keynesian economic doctrines. It also has some forerunners in the theory of finance. From the classical school, we have the teachings of Irving Fisher about the separation of financial and production decisions. Alfred Marshall provided the basis of partial equilibrium on which Modigliani and Miller built the foundation of the M&M theory. In the Keynesian model, we have the macroeconomic foundation of the investment-demand curve, depicting an inverse relation between the rate of interest and investment.

Precursors to the M&M Hypothesis

In a footnote, Modigliani and Miller[4] made references to J.B. Williams (1938), David Durand (1952), and W.A. Morton (1954) as precursors to the first of the M&M propositions. We provide a brief description of the works of the three authors.

John Burr Williams[5] considered a case where one person or an institution owns all the stocks, bonds, or warrants. Then, the company's ability to pay would not depend on whether it pays interest or dividends, and the company could issue stocks to pay off bonds, leaving the company's investment value unchanged. The value of investment remained constant just as physicists speak of the constancy of the law of conservation of mass and energy. Williams wrote that "Clearly, if a single individual or a single institutional investor owned all of the bonds, stocks and warrants issued by the corporation, it would not matter to this investor what the company's capitalization was (except for details concerning the income tax). Any earnings collected as interest could not be collected as dividends. To such an individual it would be perfectly obvious that total interest- and dividend-paying power was in no way dependent on the kind of securities issued to the company's owner. Furthermore no *change* in the investment value of the enterprise as a whole would result from a change in its capitalization."[6] Williams's argument, however, was not based on the arbitrage proof.

Walter A. Morton, was concerned with the constancy of investment values. He stated that "the over-all cost of money would be unaffected by capital structure if individuals could not differentiate risks."[7] As an illustration, he wrote that "if only one security is issued, it bears all the risk whether it be called a bond, preferred stock, or common stock, and would have the same value provided that the security could share in all the earnings. ... Similarly, if one individual owned all of the various types of securities issued, his risk would be the same. Legal differences in the event of insolvency or reorganization and tax policy will modify this result."[8]

Modigliani claimed that he became interested in this hypothesis after he had attended a lecture by David Durand. "I have been intrigued by the subject ever since attending a National Bureau conference of Business Finance ... I listened to a paper by David Durand (1952) in which the possibility that financial structure would not affect the market valuation or the cost of capital was suggested, only to be rejected as not relevant to the actual capital markets."[9]

Concerning Durand's lecture, Modigliani stated in an interview that, "I gradually became convinced of the hypothesis that market value should be independent of the structure of financing."[10] As a precursor to Proposition I, Modigliani mentioned Durand's article, which was mainly concerned with refocusing attention from maximization of income to maximization of wealth. Durand wrote, "Instead of accepting the common dictum that the businessman's interest is to maximize his income, this paper counters the alternative proposal that the businessman should try to maximize his wealth."[11] In his discussion, instances of financing with equity or debt appeared. Modigliani set out to prove what Durand rejected, namely that "the possibility that financial structure would not affect the market valuation or the cost of capital was suggested, only to be rejected as not relevant to the actual capital markets."[12]

Modigliani distanced his theory from those of the above-mentioned forerunners. He wrote, "None of these writers describe in any detail the mechanism which is supposed to keep the average cost of capital constant under changes in capital structure..They seem, however, to be valuing the equilibrating mechanism in terms of switches by investors between stocks and bonds as the yields get out of line with their 'riskiness.' This is an argument quite different from the pure arbitrage mechanism underlying our proof, and the difference is crucial."[13]

The M&M theory of market valuation

The next stage of the analysis emerged when Modigliani asked what the cost of capital is to a firm. If bonds are issued, then debts are incurred at an interest rate. If a stock is sold, then the shareholders own the assets of the firm and expect to participate in profits to the extent of their equity. The stockholders are the principals and the CEOs are the agents who try to maximize the wealth or equity. The firm's capital structure is defined as a mixture of debt and equity. M&M investigates whether a combination of debt and equity maximizes the value of the firm. If there is such a combination, then we can have theories about the firm's optimal financial structure. Modigliani was led to the theory that the return must be invariant to the structure of financing – debt or equity. Modigliani said that he was "able to sketch out a proof of the possibility of arbitraging differences in valuation that are due only to differences in the liability structure." We start with the first proposition in the next section.

Proposition I

Proposition I (Invariance Principle): The market value of any firm is independent of its capital structure and is given by capitalizing its expected return at the rate ρ_k appropriate to its class.[14]

Proposition Ia (Average Cost of Capital): The average cost of capital to any firm is completely independent of the capital structure and is equal to the capitalization rate of a pure equity stream of its class,[15] [Italics original].

Several points about this proposition are worth noting. The assumptions are that the firm does not grow, that no net new investment is taking place, and that taxes are not paid. The market value is measured in terms of a stream of net operating income and a rate of return based on the riskiness of the firm. Firms are classified into homogeneous risk groups, where the shares of different firms in a group are perfect substitutes for one another.

If a firm (j) wants to acquire some debt, it can sell some bonds with a market value equal to D_j. If the value of its stocks are S_j, then the value of firm (j) can be expressed as $V_j \equiv S_j + D_j = \overline{X}_j/\rho_j$, where $\overline{X}_j$ measures expected return on assets, and ρ_j measures interest rate for a given risk class. For example, a firm can issue bonds (debt) or selling stock (equity). A naive estimate of the value of the firm is its earnings before interest and taxes (EBIT) divided by the rate of interest. If EBIT is $5,000 and a low risk interest of 10 per cent prevails, the value of the firm from the so-called net operating income (NOI) approach is $50,000. A higher risk interest of say 20 per cent would lower the value. Usually, debts are repaid first, and then the residual earnings go to the equity holders.

Proof of Proposition I: Arbitrage

Modigliani and Miller gave the concept of arbitrage a permanent home in the theory of financial economics. Hal Varian tells a story of a professor and a farmer who decided to pay $1 and $0.50 to each other, respectively, if they could not answer a question posed by the other. The farmer asked the first question that did not have an answer. The professor confessed he did not know the answer, and the farmer confessed his ignorance as well. However, the payoff must happen: the farmer took the dollar and paid back 50 cents to the professor, thereby making a profit. Arbitrage, therefore is defined as "arranging a transaction involving no cash outlay that results in a sure profit."[16]

Modigliani based his original proof of Proposition I on arbitrage as follows: " ... an investor can buy and sell stocks and bonds in such a way as to exchange one income stream for another ... the value of the overpriced shares will fall and that of the under priced shares will rise, thereby tending to eliminate the discrepancy between the market value of the firm"[17]

Columns 1–4 of Table 5.1 are self-explanatory. Column 5 designates the holdings of the investors of each firm's stock; for instance, an investor in firm 2 is holding s_2 dollars worth of a company stock, αS_2. In column 6, we show the return to the investors. Since D_2 represents the debt of the firm, the residuals of the earnings of the firm over debt payments are available to the shareholders. We can drop the subscript from the X_2 variable, representing earnings, by the 'homogeneity' assumption above.

M&M argued that the value of the firm as shown in the last line in Table 5.1 will be the same. By column 6, if an investor wants a 5 per cent return on X, the investor can buy 5 per cent of the stock of the unleveraged firm, holding 0.05 X. Alternatively, the investor can buy the leveraged firm's stocks and debts, i.e., 0.05 $(X_2 - rD_2)$ of stocks, and 0.05 rD_2 of debts. The two alternative portfolios should yield the same payoff 0.05 X after arbitrage.

Table 5.1 Properties of the MM propositions

Col. 1	**Col. 2**	**Col. 3**	**Col. 4**	**Col. 5**	**Col. 6**	**Col. 7**
Firm	Type	Expected Return	Total Return	Investor Holdings	Investor Dollar Return on Portfolio	Value of The Firm
1	Unleveraged	$\overline{X}$	X_1	$s_1 = \alpha\, S_1$	$Y_1 = \alpha\, X_1$	V_1 = Value of Equity
2	Leveraged	$\overline{X}$	X_2	$s_2 = \alpha\, S_2$	$Y_2 = \alpha\ (X_2 - rD_2)$	$V_2 = D_2 + \alpha\ (X_2 - rD_2)$
Value			$X = X_1 + X_2$		αX	αX

To explain how arbitrage works, if the leveraged company (firm 2) has a value higher than the unleveraged company (firm 1), the investor will want to sell his/her holding of equity in firm 2. The investor would want to invest the proceeds plus any borrowings into firm 1 stock. The term "homemade leverage" is specifically applicable here. The main point about such leverage is that if a firm thinks it can increase its value by manipulating its debt/equity finances, the individual stock and bond holders will find it profitable to adjust their debt/equity holdings in their portfolios in order to undo the leverage that the firm thought it might have. In other words, individuals would be able to borrow funds under the same conditions as the firm and be able to imitate perfectly the advantages the firms thought they would have. The point is that "investors are able to substitute personal for corporate leverage."[18] Because this type of arbitrage is possible, the M&M hypothesis maintains that the value of the two firms cannot be different. Modigliani and Miller used the metaphor of whole vs. skimmed milk to clinch this point. Because of the nature of arbitrage, it will not be possible to separate the cream from the skimmed milk and sell them separately, "for what would be gained from selling the high-priced butter fat would be lost in selling the low priced residue of thinned milk."[19] Samuelson provided another illustration. If chicken were sold in whole pieces, someone would find it possible to buy the whole piece and sell the parts separately for pure profits.[20] The value concept arising from these metaphors are easily visualized. Imagine two circles each alike in size, representing the value of a firm. No matter what the equity or debt shares we divide the two circles into, the size representing the value of the firms will not change.[21]

As a preparation for the original exposition of the M&M invariance principle, we restate Samuelson's syllogistic-cum-axiomatic exposition of the M&M hypothesis. In order to clearly grasp the argument, we spread out the premises sentence by sentence below.

Modes Ponen Argument

Firm A has much debt. Much debt makes common stock earnings risky. Firm A cannot possibly pass this risk on to risk intolerant investors. Risk intolerant investors have alternatives. Risk intolerant investors can buy equity from a zero-debt company. Risk intolerant investors can raise the cash needed through margin purchases, collateral loans at the bank, or by selling shares they own at some leveraged firms.

Modes Tollen Argument

Firm A has no debt. No debt might signal that the firm stock earnings are not risky. Firm A cannot necessarily sell its stock at a premium. Risk intolerant investors have alternatives. They can put their money into risk-free overnight investments, or they can put one-half of their money into stock and the other half into a risk-free venture.

Inference from Arguments

In both cases investors have been able to duplicate the leverage activities of the firms. In the *modes ponen* argument, the investors duplicate a "high mean-return-cum-high-volatility" leverage of the firm. In the *modes tollen* argument, the investors duplicate a "premium free" leverage of the firm. As an axiom, therefore, the value of the firm is invariant, independent of the leverage structure of the firm's capital structure.[22]

In regard to the situation where the leveraged firm sets its value above the unleveraged firm, the investor will get αS_2 amount from the sales of equity of firm 2, and it will raise αD_2 amount of debt from borrowing using its holding in firm 1 as collateral. Therefore, the investor will hold $s_1 = \alpha S_2 + \alpha D_2$ of firm 1 earnings and shares. We can divide by S_1 to get a fraction of the share of firm 1 that is held. The value of firm 1 can now be expressed as:

$$Y_1 = \frac{\alpha(S_2 + D_2)}{S_1} X + r\alpha D_2 = \alpha \frac{V_2}{V_1} X - r\alpha D_2 \qquad (5.1)$$

From equation 5.1, as the investor sells the shares S_2, the value of firm 2 which was higher than that of firm 1, $V_2 > V_1$, will decline. Conversely for firm 2, as the investor buys the shares S_1, the value of firm 1, which was lower than firm 2, $V_1 < V_2$, will increase. The tendency will be for $V_1 = V_2$. Therefore the conclusion is that "levered companies cannot command a premium over unlevered companies because investors have the opportunity of putting the equivalent leverage into their portfolio directly by borrowing on personal accounts."[23]

To complete the arbitrage proof, we now have to consider the case where the unleveraged company (firm 1) has a value higher than the leveraged company (firm 2). In this converse situation where $V_1 > V_2$, the investor will sell part of his/her holding, $s_1 = \alpha S_1$ in equity of firm 1. The investor can buy a fraction of the equity and debt of firm 2, undoing the leverage to obtain the values:

$$\frac{\alpha V_1}{V_2} r D_2 + \alpha \frac{V_1}{V_2} X - r\alpha D_2 = V_2 \tag{5.2}$$

In both instances, therefore, arbitrage will make the value of the two firms tend to equality, where $V_1 = V_2$.

Proposition II

Proposition II (Linear in Debt/Equity): The expected yield of a share of stock is equal to the appropriate capitalization rate ρ_k for a pure equity stream in the class, plus a premium related to financial risk equal to the debt-to-equity ratio times the spread between ρ_k and r,[24] [Italics original].

$$i_j = \rho_k + (\rho_k - \mathrm{r})D_j/S_j \tag{5.3}$$

Proposition II is about the rate of return on stocks of a firm with some debt. The cost of equity is linearly related to the firm's debt/equity ratio. This conclusion is derived from the proposition through some simple algebra. The equity return for the ith form is $(X - rD_j)/S_j$ from Proposition I. Now, $X = \rho_k V_j = \rho_k(D_j + S_j)$, which by substitution yields equation 5.3.

To explain equation 5.3, and show its link with Proposition I, we use an example.[25] If $\overline{X} = 1000$, $D = 400$, $r = 0.05$, and $\rho_k = 0.1$, we can show the relationship between Propositions II and I in Figure 5.1. From Proposition I, $\mathrm{V} = \overline{X}/\rho_k = 10{,}000$. Since $\mathrm{V = D + S}$, then $\mathrm{S} = 600$. Inserting these numbers into equation 5.3, we get the value of $i_j = 0.1 + (0.1 - 0.05)\frac{400}{600} = 0.1333$. The values of these returns are plotted against the debt/equity ratio in Figure 5.1. The wedge between the i_j and ρ_k line measures additional cost to the firm because of leverage. If leverage is captured by the β value of the stock and debt, then $\beta_A = \beta_e{}^*\frac{S}{S+D} + \beta_D{}^*\frac{D}{S+D}$, implying that

$$\beta_e = \beta_A + (\beta_A - \beta_D)\frac{D}{S}.$$

In terms of the skimmed milk example above, this representation of Proposition II implies that "the price per gallon of thinned milk falls continuously as more butter fat is skimmed off."[26] This is obvious from solving the equation:

$$p_\alpha(M-\alpha B)+p_B\alpha B = p_M,\quad 0 \leq \alpha \leq 1,$$

for the price of skimmed milk, where M,B,p_α,p_B, and p_M represents whole milk, butter fat, price of thinned milk, price of buttermilk, and price of whole milk, respectively.

In Figure 5.1, the line MM' represents equation 5.3. The segment *ML'* is a measure of the reasonable maximum of D/S leverage. An alternative assumption holds that the segment should rise as shown by *L'G* because the market discounts more trading on stocks. The alternative position contradicts the independence of return to D/S, implying that returns will decrease with D/S, translating to the idea that debt is to a certain extent cheaper than equity. However, the M&M position is for a flat line.

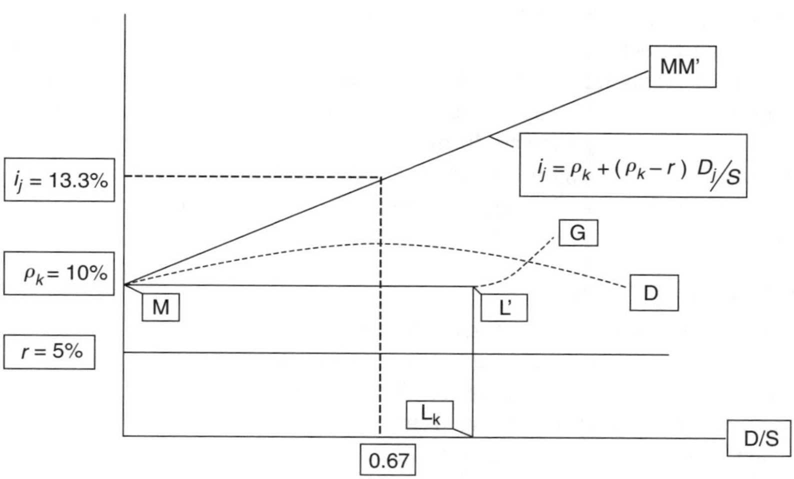

Figure 5.1 Returns on debt and equity

The line MP shows that in some instances, there is a sort of diminishing return to the mixture of debt and stocks.

Proposition III

Proposition III (Investment): The cut-off point for investment in the firm will in all cases be ρ_k and will be completely unaffected by the type of security used to finance the investment,[27] [Italics original].

Modigliani illustrated this with three examples related to bonds, retained earnings, and stocks. We present his ideas in Table 5.2 with comments for bonds and stocks. The two comment columns clarify the assumptions and/or treatment of the data for bonds and stocks. According to Proposition III we need to show that the use of bonds or stocks do not affect the way analysts evaluate investment decisions. To do so, we take information on these two instruments and indicate how investment decisions are made. The first three rows of Table 5.2 provide identical information for both bonds and stocks. Using the information on bonds alone, a decision maker will expect a return of $10,000. Using stocks and bonds on a 50:50 split, with 1,000 outstanding shares, the return on stocks will be $5,000. The rest of the table demonstrates how the decision-making is done for varying assumptions.

Besides the treatment of corporate taxes, other problems dealing with bankruptcy and the economics of information have encouraged much research in the literature. Corporate taxes have disproportional effects on equity and debt. One concern is how increases in the debt/equity ratio will affect the probability of bankruptcy. When a firm takes an action, it emits informational signals. If a firm sells equity, the signal might be that its shares are overpriced. A firm might also face an imperfect credit market where credit might not be as available as it would like. These have been ongoing issues with the M&M model that have led to frequent revisits, and divergent paths of research taken by the original authors.

Corporate tax effect

Part of the reason for introducing Proposition II is to consider the effect of corporate tax rates. Adjusting the proposition for corporate taxes yields a value of total income net of taxes. The unleveraged firm is $V_U = (1 - \tau_c)\frac{\bar{X}}{\rho_k}$ and the value of the leveraged firm is $V_L = (\bar{X}_j - rD_j)(1 - \tau_c) + \tau_c rD_j$, where τ_c is the corporate tax rate, and the whole of the first term is just V_U.[28] The introduction of the corporate tax rate changes the value of the firm, "With the corporate rate nearly 50 percent at the time of our writing,

Table 5.2 Comparison of stocks and bonds returns

Variables	Bonds	Comments on bonds	Stocks	Comments on stocks
ρ_k	10 %		10 %	
r	4%		4%	
$\overline{X}$	$1,000		$1,000	
Debt/equity:		Debt only	50:50	Capital structure
Outstanding shares		No stocks	1,000	
$V = \overline{X}/\rho_k$	$10,000 = 1000/0.1	Prop. 1	$5,000	Prop. I
Interest bill			5000*.04 = 200	
Yield on stock			800/5000 = 16%	(1,000−200)/5000
New investment ($\Delta K = I$):				
I	$100		$100	
ρ^* (yield on I)	8% (2r)		12	0.12*100
Change in income			$1,012	1000+12
Value of stock			$5,120	
Change stock price			$5 to $5.02	
Fall in earnings per share			$0.80 to $.796	Share price increases by more than fall in earnings
Borrow at r	4%			
V	$10,080	1000/.1+(100*.08)/.1	$10,120	
Reduce new market value by the amount of debt	10,080−100 = $9,980			

a dollar of debt would raise the market value of the firm by roughly 50 cents."[29]

The introduction of corporate taxes makes 100 per cent debt financing optimal. When a firm incurs debt it can deduct the interest charge from its tax return. This argument can be generalized to say that the firm pays less taxes when it carries more debt, leaving more money for the stockholder. Figure 5.1 indicates this 100 per cent debt line.

Personal tax effect

Merton Miller later argued for the inclusion of personal income taxes in the M&M hypothesis as well. He advanced this succinct formula:

$$G_L = \left[1 - \frac{(1 - \tau_c)(1 - \tau_{PS})}{1 - \tau_{PB}}\right]B_L \tag{5.4}$$

where B_L is interest that can be deducted for debts by the leveraged firm, G_L is joint personal and corporate tax gain, τ_c is corporate tax rate, τ_{PS} and τ_{PB} are personal tax rates for stock and bonds, respectively.[30]

Miller explained how the equation 5.4 was derived as follows. Return to the leveraged firm, $\alpha(\overline{X} - rB_L)$, will be taxed at the two rates $(1-\tau_c)$, and $(1-\tau_{PS})$. The investors will get a share of that, α. Alternatively, the investor could have bought the unleveraged firm's stocks and bonds. The return from the alternative would be αX times the two rates for stocks, plus αBL times the two rates, discounted by $(1-\tau_{PS})$ for borrowing. Because we can deduct interest from personal income taxes, the net cost of borrowing will be αrBL times the two rates, matching the original leveraged stream of returns.

Based on equation 5.4, setting all tax rates to zero will yield the M&M no tax situation. When the personal rates from bonds and stocks are the same, the results are identical, as if the tax is only imposed on corporations, $\tau_c B_L$. When the tax rate from stocks is less than the tax rate from bonds, leveraged gains will be less than $\tau_c B_L$, or mostly negative.[31]

An integral point to Miller's argument was that personal and corporate tax rates will cancel out, leaving the value of the firm invariant. He stated that investors belong in either the tax-exempt or high tax bracket category. They would want to hold bonds or stocks, respectively. Firms generally have an eye on one or the other of these two types of investors. They may want to alter their capital structure to accommodate them by, for example, issuing more debt if the tax-exempt investors are dominant. This process will continue until the last incremental debt that is issued cannot find a tax-exempt buyer and must be sold to the high-tax bracket buyer. Then we know that an equilibrium is reached between the two rates. This argument is equivalent to the assertion that the marketing of a firm's securities is just like the marketing of a product. In marketing, firms may see a niche in the market for more of a particular security. The firm may want to increase the supply of that security if it can. It is important to note that counter arguments exist which may create a net tax effect on personal and corporate taxes. The idea that the tax rate on stock income is zero is not tenable in practice. Investors do receive dividend and capital gains on which they pay taxes.[32]

Dividend policy irrelevance

The irrelevant argument for debt and equity can be extended to dividend policy. When we enter the study of dividend policies, the firm has already decided on its investment decision, which determines its cash flow or net profit, $X(t)$, where t is time. "If the firm raises its dividend at t, given its investment decision, will the increase in the cash payment to the current holder be more or less than enough to offset their lower share of the terminal value?"[33] That statement is transformed into the question as to whether it would be better to finance investment through retained earnings, or through new investment via floating new shares. New investment, $I(t)$, is new shares, $m(t+1)$, times its ex dividend closing price, $p(t+1)$ plus cash flow, $X(t)$, less dividend, $D(t)$ which yields:[34]

$$m(t+1)p(t+1) = I(t) - X(t) + D(t) \tag{5.5}$$

Since the firm's value is given by:

$$V(t) = \frac{1}{1 + \rho(t)}[D(t) + V(t + 1) - m(t + 1)p(t + 1)] \tag{5.5a}$$

Substituting equation 5.5 into 5.5a yields:

$$V(t) = \frac{1}{1 + \rho(t)}[X(t) + I(t) + V(t + 1)] \tag{5.5b}$$

The absence of the $D(t)$ term in equation 5.5b leads to the desired conclusion that "the value of the firm must be independent of the current dividend decision."[35] The difficulty in perceiving that deduction has been overshadowed by many equivalent ways to express equation 5.5a, such as discounted cash flow, investment opportunity, and streams of dividends and earnings.

As cash flow grows, the value of a firm grows in proportion. The growth of dividends per share will depend on whether the firm is relying on outside earnings to pay out high earnings. The M&M hypothesis states that "the growth rate of dividends per share is not the same as the growth rate of the firm except in the special case in which all financing is internal."[36]

Moving to a world of uncertainty, the cash flow variable would be random, and the discount factor would be probabilistic.[37] Modigliani and Miller asserted that "even without a full-fledged theory of what does determine market value under uncertainty we can show that dividend policy at least is not one of the determinants."[38] To establish the invariance principle under uncertainty for dividends, we extend the argument under equations 5.5 to 5.5b for two identical firms with the same cash flow, $\tilde{X}(t)$, and investments, $\tilde{I}(t)$, for period 0 to infinity, and the same dividend policy, $\tilde{D}(t)$, for period 1 to infinity. We wish to find that the firm's rate of return, $\tilde{R}(t)$, is independent of dividend policy. For that, two assumptions are necessary: imputed rationality where we impute to all traders that they prefer more wealth to less wealth, and symmetric market rationality where the traders treat each other as rational. These concepts relate to the traders and their expectations of one another, and these range over the whole market. The equivalent results to match equation 5 to 5b will be 5.6 to 5.6a, which shows independence of dividends from the financial structure.

$$\tilde{R}_1(0) = \tilde{D}_1(0) + \tilde{V}_1(0) - \tilde{m}_1(1)\tilde{p}_1(1) \tag{5.6}$$

$$\tilde{m}_1(0)\tilde{p}_1 = \tilde{I}_1(0) - [\tilde{X}_1(0) - \tilde{D}_1(0)] \tag{5.6a}$$

and by substituting 5.6a into 5.6, we find the rate of return is independent of dividends.

$$\tilde{R}_1(0) = \tilde{X}_1(0) - \tilde{I}_1(0) + \tilde{V}_1(1) \tag{5.6b}$$

A similar analysis for $\tilde{R}_2$ can be derived.

Implications of dividend policy irrelevance

Miller raised the question that "If dividends are a 'mere financial detail,' … why are announcements of dividends increases typically followed by stock price increases, sometimes spectacularly so?"[39] The argument pivots on the diffusion of information. While the M&M model irrelevance hypothesis is based on full information, agents may not have the information immediately when the dividend is announced. Investors may have credited the announced increase in dividends to increases in earnings of the firm to which the price increase was reacting.

The idea that dividend policies may act as a signal, in the sense of a signal game leading to increases in price was much developed in the literature. The M&M value hypothesis model in this sense can still be shown to be independent of dividends and securities as delineated by Miller's question.[40]

$$V_1 = X_1 - I_1 + \frac{1}{1+i}[F(I_1) + E(\tilde{\epsilon}_2)] \tag{5.7}$$

where V_1 is the value of the firm, X_1 is the firm's earnings, which is dependent on investment at time zero affecting two components of output – a deterministic component, $F(I_0)$ and a random component $\tilde{\epsilon}_1$, and i is the one period discount rate.

The outcome varies if we consider that transaction cost in securities is significant. Minimum transaction cost occurs if the firm pays dividends from its excess of earnings over its investment requirements. In that case the transaction cost is lower since the firm does not have to sell securities. Conversely, if the firm does not have enough earnings to cover its investment requirements, then it will incur some cost in its financial transactions to fund its dividend payments. The analysis is not as clear-cut as presented here, for not only a dividend signal is sent out to investors, but investment and security purchases signal as well, which is a case of complex signaling. Some complexities are added if the tax rates on dividends are higher than tax rates on capital gains, which varies with the degree to which investors seek cover under tax shelter investments. The idea that the paying of dividends sends a positive signal that enhances stock prices is still being researched. Moreover, the frequent changes in tax laws since the 1980s make the examination more challenging.

Bankruptcy and defaults

When a firm goes bankrupt, it incurs costs. Under U.S. bankruptcy laws, the firm can either be liquidated by filing a Chapter 7, or reorganized by filing Chapter 11. In the former, the creditor receives a part of the firm's assets on some priority basis. In the process transaction costs such as court and attorney fees can lower its value. On the other hand, if the firm reorganizes, its value may be enhanced even in the face of reorganization costs.

Modigliani recognized the possible effects of bankruptcy and defaults on the value of a firm. He noted one of "four major ways in which leverage could unfavorably affect the market value of the firm ... through bankruptcy costs which reduce the expected flow to all concerned ... through agency costs, resulting from the arrangements needed to protect the creditors ... moral hazard or foregone valuable opportunities ... A fourth ... debt is valuable in so far as it serves to shelter income from taxes."[41] Debt holders expect to be repaid. If firms cannot repay the loans to the debt holders, the lenders can initiate bankruptcy proceedings. The probability of bankruptcy increases with debt, because more debt means more fixed payment obligations are incurred.

Even with risky debt, the M&M hypothesis will remain intact, but the transaction cost of bankruptcy is carried by the bondholder, which affects value.[42] The effect of transaction cost channels through the mechanism whereby bond holders would require a higher return to cover the probability of bankruptcy, before they carry the debt. Shareholders in turn would require higher returns to compensate for the probability of bankruptcy. Therefore, the return vs. debt-equity relationship will be steeper with bankruptcy than without bankruptcy costs.

Stiglitz has studied the effect of bankruptcy on value. He argued that because of bankruptcy "the nominal rate of interest which the firm must pay on its bonds will increase as the number of bonds increases ... Second, if a firm goes bankrupt, it is no longer possible for an individual to replicate the exact patterns of returns, except if he can buy on margin, using the security as collateral, and if he defaults, he only forfeits the security and none of his other assets."[43] Stiglitz cast his argument in terms of state-space general equilibrium, which we develop below. The essence of the argument is that as a firm acquires more risky debts, it creates a new security or destroys an old one. The effect on value can be that the investors may not be able to imitate the new capital structure in the economy and prices and discount rates will also be altered in the process.[44] Because concerns over bankruptcy and defaults have spiraled, there is a large volume of research work within a general equilibrium (GE) framework. We discuss that framework in the next section.

Bankruptcy and defaults in time and state preference GE model

We take it as an axiom that the present is certain and the future is uncertain. Following Kenneth J. Arrow, we can characterize the future by various states of the world that may prevail. To do that, we need to think of all of the future as a single point. At that point, a state of affairs of the world will exist. Arrow postulates a security for each such state of affairs in the future. If a good state occurs, the security pays, say \$1, and \$0 otherwise. The return for the good state can be written as a pay-off vector.

The state of the world concept has immediate application to the M&M hypothesis. For the leveraged firm, an amount of debt or bonds will be outstanding. A good state would mean that no default or bankruptcy or economic downswings has occurred. The good state will have a payoff to the bond holder in the amount of $(1+r)D$. We will have to take the present value of this to know its worth today. Once the value of debt is found, we can calculate the present value of equity. The equity holding will be the total return, $X(s)$, which is state dependent now, less the present value of the bonds, $(1+r)D$.

We can now sum the present values of equity and bonds. This will be equal to the present value of $X(s)$. It states that the sum does not depend on the debt-equity ratio, precisely what the M&M hypothesis asserts.[45] The expected return on securities depends on the state of the economy. Return in the M&M hypothesis relates to contingent interest and principal payments on bonds (debt), and the contingent cash dividends on equity. To the returns a probability is associated; and to the security a price is associated. We can then determine the investor's utility function, and, therefore, his/her demand for the security.[46]

The general equilibrium approach captures many of the new challenges to the M&M hypothesis. It represents an improvement on the M&M paradigm in many ways. The starting point of a general equilibrium model is to give each investor an expected utility function to maximize. The investor, therefore, expects a return, which can be characterized by R_{is}, which associate the $i = 1, \ldots, m$ securities and the states as defined above. To get to the utility function, we need to know the price of the security $P_i = R_{is}/(1+r)$, the probability that a state will occur, π_s, and the amount of the $i-th$ security that the investor purchases, X_i.

Financial theories work with a utility function that restricts preferences to reflect probabilities and behavior towards risks. The utility function is dependent on the state of nature. The utility function is also made additive-separable by including utility at time zero as well. From the financial point of view, therefore, it is written as follows:[47]

$$\sum_{s=1}^{S} U(x_0, x_s)\pi_s = U(x_0) + \sum_{s=1}^{S} U(x_s)\pi_s \qquad (5.8)$$

Thus, investors optimize their utility subject to a wealth constraint.

We can now assess the effects of bankruptcy and default effects on the value of a firm.

For this purpose, we will use Dubey et al., (1994) general equilibrium (GE) model that is capable of addressing many issues in the area. The model has agents who promise to make a payment, A, with a penalty for default, λ, and some limitations on output, Q. We represent such a GE model by a triplet function, $GE(A,\lambda,Q)$. The standard GE model does not allow agents to break their promises, and they cannot spend more than their endowment. Assuming three states, initial endowment of $e^1 = \{0,1,1\}$, $e^2 = \{1,0,1\}$, and $e^3 = \{1,1,0\}$, for each agent in each state, and three agents with the same utility function $u(x_1,x_2,x_3) = \sum_{s=1}^{3} log(x_s)$, then we can derive commodity price p = {1,1,1}, and allocation x = {2/3, 2/3, 2/3}.

We now will adopt the situation to the GE economy. The GE is now expressed as $GE(A,\lambda,Q,K,x,\theta,\varphi,D)$, where K is the expected fraction of payments expected to be delivered of an asset in a state, θ is the amount of assets each agent purchased, φ is an alternative asset, and D is the amount of assets delivered. Then, the equilibrium price $p = \{1,1,1\}$ is attained through the following values:

$$GE(A = 1^j,\lambda = \infty,Q = \infty,K = 1,x = 2/3^h,\theta = (2/3)1^h,\varphi = (1/3)e^h,D = 1/3).$$

In this example, if we allow the alternative asset prices to be the agent's endowment, then asset prices would remain the same.

The GE model allows us to view defaults from several angles. Setting the default parameter to infinity means that default is not allowed, yielding an efficient outcome. In reality, we find that defaults are allowed, which means that the default parameter is set to a value less than infinity. Allowing a firm to default has some benefits. It allows a firm to substitute one security for another by being allowed to pay a default penalty. Agents can substitute a wide number of assets that fit their needs for one asset that does not. This allows a widening of the asset span, allowing agents to hold more assets than were intended. In other words, we can add an asset $J+1$, to the already $j = 1. \dots$ J, existing assets in the economy, each paying a dollar in every state. The broader asset base can improve welfare depending on the extent of the default penalty.

The M&M invariant proposition is not in question if the firm is not allowed to default. We would like to know its status when default is allowed under a GE setting. To fit the model into the GE framework, we let junior debt represent equity, as equity is not explicitly introduced into the model. Borrowers need not be indifferent to junior and senior debts.

Given two different assets, A^i and A^j, where "j" is the junior debt, and we let the default penalty be only slightly larger on the junior debt, the agent is likely to choose the same total default on the junior plus senior debts despite the proportion in which the agent sells them. The M&M proposition is likely to hold under partial equilibrium. However, in a GE setting, different assets allow agents different ways to spread risk. Another way of looking at the difference in GE is that by holding a different proportion of junior and senior debts the span of assets will change. This changes the interpretation of M&M hypothesis where "The conventional argument in favor of Modigliani-Miller suggests that investors who had purchased the original issues of a firm could compensate in their own portfolios for any changes in the debt issuance of the firm. But that argument ignores the implications of default. There may be no such available asset an investor could purchase or sell that would make up the change in the firm's debt deliveries."[48]

This GE argument encompasses Stiglitz's thoughts relating to bankruptcy.[49] According to Rubinstein, Stiglitz's idea amounts to stating that "if risky debt is created as the capital structure is shifted more towards debt, in an incomplete market, a fundamentally new security can be created or old security destroyed (one which cannot be replicated by a portfolio of pre-existing securities in the economy) and this may alter state prices which will in turn change the discount rates used to determine the present value of the sum of the cash flows to debt and equity."[50]

Inflation and valuation

The M&M hypothesis has the power of explaining the effect of inflation on the value of a firm. Inflationary effects on valuation show up if "investors capitalize equity earnings at a rate that parallels the nominal interest rate" or "investors fail to allow for the gain to shareholders accruing from depreciation in the real value of nominal corporate liabilities."[51] Inflation can depress a leveraged firm's earnings from profits into losses, unless the firm increases its debt at the level of the rate of inflation. In this way, "the funds obtained from the issues of debt needed to maintain leverage will precisely equal the funds necessary to pay interest on the debt and maintain the firm's dividend and reinvestment policies."[52]

We can start accounting for inflation on valuation by adjusting the unleveraged firm nominal earning stream at the rate of inflation, $X(t) = X(0)e^{pt}$, where p is the rate of inflation, and t is time. The nominal interest rate, $R(t)$, equals the real interest rate, $r(0)$, plus the rate of inflation, p. When we capitalize the inflated adjusted earnings, we get $V(t) = X(t)/\rho = X(0)e^{pt}/\rho = V(0)e^{pt}$, implying that the value of the firm at time zero is equal to its value after the inflation started at time zero and beyond. In other words, inflation does not affect the real rate of return.

For the leveraged firm, the income stream without inflation is $X(0)-rD(0)$. The appropriate capitalization rate will be $\rho+d(\rho-r)$, where d is the share of debt to total value. With anticipated inflation, the rate in the income stream must be modified to $r+p$. Appealing to the original M&M hypothesis "that the market value of the firm is independent of leverage, it follows that [the value of the firm before inflation] equals its [value after inflation] ... so [the amount of debt before inflation] equals [the amount of debt after inflation]."[53]

One problem in market valuation with inflation is on the side of profit computations. We need to "recast the earning-price ratio on a nominal base by adding back expected inflation, before averaging it with the nominal rate, and compare the resulting '*nominal* required return' with an estimate *nominal* cash flow ... or convert the nominal interest rate to a real basis before averaging with the earning-price ratio and perform all calculations in real terms," [Italics original].[54]

Another problem in market valuation is on the side of equity computations. As debts devalue, we need to make corrections. "In the United States where both inflation and leverage are moderate, this error in recent years has amounted to perhaps 30–40 percent of profits."[55] Some errors creep in because the price-earning ratio is treated as a nominal, whereas it should be treated as a real rate: "Equity is a claim to a real asset, whose value should grow at the rate of inflation – at least as long as inflation does not have an adverse long-run effect on real profits."[56]

Pooling the errors in market valuation with inflation, Modigliani argued that during 1978–1979, the values of equities in the United States were undervalued by approximately 50 per cent, which represented "an enormous destruction of wealth and well-being."[57]

Comments on the propositions

The role of arbitrage

According to Miller's recent assessment, some 30 years later, Proposition I with its arbitrage proof, is well accepted in the economics world today, but less so in corporate finance.[58] One angle of differences surfaced from the arbitrage proof. The arbitrage theorem is considered the fundamental theorem of modern finance.[59] It specifies the simple condition that the prices of assets can be determined for arbitrage to exist. Such prices are different from the ones economists usually calculate from equilibrium analysis, but are useful for calculating them where arbitrage will not take place. For example, Neftci considered a stock with payoffs of \$100 and \$150, a risk-free investment that pays 10 per cent, and a call option, C, with a strike price of \$100. In equation form, the dividend and yield equation is as follows:

$$\begin{bmatrix} 1 \\ 100 \\ C \end{bmatrix} = \begin{bmatrix} 1.1 & 1.1 \\ 100 & 150 \\ 0 & 50 \end{bmatrix} \begin{bmatrix} \Psi \\ \Psi_2 \end{bmatrix} \tag{5.9}$$

If we set a premium price of \$25 for C, then we cannot find unique values for the yields, ψ_1, ψ_2, which implies that the possibility for arbitrage exist. On the other hand, if we solve for the yields in the first two equations, and then for C, no arbitrage possibility exists.[60]

A variety of solutions

In 1969 Joseph Stiglitz[61] listed five limitations of the M&M hypothesis. One limitation is that the "risk class" assumes an objective probability distribution over outcome. Another is the need to look at the hypothesis from the general equilibrium rather than from the partial equilibrium point of view. Other limitations are the need to consider more elaborate competitive market points of view in a GE setting, and the need to clear up the influence of bankruptcy and defaults.

As surveyed by Milne,[62] others have advanced different methods of proofs. They include proofs that replace the concept of "risk class" with perfect markets that use the concept of Arrow's securities that decompose production processes to establish competitive equilibrium, and proofs that use mean-variance models. Arrow's securities require general equilibrium analysis that Modigliani did not examine. Also, Modigliani did render his proof in terms of mean-variance ratio, and provided additional modifications to it.

Modigliani and Miller did not accept the mean variance approach that is seen as an alternative way to discuss the M&M hypothesis. They wrote:

> Why anyone would want to introduce the variance of returns into the proof is particularly hard for us to understand since the essential motivation underlying our original arbitrage proof, after all, was

> precisely to avoid having to establish tradeoffs between the moments of the probability distribution of returns. Instead, we were able to show that unless the equilibrium conditions were met, one distribution of returns would completely dominate the other.[63]

Baldwin and Velk were among the first to advance an argument of a probability distribution on how returns are scattered over equity and bonds.[64] They asserted that if the value of the leveraged firm is greater than the value of the unleveraged one, $V_2 > V_1$, then we expect that the variation of returns on stocks of the leveraged firm would also exceed the variation of the stocks of the leveraged firm, $\delta_2 > \delta_1$. They went on to show the necessity of the argument that the income of firm 1, Y_1, will be smaller than the income of firm 2, Y_2, in this situation, i.e., $V_2 > V_1 \supset Y_1 \geq Y_2$, provided that no negative return, X, is expected.

Modigliani and the classics

Although Modigliani did not use a general equilibrium state preference framework for the M&M hypothesis, we know he was not averse to this line of thinking as he used it in giving his LCH hypothesis a classical foundation. The classical source of this approach can be traced to Irving Fisher's separation theorem.

Fisher, a classical economist, was concerned with keeping the decision to invest, I, separate from the decision to consume, C, over time. I-decisions depend on prospective earnings and the rate of interest, while C-decisions depend on wealth, personal preferences, and interest rates.

An investor contemplating a project will draw up a *pro forma* statement about the prospective yield of the project. Usually, the *pro forma* would show expected revenues against expected costs for five to ten years. An investor is likely to have a number of planned projects. Comparing the prospective yield of those projects against the cost of funds, the rate of interest, will result in the determination of the investment demand schedule. Investment demand is inversely related to the rate of interest because when the rate falls, more projects will become attractive, and additional investments will take place. Usually, if the Net Present Value (NPV) is positive, i.e. if present value less initial investment is positive, the project will be worthwhile.[65]

Fisher's theory focused on sources of funds for investment. It examined the opportunity cost of engaging in the project. If, for instance, the funds are from personal savings, then the alternative costs will be what the investor would have done with the savings. Most likely the investors would wish to buy consumption goods, and so the alternative cost would be impinging on the investor's personal preference about how soon it should be consumed or what we call the C-decision. If the investor wanted to borrow the funds, then repayment would most likely be from the expected earnings of the business, or what we call the I-decision.

Fisher's contribution to the cost of fund theory is to keep these decisions apart. This requires the assumption of a perfect capital market. The requirement relates to both the I-decision and C-decision approaches. Under the C-decision approach, investors will be concerned about the interest rates they could get from investment of their savings. Under the I-decision approach, investors would be concerned about the interest rates at which they can borrow funds for a particular project. If the two rates are the same, all parties, investors and lenders, would have the same terms, necessitating the assumption of a perfect capital market.

The M&M hypothesis has moved away from the classical direction in a number of ways. "The first extension of the Fisher Separation Theorem to a setting with uncertainty was made in the well-known paper of Modigliani-Miller (1958): they showed that the market value of a corporation depends only on its profit stream and not on the way the claims to the income stream are divided between debts and equity holders."[66] Modigliani and Miller mentioned some precursors that set the stage for this first portion. We discuss them briefly next.

Modigliani and modern portfolio theory

Earlier in this chapter, we expressed Modigliani's concern about modern portfolio theory. He did not want to get into "tradeoffs between the moments of the probability distribution of returns."[67] In subsequent writings however, he did entertain some variant of it. As it turned out, the modern portfolio approach also leads to a proof of the M&M hypothesis.[68] Somewhat earlier, the mean-variance ratio approach also proved the M&M hypothesis.[69] According to Leah Modigliani, the granddaughter of Franco Modigliani, "Morgan Stanley is calling our measure the Modigliani-Modigliani measure of risk-adjusted performance, or M^2 for short."[70]

In a joint paper with Leah Modigliani, a close link with the modern finance theory was achieved. They measured "the performance of any managed portfolio against that of a relevant unmanaged 'market' portfolio ... after properly adjusting for the portfolio return for risk."[71] To facilitate this, we need the portfolio return and risk dispersion. Leveraging means increasing investments through borrowing. Unleveraging implies selling a part of the portfolio to purchase a more risk-free asset. In the process, the portfolio risk is made equal to the market risk.

The traditional method of appraising a managed portfolio is to compare it with one that is not managed and that is chosen at random. Such a methodological approach includes efficient criteria as well, meaning that the performance of the portfolio is measured against standards such as portfolios in the unmanaged market, or portfolios that are weighted averages of the whole market, where such weights can be the rate of capitalization. The Modiglianis shifted the appraisal onto a risk criterion, one that can bias total returns up or down depending on the level of uncertainty in the managed portfolio. In particular, they give managers an opportunity to trade-off risk, measured by the dispersion of a portfolio, δ, against expected return. A major goal of such a decomposition of a portfolio by risk level is to source the return of the managed portfolio to either a risk-premium due to plunging or to management efficiency due to strategy and insight.

The alternative measure of Leah and Franco Modigliani is termed risk-adjusted performance (RAP). It has properties that sets it apart from the Sharpe ratio which "converts total returns to excess returns by subtracting the risk-free rate, and then divide the result by a common measure of dispersion, the standard deviation or sigma, to get a measure of 'reward per unit of risk.'"[72] RAP adjusts all random unmanaged portfolios to a market level of risk derived from the S&P 500 for instance. RAP for the portfolio, $RAP(i)$, can be compared to another portfolio, $RAP(j)$, or to a market portfolio for the same timeframe, r_m.

Three measures of RAP are advanced. One measures the extent by which RAP exceeds the market, $RAP(i) = 100(r(i)/r_m) - 1)$. Another measure re-expresses the first in terms comparable to the Sharpe ratio, $RAPA(i) = 100(e(i)/e_m)$, where e measures the average return of the portfolio from its short-term risk free rate. A third measure assesses the difference of RAP on the market in terms of a percentage of the market return, $RARP(i) = 100(e(i)/e_m - 1)$. These measures were shown to be very practical.

Early reception of the M&M hypothesis in finance

Modigliani was skeptical about how practitioners of finance would receive the M&M model. As a result, he remarked that they had to provide a "laborious" proof of some 30 pages long because it went against the existing teaching in corporate finance.

The adoption of the M&M hypothesis has been overwhelming. Modigliani himself discovered that young cab drivers in the Washington, D.C. area were well informed of the M&M hypothesis.

However, it is also important to mention that most cab drivers in the area at the time (with a foreign accent) were MBA students.[73] In MBA textbooks, and in the programs, students are taught how to calculate the discounted value of a unit of debt to the present time, add that to the value of equity in the marginal unit of capital, which is a residual equal to the marginal unit of capital less the amount paid to the bond holders, and consider the value of many financial assets besides debt and equity, and test the value-invariance principle with and without taxes on profits, and tax deductions on debt interest.[74] It is interesting to note that the robustness of the M&M hypothesis stood up to the popular put-call parity analysis, or the Black-Scholes capital structure model: "The familiar Put-Call Parity Theorem ... is really nothing more than the M&M Proposition I in only a mildly concealing disguise!"[75] However, the M&M model had to confront a series of empirical distortions, which according to James Tobin[76] " ... include corporate income taxation, which is not neutral as between debt interest and dividends; the implications of leverage for probability of bankruptcy and loss of control; and economies of scale in borrowing which enable stockholders to borrow more cheaply through the corporation than individually." While looking at some regression results for 1960–1974, Tobin[77] found a negative sigma coefficient, a dislike for dividend protection, and indifference or a rejection of fixed debt service obligations, implying overall that " ... the stock market likes leverage, and prefers pay-out rather than retained earnings." Another study, by Stiglitz,[78] examined more general conditions under which the M&M hypothesis may hold, including Arrow-Debreu general equilibrium conditions, where securities are held based on varying states of the economy. He asserted that " ... in the context of a general equilibrium state preference model that the M&M theorem holds under much more general conditions than those assumed in their original study ... . Except that they must agree that there is zero probability of bankruptcy."

In response to the critics, Miller pointed out that they were considering a general equilibrium approach from the inception, having drafted up an appendix to the original paper, but that the approach later took the form of three separate papers.[79] An additional criticism was addressed towards various parameter assumptions of the model. For instance, varying dividend policies were accommodated either by a random error term that bridges the theoretical model to reality, or by a firm's "payout policies" which would tend to attract a certain "'clientele' consisting of those preferring its particular payout ratio."[80] Another adjustment was made to the "method of taxing corporations on the valuation of firms", which was based on whether a firm should seek to maximize debt financing in their capital structure because of the tax advantage. In the philosophical sense of the argument, the authors did not find debt and equity financing to be "either or" propositions, for they asserted that retained earnings can be a cheaper alternative. While Miller[81] thought of the Tax Reform Act of 1986 as rare "supershocks" whose validation of a theory is yet to be seen, Modigliani[82] thought it did point to a validation of the original position on taxes.

The GE approach that complements the partial equilibrium approach has spinned off the model in many new directions. A summary of the new developments is found in Magill and Quinzii.[83] Essentially, the developments have likened the M&M hypothesis to the primitive assumption of the CAPM models, and "optimal choice of production plan for the multi-owner firm",[84] and a firm's optimal financial structure as it relates to inside vs. outside equity holders, and bond holders.[85]

Conclusion

Modigliani received the Nobel Prize based partly on his work on the M&M hypothesis. Over time he had revisited the M&M propositions frequently, addressing critics and new issues of applying and extending the hypothesis. He had expressed to one of the present authors his desire to revisit the hypothesis once more just two months before his death. We cannot speculate as to what materials he would have included, but we know from past reappraisals that we have missed something of deep thought and thoroughness on everything his critics had to offer, including the recognition of divergent views of his friends as exemplified by his co-author on points of taxation.

We have basically presented research molded in the framework of the original propositions. The work of Milne[86] surveyed general equilibrium frameworks from that foundation and was also included in Dubey, et. al.[87] Magill and Quinzii's[88] surveyed works done under more primitive assumptions for the CAPM models. Both the general equilibrium view, as represented by Dubey, et al, and the partial equilibrium view, as represented by the propositions of M&M, are delineated in this volume. The joint work of Leah and Franco Modigliani pits the M&M hypothesis in the domain of the modern theory of finance. Based on the theories covered in this chapter, the M&M hypothesis is a progressive research program that could provide practitioners of corporate finance and economics with future research problems.

6
Forecasting: The MPS Model

Introduction

Modigliani studied statistics with Abraham Wald, who was also a mathematician, and a general equilibrium theorist. Modigliani taught econometrics and had the reputation of forming theories that clearly explain reality. His reputation as a forecaster started with early collaborative work with his teachers at the New School on the specification of international trade functions. By far, however, Modigliani's work on the FRB-MIT-SSRC model, which took on a large-scale econometric view of the macro economy, is his most important contribution to econometric forecasting. In that model, Modigliani flirted with an early version of the Rational Expectation Hypothesis (REH). He made many econometric forecasts for foreign countries based on that model. We will discuss his essential contributions to forecasting in this chapter.

Specification of import and trade functions

While at the New School, Modigliani co-authored a volume with Hans Neisser on forecasting.[1] Essentially, they were concerned with the flows of imports and exports between the United Kingdom, the United States, Germany, France, and the rest of the world (ROW) in raw materials, food, and manufacturing. As Brems explained, the focus was on linear homogeneous relationships between imports and exports.[2] The modern concerns with the global economy have roots in these foundational works. Next, Modigliani's early version of the consumption function was about forecasting savings. Also, as we mentioned earlier, Klein and Ozmucur have recently reworked that model and found it robust.

The preface to the book by Neisser and Modigliani states that "Professor Modigliani joined the project in the fall of 1944, and devoted to it most of his time during the subsequent four years. He was a general adviser in the investigation of import functions, and he made an important contribution in reformulating the underlying model of international trade."[3] Modigliani formulated linear homogeneous specifications for a country's balance of payments. Commodities such as raw materials, food, and manufacturing products were fitted for various regions including the United States, the United Kingdom, Germany and France. Imports into industrial countries were made dependent on income, prices, net stock change, net capital flow, and food production. For non-industrial countries, imports depended on exports plus industrial output, prices, net stock change and net capital flow. Exports were defined uniformly as dependent on imports of all other countries, prices, net stock change, and net capital flow.[4] All 36 equations with 36 unknowns were fitted for the international sectors. The model was first concerned with the question of how a change "in the income of a certain industrial country, *i*, with no change in any other exogenous variables ... [and how] the change in *i´s*, caused by the income change in *i*, has repercussions on the other countries' income, but no further effect on *i´s,* income,"[5] [Italics original].

The early saving forecasting model

Modigliani was also a pioneer in the specification of saving functions. We have covered some aspects of the saving function in chapter 4. Here we examine its ability to forecast.

Among the factors important in appraising a forecasting function, the ability to incorporate *a priori* information and assumptions is prominent. Modigliani built his saving function on the foundation laid by Keynes's psychological law. It states that people will tend to save an increasing proportion of their income as their income increases. At the time, post-WWII models were faced with many counterfactuals to be reconciled, and the model was supposed to explain anomalies, plus present some novelties. The size of the saving coefficient was one such anomaly. An explanation of consumer behavior during cycles was another. Modigliani integrated both these phenomena into his early saving model.

The FRB-MIT-Penn-SSRC model, 1969–1995

The FRB-MIT-Penn-SSRC model was initiated in the mid-1960s when the Federal Reserve Board asked Modigliani to develop one to forecast and analyze economic policies.[6] In 1964, Chesney Martin, the then president of the Federal Reserve, had initiated the request. Arthur Burns who succeeded Martin was not convinced of its efficacy. Yet Modigliani pressed on. He invited Albert Ando, a former student of his at Carnegie Institute of Technology, who had co-authored the life cycle hypothesis project with him, to join in the effort. Together they completed the model in 1969.

Modigliani explained the slant of the model as follows: "Ando and I developed our model of the American economy along essentially Keynesian lines–but our sort of Keynes, where money is very important. Indeed, we discovered that it was given more importance than we thought, owing to the interaction between my consumption function and monetary policy. Since my consumption function shows that consumption depends on income and wealth, and since rates of interest influence wealth, we found an additional channel through which monetary policy can influence income ... the channel was faster than the traditional one that passes through investments and implies several delays."[7] These thoughts framed the discussion we present now on the MPS model.

The delay of the model from its original request by the Fed in 1964 to its delivery in 1969 was partly due to specification problems. Among the problems at that time was the need to address inflation. The early model was grounded on the IS/LM system, which determines interest rates and output. The Phillips curve determined wage-inflation and a mark-up equation determined price inflation.[8] But inflation was a new phenomenon. As Modigliani described it "until the Vietnam War inflation had been low and stable. But the situation changed in 1966 and continued to get worse until 1970, when inflation reached 6 per cent. We were thus forced to revise the model, making a more careful distinction between nominal and real variables."[9]

Following Modigliani's Keynesian framework, the MPS model has two major divisions, a real sector that is influenced by fiscal policies, and a financial sector that mainly links with the real sector through monetary policy. In building the model, Modigliani also drew on partial econometric models, such as the one he and Neisser created for the open economy, and on work that he was doing simultaneously starting in 1966 on an econometric model for the Italian economy.[10] In a 1972 version of the MPS model, Modigliani discussed relationships between money (nominal and real) and labor markets to output and income.[11] He emphasized that in the short-run, which is the relevant timeframe for stabilization policies, "monetary and fiscal policies have powerful effects, first on real output and, more gradually, on prices, with the relative size of the two effects dependent on the degree of slack in the economy."[12]

The 1968 version of the model was discussed under many names–FMP, MPS, FRB-MIT-Penn-SSRC, depending on the sponsorship. The last financial supporter was the Social Science Research Council (SSSRC). The 1968 version had 171 endogenous and 119 exogenous variables, and was concerned mainly with the monetary and financial sides of the economy.[13] Modigliani was concerned with discretion rather than policy rules in framing the model. The original specifications and predictions of it will be discussed below. We will investigate the dynamic realities the model had to confront in its predictions, estimations, particularly with regard to stagflation of the 1970s.

Specification, prediction and explanation of the MPS

The MPS model is large-scale, and, therefore, cannot be discussed comprehensively. We will follow the example of others in selecting small imitation models of its behavior to gain insight into the whole model. Albert Ando, a collaborator on the model, has provided a system of 25 equations as a small-scale replica.[14] The main sectors are Demand for Output, Income Identities, Labor Markets, Financial Markets, and Government. McElroy[15] and Christ[16] have suggested the ways in which the essence of large scale models can be presented. In this section, we will incorporate these approaches in discussing the financial as well as the other major sectors of the MPS model.

The financial market

We start with the money and security markets where monetary policy makes its initial appearance. The model is intricately linked with a network of feedback mechanisms. In the opinion of some major analysts at that time, the FRB-MIT-Penn model has "the most elaborate financial sector of any econometric model so far constructed and represents the 'state of the art' model building."[17] At the heart of the model lies a transmission mechanism of how monetary policy affects employment, income, and prices. It is possible to describe the mechanism through which this change takes place from the perspective of interest rates. The interest rate mechanism takes on a term-structure to the extent that short- and long- run rates prevail. In short, "the financial sector of the MPS model was designed primarily to provide input for real sectors of the model, thus enabling us to analyze the impact of financial conditions on the overall performance of the economy."[18] The approach in the MPS was to study excess demand for various assets.[19]

A first step toward unraveling the casual relations in this sector is to list its equations in normal form. According to econometric practice, each equation should have only one endogenous variable on the left hand side (LHS).[20] This is also the method recommended by Carl Christ.[21] Based on a very early version of the MPS model, Table 6.1 shows only the main equations for the major sectors for the 1969 version of the MPS.[22]

As shown in Table 6.1, the financial sector has the largest number of equations. The development of the equations in the financial sector start with the net worth of consumers, A, being equal to the market value of existing real assets, V, and dependent on several rates of returns. In the short-run, net worth is equal to the real value of money, M, and government debts, D, i.e., $A = (M + D)/p$. The demand for money, M, depends on the nominal interest rate and the current value of international products.[23]

We now discuss the way in which monetary policies affect output and employment. First, we enter the financial model at the point where unborrowed reserves, *UR\$*, reserve requirements, *RR*, and the discount rate, i_d, affect the short-term money rate of interest, i_s, and the nominal money supply, *M\$*. Here, unborrowed reserves are total reserves, which are required reserves for demand and time deposits plus surplus or excess reserves and loans in federal fund market, less borrowing from the FRB and the federal fund market. This must be distinguished from the free reserves, which are surplus, or excess reserves less borrowings. In other words, the concept of free reserves does not include the required reserves.

Second, the short-term rate and nominal money supply ripples through the financial market. The i_d competes with the long-term rate, i_L, and the rate on savings deposits, i_{SL}. Third, the long-term rate will have a direct effect on the rental rate, RD^*, of durables in the real sector, affecting the desired stock of durables, KD^D, and investments in durables, *ID* in that sector. The long-term rate will also have a direct effect on the real rental rates on plant, *RP*, the real rental rate on capital, *RE*, the real rental rate of the state and local government stock of capital, *RSL*, and the market prices of houses, *PH*, that would in turn affect output and employment.

The long-term interest rate has many indirect effects on output and employment. From the equity market side, the long-term rate will have indirect and direct effects on the real sector. It will affect the mean anticipated real rate of return on equity, i_E, which in turn affects the market value of equity, V. The effect of i_E will augment changes in *RP* and *RE* in

Table 6.1 Causal structure for main equations of MPS, 1969

Equation number and sector.	LHS endogenous variables	RHS endogenous variables	Predetermined and exogenous variables	Comments
1. Consumption	*CON/N*	*YD, VCN / CON,*	$YD_{t-i} / N_{t-i}, VCN_{t-i} / CON_{t-i}, Ra$	1 of 6 eqs.
2. Investment	*OPD*	VPD_{t-1}	$VPD_{t-i} * XB_{t-i}$	1 of 19 eqs.
3. Housing	*HS1$*	*CON / N, RCH*1	$RCH_{t-i}, (D-DSL)_{t-i},$ $KH1, (PCON / PHCA)_{t-i}$, Time.	1 of 10 eqs.
4. Government	*EGSC$*	$\theta, \theta^* RSLG,$ $\theta^* PS / POBE,$	$GFS\$, \theta_{t-12}, \theta_{t-3} * RSLG_{t-3},$ $\theta * 100(PS_{t-i}-PS_{t-j}/PS_{t-j}),$ $KSL_{t-1} * PS * N$	1 of 6 eqs.
5. Inventory	*I*	*ECO, OPD*	$ECO_{t-i}, I_{t-i},$ $EGDP_{t-i}, ECO_{t-i}, NDI_{t-i},$ OPD_{t-1}	1 of 2 eqs.
6. Imports	*EIM*	*XOBE, XB / XBC*	*JCAA, JID, JIA, JIB*	1 of 2 eqs.
7. Labor	*LMHT*	*XBNF, XB / XBC, ULC*	$XBNF_{t-i}, JR, JT, R_a$	1 of 10 eqs.
8. Money	*MC$*	*ECO$, RTP*	$MC\$_{\Delta-1}, R_a$	1 of 35 eqs.

CON is Consumption, *N* is population, *YD* is personal disposable income, R_a is autoregressive structure, *t* is time, *i, j* are different period lags, *HS*1$ is single family starts, *RCH*1 is cost of single family capital, (*D* – *DSL*) is flow of funds into savings, *KH*1 is single family stock, *PCON* is price deflator for *CON*, *PHCA* is construction cost adjusted, $\theta = YS\$ / N * POBE * .00001$, *YS$* is GDP net of federal taxes and transfer, *POBE* is GNP deflator, *EGSC$* is state and local government construction expenditures, *RSLG* is municipal bond rate, PS is price deflator for *EGS*, *GFS$* is Federal Grants to state and local governments, *KSL* is stock of capital of state and local governments, *ECO* is personal consumption expenditures, *NDI* is man-hours idle due to major strikes, *I* is inventory, *EIM* is Import, *XOBE* is GNP, OBE definition, *XB* is GDP business product, *XBC* is production capacity of producers' durables, *JCAA*, *JID* , *JIA* , *JIB* are dummy variables, *LMHT* is man-hours, XBNF is nonfarm business and household products, *ULU* is unemployment rate, *JR* is productivity time trend, *JT* is strike dummy, *MC$* is currency outside banks, *RTP* is rates on passbook savings deposits at commercial banks, a $ sign means the variable is in nominal form.

the financial market and will have the effect described above on the real sector. The effect of *V* directly affects net worth, *NW*, in the real sector, leading to effects on output, *X*, and employment, *E*. Change of the long-term rate will also affect the rate on saving deposits, commercial loans, and mortgages, where investment in housing stands to gain, which translates into output and employment effects.

An early empirical fit of the monetary segment took the form of five equations.[24] They show "the major sources of exogenous influences upon the sectors (1) gross national product through the demand side of the market; (2) the instruments of monetary policy, unborrowed reserves, the discount rate, and reserve requirements through the supply side; and (3) the time deposits and commercial loans which are exogenous".[25] The fitted money demand and supply equations are:

$$M_d = -0.0021iY - 0.0043r_sY + 0.542Y + 0.0046NP + 0.833Md_{t-1} \tag{6.1}$$

$$\begin{aligned} FR = {} & (0.001 - 0.00204S_2 - 0.00237S_3 - 0.00223S_4)\overline{D}_{t-1} + 0.00122i\overline{D}_{t-1} \\ & + 0.00144d\, d\overline{D}_{t-1} + 0.646(1-\delta)\Delta RU - 0.502\delta\Delta CL \\ & + 0.394RD + 0.705\, FR_{t-1} \end{aligned} \tag{6.2}$$

where M_d is demand for deposits held by the public, Y is GNP, r_s is the savings deposit rate, i is the available returns on short-term assets, P is expected profits, FR is free reserves, S_i are seasonal adjustments, $\overline{D}$ is the expected value of the stock of member banks deposits, RU is unborrowed reserves, CL is commercial loans, RL is a reserve release term, and δ is a constant.

The equations 6.1 and 6.2 are clearly sprinkled with lags and expected variables. This had been a virtue in the early phase of their developments, but a vice when more sophisticated expectations beyond the Koyck lags, and adaptive hypotheses were necessary. Koyck lag is a way to achieve gradual adjustment by weighing the coefficients of lagged variables in an exponentially declining way. We shall discuss adaptive types of adjustments later, but for now we note two types in the MPS model. "The first type of delay is the usual stock adjustment, reflecting the time it takes for the public to adjust their cash balances to the desired level. A second source of delay might be expected to reflect the time it takes for the desired cash balances, or more precisely, for the desired ratio of money to transactions to respond to changes in interest rates."[26]

Modigliani had argued that the response from a change in unborrowed reserves to GNP works through lags, and is subject to some delayed effects. He wrote: "The response is clearly rather slow, as the money supply responds but gradually to the increase in reserves and in turn GNP responds gradually to the change in M."[27] It appears that the delay is mainly due to the approximately 16 period lags involved between the long and short-term interest rates. The specification for this relationship is as follows:[28]

$$R_t = \alpha + \beta_0 r_t + \sum_{i=1}^{m} \beta_i r_{t-1} + \eta(t) \tag{6.3}$$

where R_t is the long-term rate of interest, r is the short-term rate of interest and $\eta(t)$ is a stochastic error term.

Equation 6.3 follows Modigliani's several theoretical positions. It mirrors effects of the LCH in that people who save earn the short-term rate over several periods. In the short-term the market may be segmented so that people hold an asset that matches up with what they want to do at their age—saving either for retirement or for their children's education. On the other hand, we know that Modigliani harbored a preferred habitat theory as well, which states that people can invest in less preferred maturities if they get a risk premium to compensate them for that risk. The risk premium can be attached to the equation.

The question of lagged responses has invited several criticisms from the monetarist camp on the validity of stabilization policy. Monetarists take the position that monetary policy can not have a real effect on the economy. They argue that because the length of a lag is uncertain, a discretionary policy can turn out to be destabilizing. Because the lags are not known for certain, the monetarists argue, a new wave of discretionary policy being layered on a lag that is working its way through the economy will be destabilizing.[29] The monetarists, therefore, try to avoid lag structure in their models, vying more for adaptive and rational expectation specifications.

Modigliani embraced much of the rational expectation hypothesis in his term structure of the interest rate model. One model he used combined the "'Preferred Habitat' version of the Expectation Theory with a simple and readily tractable model of the formation of expectations, a model in which expected future rates are represented by a linear function of past rates."[30] This model was extended to include changes in the price level as well, and its results were compared with those of the rational expectation hypothesis. Central to this model is that "(1) the long rates were an average of expected future rates ... and (2) the expected future rates tended to represent optimal forecasts–as called for by the rational expectation hypothesis."[31] Modigliani tested these views by first estimating a fit for equation 6.3 to yield the following estimate for the MPS model using data for 1954:4 to 1966:4.

$$RS = 0.99 + 0.73RCP + 0.07P + 0.07S \tag{6.4}$$

where *RS* is Moody's Aaa corporate bond yield average, *RCP* is 4–6 month prime commercial paper rate, *P* is annual rate of inflation, and *S* is eight quarters moving standard deviation of *RCP*. The coefficients of inflation and commercial rate are the sum for 19 period lags.

Modigliani built in two adjustments to equation 6.3 to obtain the estimates of equation 6.4. The two adjustments are $p \equiv \Delta p / p$ for the rate of change in prices, and $i_t = r_t - p_t$ for the real interest rate. With these definitions, we can at the present time express the short-term rate to prevail at a future date "as the sum of an expected real rate, and an expected rate of changes of prices for that period."[32] The result is an improvement in the fit of the model: "What is most relevant for present purposes is that the contribution of the price variable remains substantial, with several coefficients again having t-ratios in the order of 3 and 4."[33]

Finally, Modigliani compared his results with a rational expectation version. The rational expectation model tested used Bayesian methods of estimation to graft information into the price and interest rate variables. Forecasts were obtained for the regressions of RCP on itself lagged several periods, and on $I = RCP - p$ and prices. The results were expressed in general terms such that "rational expectations of future *r* should take *p* into account,"[34] and that conditions that should be satisfied if the long-term rates are to be considered rational were "broadly satisfied."[35] The issue of whether lag structure captures rational expectation appears to be inconclusive. We shall take another look at this issue in the adaptive and rational expectation in relation to MPS.

The investment block

Following the Keynesian tradition, the investment segment of the MPS collects all the autonomous expenditures. They include "housing, producer's equipment and structures, and the expenditures and taxes of state and local governments. All of these items are relatively insensitive to the current quarter's income and relatively sensitive to interest rates and relative prices."[36]

The investment block observes investment in plant and equipment, the housing sector, state and local government investment, and taxes. The specifications for producer durables follow a neoclassical model that operates through capital-output ratios varying due to changes in interest rates, tax regulations, and relative prices. The "putty clay" specification, to the extent that permanent changes in interest have gradual influence over the lifetime of the investment, was found particularly suited for producer's equipment. A CES rather than Cobb-Douglas specification is used, and both actual or expected prices and output are incorporated into the specification of producer durable goods.[37]

The housing sector provides a flow of services for residents and equity for owners. The rental price in this sector varies with real income and population, and the supply of houses. Houses and mortgages are not assumed to be perfect complements as the rate of return does not adjust equiproportionally to mortgage rates.

The consumption-inventory block

This sector contains the analysis of consumption, inventory investment, imports, personal income, and taxes. "The multiplier sector would be an appropriate title for this block" of factors mentioned above.[38] The consumption sector of the MPS was built on Modigliani's life cycle hypothesis. One adjustment was made for temporary equilibrium because consumers will attempt to balance their portfolio after they purchase consumer durable goods. Another adjustment was to make labor and property income one variable measuring the net worth of households. For the period of 1953 to 1965, the model, as illustrated in equation 6.5, contains *CON* as aggregate consumption, *YD* as disposable income, *R* as relative rental rate of durable goods, *KC* as consumer asset portfolio, and the sum of the βs as 0.429.[39] It was difficult to fit the wealth variable in explicitly, but the lagged income variable is a partial substitute for a direct wealth variable.[40]

$$\frac{CON}{YD} = 0.3531 + 0.28\left[\frac{KC_{t-1}}{YD}\right] + 0.0419R + \sum_{i=1}^{10}\beta_i\left[\frac{YD_{t-1}}{YD}\right] \qquad 6.5$$

The consumption block distinguishes between several types of consumption such as consumption on nondurables and services, the imputed services of autos, and other durables. Those consumption expenditures vary with interest rate, population, relative prices, and stock of durables. The total estimate in equation 6.5 is constrained since the independent variables affect several categories of total consumption, yet do not affect total consumption.

The money, investment and consumption sectors

In putting together the three sectors discussed above, portfolio analysis becomes pivotal in the MPS model. This combination takes demographic variables such as population, government expenditures, taxes, money variables and exports as exogenous. In the early stages, a labor market was not yet specified, so wages and prices, excluding housing prices and rents, were considered exogenous as well.[41]

The combined three sectors were simulated for 1965:3 to 1966:4. One critical equation resulting from the combination was corporate dividend payments which channel through stock prices and personal income. A simulation of the model without the labor market did not capture a small level of growth that took place in 1966:4, and had a large error in predicting the treasury bill rates for 1966:2. Demand deposits failed to capture the decline in 1966. In other simulations for changes in unborrowed reserves, defense spending, and taxes, fiscal policy reacted differently from monetary policies in the specification of lags, which is pointed out later in this chapter. The model was thus in need of some respecification.

MPS and the tax incident problem

One traditional test of a model is to determine how it handles a change in taxes. Modigliani and Steindel[42] assessed the impact of the tax rebate on the consumption sector, when $8 billion was rebated in the second quarter ($32 billion annual rate) of 1975. They also revisited the tax reduction of 1964, and the tax surcharge of 1968. They did so using a traditional MPS specification, and a special one with independent variables including labor and property income before and after taxes, the unemployed, OASDHI (Old Age, Survivors, Disability, and Health Insurance) and transfer payments, consumer's net worth, windfall OASDHI payments, labor and property taxes, and a one period autoregressive structure. They fitted two equations for consumption, and two for consumer expenditures for the period from 1955:4 to 1975:1.

The MPS model showed that approximately 30 per cent of the 1975 rebate was spent during the second and third quarters of 1975. When adding two more quarters, 1972:2 and 1976:1 to the sample, approximately 61 per cent of the rebate was spent. The overall conclusion was that "there is strong, though not uniform, evidence that a rebate is not a particularly effective way of producing a prompt and temporary stimulus to consumption." Modigliani did not think that a permanent tax cut would do any better. Rather, he felt that change in sales and excise taxes would have stimulated consumption more.[43]

MPS and simulation

Zellner and Peck[44] put the MPS model to a test for the period 1964:1 to 1966:2. Their simulation examined the final demand and financial sectors. They looked for effects of symmetry and depression. "In the first set of experiments, we subject the model to symmetric increases and decreases in an important monetary and then a fiscal policy control variable. Our objectives are to determine the extent to which induced changes in the model's endogenous variables are symmetric and/or linear ... In the second set of experiments, we set up conditions such as to make the model produce a major depression. Again, the objective is to provide a check on the global properties of the model and to discover possible weaknesses in its formulation."[45] Policy effects in the MPS model are channeled through unborrowed reserves and currency in the hands of the public, *M*, personal income tax rates, *T*, and government expenditures, *G*. The simulation was based on changing *M* by one to five billion dollars, and T by two to five percentage points in the positive and negative directions.

Zellner and Peck found symmetric responses of output to one billion dollar changes in *M*, but asymmetry in the response of the general price level variable measured by the implicit GNP deflator. Perhaps there was a "nonlinear asymmetric dependence of the employee compensation variable on the unemployment rate. Since the general price level is related to the employee compensation variable in a 'mark-up' equation, the effects of the aforementioned asymmetric nonlinearity are reflected in the behavior of the general price level."[46] The simulation test shows asymmetry in the 5 per cent tax reduction, and reinforces the asymmetric changes in the price level. The symmetric test for output did not converge for a three and five billion dollar increase in the money supply. The simulation found that price changes depart from linearity for changes in taxes and money. For a "3 points or less in *T* and downward changes of about 2 or 3 billion in *M*, the variables that we studied responded almost linearly with the exception of the general price level variable."[47]

Inducing a depression by a strong decrease in *M* of 5 per cent per quarter for 5 quarters resulted in more than a doubling of the unemployment rate from 5 to 12 per cent. Some anomalous results in price, interest, and government deficits took place. In particular, price remained stable at its 1963:1 level. Bonds and TB (treasury bills) interest rates moved up to an extremely high level of 15 per cent. Federal deficit, *G-T*, moved up by $50 billion, and state and local deficits increased to approximately $11 billion. Attempts to correct the deficit problems by reducing G and increasing financial aid to states did not work well–GDP fell more, prices did not fall, and the deficits increased. In terms of the IS-LM apparatus, a cut in M shifted the LM curve to the left, increasing the interest rate and lowering GNP. The fiscal effect did not increase the IS curve enough to compensate for the leftward shift in the LM curve, keeping rates of interest high and output low. Zellner and Peck speculated that " ... changes in anticipations of consumers and investors are not adequately incorporated in the model's consumption and investment equations."[48] Had anticipations been correct, the IS curve would have fully adjusted to eliminate the high interest rate and return output to its equilibrium level. This simulation is a hint that the model may be misspecified, needing some work in the area of how agents anticipate prices.

MPS and stagflation

The decade of the 1970s was dominated by simultaneous inflation and unemployment, called stagflation. Being a new phenomenon, the stagflation problem required that most large-scale econometric models such as the MPS should be respecified to take account of how expected changes in the inflation rate affect prices. At first, the attempts to remedy such omissions took the form of augmenting expectations through the Phillips Curve. Afterwards, it became debatable as to whether the MPS model based on traditional Keynesian theory should be replaced by a model based on General Equilibrium analysis of the rational expectations type.

The early 1970s opened up with two shocks, the devaluation of the dollar, and the OPEC crisis. In the context of the MPS, Albert Ando considered the shocks as an imposition of an excise tax.[49] In that context, the OPEC revenues are collected as taxes but are not spent in the economy, and the falling dollar is equivalent to a removal of export taxes and import subsidies equivalent to the removal of negative excise taxes. The estimated impact of these excise taxes was quite variable, from \$30 to \$60 billion. Using a 6 per cent growth in the money supply and fiscal policies that were ongoing in 1974, Ando forecast that from 1973:4 to 1974:4, the fall in GNP in constant prices was between the annual rates of 2.3 to 3.8 per cent and the inflation rate between 9.3 to 10.6 per cent annually. Compared with the actual fall of GNP of 3.5 per cent and the actual inflation rate of 11 per cent, the forecast was neither far off nor was it an anomaly. A similar forecast for the 1974:4 to 1975:4 period showed GNP falling from 0.4 to 1.1 per cent. This was a small decline, but the actual GNP increased by

2.4 per cent. The inflation forecast was from 6.4 to 7.8 per cent, while the actual rate was 7.4 per cent, still not enough of a difference between the actual and the forecast rate to be called a spectacular failure.

Another appraisal of the model for the 1974:1 to 1983:4 period was made with a then larger MPS model, containing 332 equations, with 123 behavioral specifications, 197 exogenous variables, and 208 identities.[50] Brayton and Mauskopf constructed a small-scale model to unveil the steady-state structure of the full MPS model. Essentially, the MPS used an autoregressive construct rather than a rational expectations specification to model expectations. The key dynamic features had lags and expectations at the center. In particular, the major functions were determined as follows:

> in the life-cycle model, consumption depends on expected future values of labour income and the return on wealth; investment depends on expected requirements for future productive capacity and the future path of the cost of capital, the long-term interest rate moves with the expected future pattern of short- term interest rate; the value of corporate equity equals the present value of future profits; wages depend on expected price changes.[51]

The 1985 appraisal of the MPS took on a distinct IS-LM block approach. The IS block contains consumption, investment, government, and net export components. Its typical response to the simulation for the 1974:1 to 1983:4 period was to overshoot, and then to settle down in a corridor around the long-run position. The LM block used the standard M1 and M2 definition of money at that time. It used an arbitrage condition that we explained in the M&M model to equate expected return on equity and bonds. Responsiveness to the M1 and M2 drivers depends on the cumulative elasticities of their lags, which are –0.11 and –0.14, respectively, at a rate of interest of 10 per cent. For example, the long run elasticity achieves its response after four quarter lags for an interest rate of less than 15 per cent.

In addition to the IS/LM blocks, the 1985 appraisal gives specifications for other sectors such as labor markets, production functions, government, net exports, income and its distribution, and prices. No new specifications for expectations were attempted beyond one accounted for by lags, adaptive mechanisms, and the inclusion of some expected variables.

Phillips curve and the MPS in the 1960s

Modigliani was aware of inflation problems in his inputs to the MPS models. He accounted for inflation through the MPS labor market segment where prices and wages are prominent, and in other sectors where expected variables are permitted. Improvement for expectation is incorporated mainly in the labor market where wages and prices are determined. Modigliani wrote that "the price level ($p\$$) is determined by an oligopolistic mark-up on long-run minimum average cost; its main component is unit labour cost determined by the wage rate ($w\$$) and long-run productivity, α ... the wage rate is determined by a fairly conventional Phillips mechanism that is, $\dot{w}\$$ is a function of the rate of unemployment (u) and the rate of change in prices, $\dot{p}\$$ .... Finally, $\dot{p}\$$ contributes to the determination of real interest rate by influencing expectations about the future rate of change in various prices."[52] Changes in the expected rate of inflation, $\hat{\pi}$ is set by some proportion, γ, between the actual inflation, π, and the expected inflation. Modigliani expressed the relationship as follows.[53]

$$\hat{\pi} - \hat{\pi}_{-1} = \gamma(\pi_{-1} - \hat{\pi}_{-1}) \qquad 0 < \gamma \leq 1 \qquad 6.6$$

To take an analogy with temperature, let's say today, which we will call Monday, *t*, we expect that the temperature will be 90 degrees tomorrow, Tuesday, *t*+1, but the temperature turned out to be 80 degrees on Tuesday. Then we have made an error of over forecasting the temperature by 10 degrees. That is our current error. We must now correct our expectation for that error. If $\gamma = 1$, then our change in the expected rate of inflation would be 10+80 = 90 degrees. Often, $\gamma < 1$, then we would only partially adjust to our current error. This type of adjustment is on the adaptive expectation side.

Adaptive vs. rational expectation in the MPS

When the MPS was under construction in the 1960s, only an adaptive expectations model was known. Phillip Cagan, invented the adaptive expectations model in his studies of hyper-inflation.[54] The adaptive hypothesis was a welcome tool in both the Monetarist and Keynesian camps. During the time the MPS was being built, policy makers used monetary restraint in 1966 and a tax surge in 1968 to counteract the inflation that had started in 1965. Monetary growth was down from 7 per cent in 1968 to 3 per cent in 1969, but inflation did not abate. The policy effort was then to accept a higher than natural rate of unemployment to stabilize prices.

In his interesting way of sizing up the problem, Cagan was neutral between the Monetarists and Keynesian ideologies in his policy recommendation. He wrote:

> Economists had already been debating whether full employment and price stability were compatible. Some argued that an inflationary bias in the economy necessitated rising prices at high employment so that, unfortunately, only some permanent level of unemployment could maintain price stability. Others argued that in the long-run the level of unemployment was not changed by the rate of inflation. But the debate did not immediately affect the policy decisions of early 1969. Consumer prices were rising by more than 6 per cent a year and the economy was operating at full capacity. Whether or not there was a long-run trade-off between unemployment and price inflation, few believed that the 1969 combination could not be improved if the economy were guided through a temporary period of reduced aggregate demand.[55]

One can speculate as to whether Cagan's neutral position was a result of both sides using his adaptive model. At that time the "expectations-augmented Phillips Curve"[56] of a short-run nature, and one of a long-run nature were in vogue.[57] Modigliani was evolving the concept of the Non-Inflationary Rate of Unemployment (NIRU). The idea that a constant rate of inflation was achieved when the Phillips Curve was vertical, the so-called Natural Rate hypothesis, was also known at the time. Modigliani argued that the "non-vertical view of the long-run Philips curve also implies the existence of a NIRU since it implies that for any given unemployment, inflation will keep decreasing as long as it is above the value implied by the long-run Phillips curve." What Modigliani said was that a "negligible" rate of inflation exists when the short- and long-run Phillips Curve intersect. This view is relevant because at that time, it was empirically difficult to provide a vertical Phillips Curve.

Following Milton Friedman (1968) and Edmund S. Phelps (1968), Modigliani recognized that the Phillips curve relationships were unstable because "they resulted from actions of economic agents induced by unanticipated price fluctuations under conditions of imperfect information. Expectational errors could persist, resulting in transitory output fluctuation, but in the long run actual and expected price changes could not deviate systematically. Consequently, in the steady state there is a unique 'natural full-employment output level which is invariant to permanent inflation."[58]

Phelps explained in detail how the economy moves to a market equilibrium through a process of changing expectations. A market equilibrium is distinguished from a competitive equilibrium in that it accounts for "vision and fears" agents may have about future prospects. Phelps' early thought in the 1960s channeled expectations through wages where output increased with demand and unemployment stayed near some temporary equilibrium. Demand increases were driven by forces that were not probabilistic, such as wars. Rational Expectations models brought in randomness and conditional expectation that ignored some of these forces. Phelps saw to it that expectations of future prospects will consider events such as public debts, productivity, and the possibility of wars. Therefore, the economy would not be reaching its competitive equilibrium.

Friedman's approach and Phelps' Phillips Curve explained employment by real rather than nominal wages. When inflation is fully anticipated, it should have an effect on real wages. But this leaves room for unanticipated inflation to affect output and employment in the short term. In the long term, when all expectations adjust, the unemployment rate will settle on its natural level.[59] The Phillips Curve then is just the right hand side of equation 6.6 plus the NAIRU. Therefore, if the actual and expected rates are equal, the economy would be in the long-run natural or NAIRU level.

The builders of the MPS models in the 1960s were aware that the augmented Phillips Curve was not predicting well. The problem as it related to the MPS was well summarized in a speech by the Federal Reserve Governor Edward M. Gramlich. Gramlich stated that the model "didn't have a forward-looking expectations behavior. In qualitative terms we all knew the difference between adaptive and rational expectations, but nobody knew how to estimate rational expectation equations ... .the modeling group was quite aware of the natural rate hypothesis then. We knew that an adaptive expectations Phillips Curve would explode if the lag coefficient was one—we just couldn't get its estimated value to be one ... our nonlinear Phillips Curves became very, very steep at low unemployment rates, implying that inflation would become uncontrollable at low unemployment rates."[60]

Empirical Phillips Curve

Given the discussion on adaptive expectation above, we can capture the existing features of the Phillips Curve in the 1960s and early 1970s in an equation. Basically, it will be a fraction, λ, of the 11.5 per cent expected inflation we estimated above, plus a fraction of the unemployment rate. The curve will be vertical if λ is equal to one. The actual curve Modigliani fitted was a " ... 'reduced form' relation resulting from the interaction of two basic equations: (1) a price equation according to which prices adjust gradually to a target level determined by unit labor costs and exogenous input price; unit labor costs in turn depend on wages and productivity; and (2) a Phillips wage equation relating changes in wages to unemployment and previous changes in prices of the basket of goods bought by workers, including food as well as non-food prices. The effect of past inflation on wages may partly reflect expectations of future inflation."[61] The fitted equation for the annual time frame 1953 to 1971 was as follows:

$$p\dot{c}x = -0.42 + 8.2(1/ua) + 0.68\, p\dot{c}x\,(-1) - 0.24\dot{\pi} + 0.081\, p\dot{m}x + 0.059\dot{p}f(-1) \tag{6.7}$$
$$\quad (0.73)\quad (2.4) \qquad\quad (0.10) \qquad\qquad (0.10) \quad (0.044) \qquad (0.033)$$

The standard errors are in brackets, the adjusted R-square is 0.88, the Durbin Watson value was 1.80, *ua* is unemployment rate, $\dot{p}$ is the rate of inflation, $\dot{\pi}$ is the rate of change in productivity, $p\dot{m}x$ is the rate of change of the price index of imports, $\dot{p}f$ is the rate of change of the index of farm products, and $p\dot{c}x$ is the change in the overall price index. The equation explains inflation by current unemployment, lagged inflation, and three exogenous variables.

Modigliani argued that equation 6.7 "fits quite well the data for the period of observations as indicated by the standard error, and, what is more important, when extrapolated to the 1970s."[62] He estimated that the lagged inflation coefficient was 0.82, which is close to one when the standard error is taken into consideration. The Natural Rate hypothesis, therefore, seems plausible, and cannot be rejected.[63] In 1974, equation 6.7 attributed approximately 60 per cent of the 10 per cent inflation rate to farm and import prices due to oil imports and devaluation.

Using the estimates of equation 6.7, Modigliani proceeded with two types of analyses–one for long-term trends in unemployment and inflation, and the other for a vertical Phillips Curve. The analysis is elevated one step further, taking into consideration lack of foresight and perfect foresight to determine the optimal unemployment and inflation policies for alternative welfare objectives. The public wants to minimize the weighted sum of deviations of unemployment and inflation from their equilibrium levels, i.e.,

$$\min w_u \sum_{t=1}^{\infty} |u_t - \bar{u}| + w_p \sum_{t=1}^{\infty} |p_t - \bar{p}| \tag{6.8}$$

Equation 6.8 is a welfare function between inflation and unemployment. It is a line in the inflation and unemployment plane with its slope defined by the ratio of the unemployment to the inflation weights, $-w_u/w_p$. If the tangency of the welfare line and the short-term Phillip Curve occur at the NIRU level, then a policy that maintains the NIRU inflation rate will result in a "gradual decline in inflation toward the target value ... regardless of the initial rate of inflation."[64]

Given values for the weight of the welfare line, we can calculate optimal unemployment and inflation policies for welfare objectives, under the Natural Rate hypothesis, and under imperfect foresight. Assume equal weights for unemployment and inflation of 0.5 in 1975, then the computed unemployment rate is 6.5, and the inflation rate is 7.77. Corresponding estimates under the Natural Rate hypothesis are 9.9 and 5.2 per cent, respectively.[65] Under conditions of uncertain supply shocks, the unemployment and inflation rates are estimates at 6.28 and 8.66 when the Phillips Curve is not vertical, and 7.92 and 6.93 per cent when the Phillips Curve is vertical.[66] Comparing these estimates with the historic data, Modigliani concluded that "at least when there is a long-run trade-off, even if quite steep, lack of foresight does not seem to be very costly and hence does not pose a serious problem."[67] Overall, the NIRU rate is estimated at approximately 4.8 per cent, giving a "negligible" inflation rate of 2 per cent.[68]

From MPS to FRB/US model,paradigm shift, extension,or micro revolution

In the world of econometrics, the prevalence of anomalies in a model is an important criterion to be used for its rejection. In theory, whether one anomaly can falsify a theory is an issue. In practice, econometricians re-specify their model to accommodate anomalies. They follow the die-hard approach that maintains the hard-core elements of their econometric program. We look at these applications in the MPS model.

Frank de Leeuw and Edward Gramlich[69] provided the first preliminary report on some results of the 1968 version of the MPS model. They identified some weaknesses of the model from the specification side. Their appraisal selected financial, investment, and consumption-inventory equations to analyze the effect of monetary policy on the economy. The model was fitted to data through 1965, and predictions were done for 1966 and 1967. The emphasis was not on the statistical properties of individual equations, but on the model's overall ability to predict. The model predicted that GNP deviated approximately by $1.5 billion from its actual level up to the 1966:3 quarter, but became as large as $9 billion for the 1966:4 quarter. The forecast of aggregate demand also shows similar divergencies for the 1966:4 quarter. The model was found strong in its monetary specifications where divergencies for the whole period were approximately $0.6 billion. The forecast of the treasury bills rate was somewhat high, varying from 25 to 38 basis points over the four quarters of 1966, but the forecasts for corporate bond rates were accurate for most of the quarters. The general conclusion of this preliminary work using policy simulations was cautionary. The "model finds monetary policy to be quite powerful–much more so than is found in other econometric models."[70] The results were selective, using only "best specification of the way monetary policy affects the economy," and the authors "caution against using them as a basis for generalizations about stabilization policy."[71]

Rasche and Shapiro[72] performed a forecast assessment of the MPS model. For the period of 1958 to 1965, or 32 quarters, the model tracked GNP closely. It was off a bit in tracking aggregate demand, particularly in forecasting consumer durables and the housing sector. They also analyzed the multipliers of the model for bank credit, defense expenditures, and personal income taxes. The levels of the multipliers after 11 periods were estimated as 10, 6, and 4 respectively. The money multiplier of 10 supported the idea that "money matters." The multipliers governing stabilization policies were low, implying that it takes a long time, approximately two years, to realize a policy effect. Defense and tax multipliers attained 75 per cent of their effect after 2–3 quarters.

Ray Fair[73] also reviewed Charles Nelson's[74] work as a standard for measuring the FMP performance from the econometric point of view. Nelson used the Mean Square Error (MSE) and an ARIMA model of his own to assess the predictive performance of the FMP. First, he obtained predicted values of the FMP model and constructed alternative predictions based on the ARIMA process. The ARIMA model used only information on the past values of variables. By neglecting the current and future conditions, its information content can be only partial. Second, Nelson regressed actual values of the variables on the two predicted variables, one from the FMP, and one from the ARIMA model. We would expect that if the FMP had used information efficiently, then the ARIMA model that contains past information would be redundant, and, therefore, its coefficient should not be significantly different from zero. Nelson found that "If the FMP model make[s] efficient use of that information, that is, if it does in fact provide conditional expectation predictions, then the ARIMA models which draw on only a subset of the same information should not be able to contribute to the accuracy of the composite predictions which combine both."[75] Nelson found that the coefficients of the ARIMA model were significantly different from zero, implying that the FMP model did not use all information efficiently. In the forecast of GNP, the MSE for the FMP model was 77.259, much higher than the MSE of 36.652 for the ARIMA model. The same relationship holds for expenditures on consumer and for producer durable goods, government expenditures for state and local government, the unemployment rate, and three different interest rates. The result points to the fact that the ARIMA model has ignored information from simple time series data.

On the prediction of actual GNP data, Nelson fitted his ARIMA model from 1947:1 to 1966:4. He found that the forecast of the FMP was low by $4.9 billion in 1968:3, and $4.4 billion in 1968:4. The corresponding numbers for his ARIMA model were much smaller, $0.5 billion and $2.4 billion, respectively, implying that the simple ARIMA model had outperformed the large-scale FMP model.

In an earlier section, we examined the simulation by Zellner and Peck for the period of 1964:1 to 1966:2. Their results pointed to the need to improve the model's specification. On the other hand, we discussed other simulations in the tax and stagflation section above where Modigliani was able to demonstrate that the model was robust in its prediction.

A study by Mauskopf appraised the FMP model for changes that had occurred in the economy up to 1990.[76] Those changes include the abandonment of fixed exchange rates in the 1970s, the integration of the global financial market, and removal of regulatory ceilings on deposits rates, large corporate debts in the 1980s, and the introduction of adjustable mortgage rates. Using the MPS model to assess these changes, the study found that output is no longer sensitive to changes in monetary policy the way it was in the 1960s and 1970s, for the first three to four years after the policy was introduced.

To assess whether the MPS model was consistent with rational expectations, McCallum[77] used a small scale MPS model created by

Albert Ando.[78] This model determines real wage rates and prices as $P = WF(L(E/X),\mu, u, P_{t-1}$, where P is price level, W is nominal wage rate per man-hours, E is employment per man-hours, X is net national product, μ is a mark-up factor, and u is the unemployment rate. Changes in the money wage level are dependent on changes in the past period prices, and the unemployment rate. McCallum reasoned, "It would seem appropriate to interpret the distributed lags of previous inflation rates as proxy for the expected rate of inflation ... . Modigliani might not approve of this interpretation, but it is certainly consistent with a very large portion of the Phillips curve literature."[79] This gives McCallum a supply equation to mesh with a demand equation consisting of consumption, investment and portfolio holdings. Finally, he added a feedback rule to the supply and demand equations. With this apparatus, McCallum found that the rational expectation hypothesis "does not hold by exhibiting a dependence of the conditional mean of output ... on the parameters of the money feedback rule."[80]

So far, Modigliani would have agreed the MPS and rational expectation hypothesis are inconsistent. He maintained that attempts to stabilize the economy by policy rules would be ineffective, and the attempt by McCallum to layer expectation and policy rules on the MPS may have borne this out. McCallum demonstrated that the inconsistency lay elsewhere. He showed that it could not be the relationship between adaptive specification and the mark-up oligopoly pricing equation. He wrote that "the failure of the MREH and MPS models does not result because of markup pricing or sluggish adjustments ... . Instead, the failure results from the joint appearance of 'mixing' of real and nominal variables in the pricing equation."[81] The point is that the supply equation should have only real variables, and this apparently is not unique only to the MPS, but to other well-known models as well.

In 1996, the FRB/US model replaced the MPS. In a recent article, Zellner stated that the "complaints were that it did not forecast well, that its outputs were not understandable, etc. Finally, the model was shut down and efforts have been instituted to produce an improved model."[82] Zellner suggested that the move was more toward models with simple solutions, rather than sophisticated large-scale models. Others have suggested that the change was to incorporate expectations more explicitly. For example, "the new model can show how the anticipation of future events, such as a legislated reduction in future defense spending, may affect the economy today. Similarly, the FRB/US model can be used to examine the extent to which the consequences of inflation of a sharp increase in the price of oil depend on the course of monetary policy anticipated by the public."[83] The FRB/US model incorporated rational and Vector Autoregression types of expectations with a view to improving forecasts. Modigliani's life cycle theory, mark-up theory of prices, and the NAIRU concepts are still standard inputs to the model, but with new expectation specifications.[84]

According to the development of the literature, some may view the replacement of the MPS by the FRB/US model as a paradigm-shift based on the way expectations are incorporated in models in general. To the extent that we now have a model that has moved from making economic reality the pillar of its specification, to a simpler model that looks at only the forecast, a micro revolution may have taken place. With regards to the foundation of expectations, the changes appear more in the nature of a counter-revolution than a revolution. We had Keynes theory that public opinion influences expectations in a manner analogous to how beauty queens were selected in his day, in that judges tried to predict the public's taste in beauty. Following this, Bayesian methods were developed to add information to a model. The development of cognitive psychology allowed expected utility theory of the game theoretic type to perform experiments. The work of the rational expectation economists takes us back to the Bayesian area by making expectations conditional upon information.

Looking over these trends in the development of expectations in econometric models, Kenneth J. Arrow has suggested "failures of the rationality hypothesis are in fact compatible with some of the specific observations of cognitive psychologists."[85] He picked up the argument from Cagan's[86] view that a simple extrapolation of the current spot price is an accurate predictor of the future spot price. This Arrow thought would mean the absence of private information.[87] Spot and future prices are random variables. Future prices would change as new information is accumulated on a daily basis. But according to the *representativeness* heuristic of cognitive psychology, people judge future prices by what present evidence they have. Future prices are also affected by framing, the *extensionality* heuristic, meaning that people consume not only according to the opportunity set that is available but also on how it is described. When we double prices and income, we say that the budget is the same, and therefore, demand will not change, i.e., it is homogenous to degree zero. However, the description of the set has changed, and experiments have shown that agents change their behavior when the description changes. One example of changes due to framing is the Allais paradox where the certainty equivalent is a large sum of money, and the lottery is framed with a small chance of death.

Conclusion

Econometricians are a die-hard group of researchers. They continue to stick with their models with the good intention of making them forecast better. From the first version of the MPS, through many respecifications, the hardcore contributions of Modigliani still resonate. As the amendments to MPS by the adaptive expectation hypothesis was progressive and then degenerative, so, too, is its amendment by the rational and the Vector Autoregression (VAR) expectations hypotheses, which are degenerating. But we invariably find that the hard core of the MPS remains intact, where money transmits to influence output, LCH, portfolio balancing, and other Modigliani specifications for the MPS or FRB/US model.

Appendix A
A Question of Identity

The thought given to this appendix is to try to illuminate some aspect of the inner Franco Modigliani even though the literal truth is that economics was his life. When it came to research activities, he was relentless, incredibly focus-driven, passionate and able to sustain extraordinary intensity. In contrast to the way Oscar Wilde describes great artists as dull in *The Picture of Dorian Grey* because they are totally absorbed in their work, Modigliani was anything but dull. Moreover, anyone who came into contact with him was taken by his infectious enthusiasm.

It was Franco Modigliani's good friend, the MIT's 1969 Nobel laureate in medicine, Salvador E.Luria, who noted that a biographer of scientists should not only explore the scholar's scientific endeavors but also capture "the more controversial, more intimate aspects of the subject's personality." As an example he mentions that "to examine Pasteur without his roots in French provincial bourgeois life or Einstein without his relation to Judaism is to diminish them."[1]

Our interest in Modigliani's identity the purpose of which is to supplement his intellectual portrait was whetted by his autobiography. The early chapters charting events prior to his arrival to the United States are punctuated with references indicating his Italian Sephardic roots. It is of interest to note that during World War II his mother found refuge in Palestine. Modigliani, however, referred to it as Israel even though the state was founded only in 1948.

As the narrative unfolds, the latter chapters are devoid of any mention of his roots or of Israel where he lectured. Moreover, he appears to exalt in his wife, Serena's and his decision not to provide any Jewish education to their children. However, in my interview with Leah Modigliani, the granddaughter, she mentioned that in her youth she was a member of Hashomer Hatzair, a Zionist leftist group.

Since most scientists tend to distrust, in the words of Jacob Bronowski, the "not-formalizable," they shy away from abstract thought.[2] This overly rational mindset guiding scientists might explain why Modigliani avoids expressing abstract emotions and feelings, such as passion, anguish or doubt toward his religion and heritage. There are many academics who have attained their success only through years of organizing their lives into chapters of almost entirely dispassionate, rational, coherent events. Janna Malamud, a Boston psychoanalyst, daughter of the famous writer, Bernard Malamud writes, "My father was frequently uncomfortable with the messy, fleshy reality of life. He rather preferred himself as a book – at least sometimes."

Janna Malamud remembers, "My father disliked the label Jewish Writer." Once when identified by a taxi driver as Jewish, "he answered stiffly, 'I'm an American Professor.'"[3] Bernard Malamud's composed demeanor and dislike for discussing his personal and religious past is plausible given his troubled childhood and his utter shame over his immigrant past. Towards the end of his life, the irreligious Malamud, who asked that his body be cremated, regretted not having a Jewish spouse and urged his daughter to marry a Jew. Modigliani, in contrast, apart from his father's untimely death, recounts his childhood as happy and uneventful, not counting, of course, his frequent boisterous tantrums. Unlike Malamud, Modigliani shows neither embarrassment nor disdain for any parts of his past, Italian and Jewish. Assuming Modigliani considered all of his past equally important – the progression and outcome of his life, why then, does he show no recognition of his Jewish heritage?

Jewish intellectuals usually make it a point to discuss in detail their Jewish identity, be it with pride or disdain, along with their religious convictions or lack thereof and all of its related consequences, such as the formation of a Jewish state and the Holocaust. At a Jerusalem symposium, Hannah Arendt, for example, openly lamented her fate of having been born a Jew. She spoke of "the misery and misfortune of my life – having been born a Jewess – this I should on no account now wish to have missed." Henry Roth, the famous author of *Call It Sleep*, who for 40 years experienced a writer's block, astonishingly suggested that Jews in America might add to the gifts they had already conferred to humanity: "the last and greatest one: of orienting themselves toward ceasing to be Jews." Aharon Applefeld, an Israeli novelist pointedly asked: "How could [one] bear to waste [one's] cultural legacy?"[4]

Nathan Sharansky, the celebrated Russian dissident refutes in his biography those who claim that Jews are focused too much on Jewish issues despite the evidence to the contrary. He tells of his Russian Jewish friends "who insisted that what was important was not saving Soviet Jewry but saving the world. Paradoxically those who tried to save the world by taking up Communism ended up creating a slave state." Sharansky cites Cynthia Ozick's story on the shofar. The shofar has a broad opening and a narrow opening "If you blow into the broad end, you get nothing. If you blow into the narrow end, you get a sound everyone can hear."[5]

While most secular Jewish intellectuals take a stance or at least display some curiosity regarding their heritage, Modigliani showed not the slightest interest. At a lecture delivered by Gershon Levy at Oxford University in 1952, the eminent philosopher and self-proclaimed agnostic Jew, Isaiah Berlin, agreed with the speaker that "We Jews are both a religion and a people. When we were liberated from Egypt – the Exodus – we entered history as a people, and when we were given the Ten Commandments at Mount Sinai we entered history as a people." He added enigmatically "we are steeped in memory. We have longer memories than anybody. Hence, we are aware of continuity and heritage more than any other surviving community in the world."[6] Robert Pinsky, who served an unprecedented three terms as U.S. Poet Laureate, seconds the statements by stating that "Jews are nothing if not memory; we are made of memory."[7]

Modigliani however does not focus on or highlight any memorable or personal experiences of any Jewish holidays, religious activities or Jewish saga. Why? Although, he supplies no evidence to assume any anger or disdain toward Judaism, inference or supposition to the contrary may not be compelling enough to merit dismissal either. Modigliani, however, barely mentions his identity, let alone discusses his Jewish past, calling himself first and foremost an Economist. He enrolled his children in Quaker schools, proclaiming himself as "free thinking" and having no intention of "reconnecting" to religious bigotry, thus, effectively disconnecting from his Jewish heritage, albeit unintentional, perhaps. He writes: "We had always been free thinkers, convinced that morality must have its own roots in conscience, not in dogma."[8] Ironically, it was Hitler who blamed Jews for creating and burdening the world with conscience. [http://www.youtube.com/watch?v=yB7x_uuxKdM&mode=related&search=]

It is of interest to note that the 17th century philosopher, Baruch Spinoza was one of the first to question the "a priori truths of organized religion in favor of interpreting spiritual values within a personal context" thus, contributing to the distinction between Jewishness and

Judaism, a distinction between the secular and the religious. [9] It appears that Franco Modigliani in contrast to his namesake, the painter Amedeo Modigliani did not make this distinction.

When Modigliani is greeted by Professor Harold Burbank, department head of economics at Harvard, after receiving a formal invitation from the economics faculty to join, we find Modigliani admit to feeling "flustered" for the first time in his life and understandably so. He says, ".... I was received by the head of the economics department, whom I discovered on that occasion to be a well-known reactionary, backward-looking anti-Semite, and opposed to anything that had even a faintly European flavor."[10]

Yet, even at this peak of anger and frustration he did not focus on anti-Semitism solely. Instead he mentioned it along with the other characteristics he couldn't find in Burbank, such as being forward looking – open minded – free thinking not bound by religion. Modigliani blamed Burbank's rejection of him not on his "internal flaws" such as being Jewish. Rather, he ascribed this to Burbank's stupidity. He did not dwell on the issue, moved on and "never looked back."[11]

Appendix B
Selected Personal Vignettes

By William A. Barnett [1]

In spring of 1963, I was a senior, majoring in engineering, at MIT. I had heard about what Modigliani and Miller were doing in corporate finance, and I knew that Modigliani's graduate course was electric. Although it was unusual for an undergraduate at MIT to be permitted to take a graduate course, especially in another field, I asked for permission, and Franco agreed. His class was an astonishing show. What he and Miller were doing (Miller was at the University of Chicago then) ran against the grain of what was widely believed in mainstream corporate finance at the time. The class was large and the graduate students in the class were very aggressive with their questions. It would not have surprised me if some of the people in the room were junior MIT faculty, rather than students, but I did not know. Franco typically walked into the room without any notes. He would walk to the board, pick up chalk and start enthusiastically deriving equations, which soon would cover all of the blackboards. When students would ask confrontational questions, he would light up and start deriving more equations on the board. Clearly he loved to be challenged and was enormously impressive to everyone in the room.

As an undergraduate in engineering, most of my other classes had been in engineering, science, and mathematics. Those classes at MIT were intense and certainly not unimpressive. After graduating, I went to work for Rocketdyne in Los Angeles. Rocketdyne produced the rocket engines for the Apollo project, and I worked on the development of the F-1 rocket engine, which was the booster engine that got the vehicle off the ground. My colleagues were formidable high-tech engineers. But despite all of the outstanding engineers and scientists under whom I had studied and with whom I worked, the memory of Franco's course stood out in my mind, along with his statement to me at the end of the last day of class that I should write to him in the future. I wrote to him from Rocketdyne a few years later, and that was the beginning of my drift away from engineering into statistics and economics. In short, it was the inspiration of Franco's electric course to which I am indebted for the direction of my subsequent graduate study and then my career as an economist and econometrician. Few other economists or scientists have ever impressed me in the same way that Franco did in his amazing class in 1963.

I was on the staff of the Federal Reserve Board in Washington, DC. from July 1973 to September 1981. Twice a year, there was a big show in the Board Room. The Governors met with the "Academic Advisors" to hear what they had to say and to ask them questions. They were eminent economists who were invited by the Board. Certain of them clearly stood out in my mind, including two about whom I had heard but never saw at one of those meetings.

Milton Friedman had, a long time ago, been among them. But we were told that during one of the those meetings he stood up, said it was a waste of his time since he was not being listened to, and walked out, never returning to one of those meetings. This happened before I arrived, so I never did see him at an Academic Advisors' meeting. Another was Karl Brunner, whom I also never saw in one of those meetings. I asked my colleagues why. They told me that the Board was so angry at some of the things Karl had said that they had given instructions to the guards at the entrance to the building to never again permit him into the building. When I asked Karl about that at a conference, he said that the ban had done wonders for his career.

Of those whom I did periodically see at those meetings, three were clearly particularly influential. One was Ben Friedman from Harvard. Another was a somewhat puzzling person. We had never seen any of his publications, he was not at a university, and he worked for a consulting firm that had an econometric model that was not taken seriously by the Board's staff. Nevertheless, at the Advisors' meetings, he appeared to be surprisingly knowledgeable. His name was Alan Greenspan.

But it was clear who was the most respected of the Academic Advisors. It was the person who had played the primary role in the creation of the Board's own quarterly econometric model, called the FRB-MIT-PENN model. It was Franco Modigliani.

As editor of the Cambridge University Press journal, *Macroeconomic Dynamics*, I publish occasional interviews with famous economists.

I do not conduct the interviews myself. A collection of many of those interviews will be reprinted in 2006 by Blackwell in the book, William A. Barnett and Paul A. Samuelson (eds.), *Inside the Economist's Mind: The History of Economic Thought, as Explained by Those Who Produced It*. The interview with Modigliani was to be by his friend, Robert Solow. But there were problems with the transcript of Solow's interview with Modigliani. As a result, the usable parts of the interview would only be about half the length of a normal interview in *Macroeconomic Dynamics*. Because of the role that Franco had had in the direction that I followed in my career, I felt a special obligation to see to it that his interview was completed. Because of his advanced age at the time, I decided to complete conducting the interview myself without delay.

I flew to Boston from my office at Washington University in St. Louis and spent two days conducting the interview in Franco's condominium apartment near Harvard Square. The interview was completed November 5–6, 1999. The Franco with whom I conversed during that interview was not the vibrant young man who had so excited the room in the class I took from him in 1963. His health clearly was declining, and he walked with a cane. But, indeed, below the changed exterior, it was the one and only Franco Modigliani.

His phone rang repeatedly with calls from Congressmen and their staffs in Washington, DC, some of whom he dismissed out of hand. When he drove me to lunch, I was astonished to find that such an old man was driving a high-powered European car, which he proudly explained was consistent with his life-long preference for "sporty" cars. While in his apartment, food was served by his dynamic and charming wife, Serena. But not the coffee. Franco took great pride in the high-end espresso machine that had been given to him by a former student, and Franco took me over to that machine to watch, each time he made a cup of espresso. Clearly this was more important to him than some of the Congressmen who periodically called him.

During the interview, Franco stated in the clearest possible terms that the stock market was on a bubble and would surely drop 25 per cent soon, when the bubble burst. That statement is contained in his interview that I published in *Macroeconomic Dynamics* in 2000. Of course, he was right. Robert Shiller, whose book predicting that bubble's bursting is more widely known than Franco's prediction, has said of Franco, "He is my hero." Shiller was one of Modigliani's students at MIT. Indeed there was only one Franco Modigliani.

By Alan S. Blinder[2]

I was a young kid when I showed up at MIT in the fall of 1969 and wound up taking Monetary Economics from the great Franco Modigliani. Modigliani's intellectual achievements were, of course, legendary. And we students all held him in a bit of awe. Locally, his infectious enthusiasm for the subject – an enthusiasm that clearly infected Franco himself – was also legendary.

Franco's lectures routinely ran over their allotted time. I don't think he even heard the buzzer announcing the end of class, so enraptured was he in the intricacies of, say, money demand. So we students grew accustomed to arriving at our next class, or wherever we were going, 5–10 minutes late. But one day, the 5 or 10 minutes stretched … and stretched … and stretched. One by one, students rose from their seats and walked out of the room, heading (very late) to their next destination. Franco gave no sign of noticing the gradual exodus.

So there I was, at the tender age of 24, needing to leave the room but thinking that it was borderline sacrilegious to walk out on the great Modigliani. I therefore stuck it out – until only two students remained. At that point, my fear of being the last person to exit, thereby leaving Franco talking to an empty room, began to overwhelm my sense of politeness. So I seized an opportune moment in which Franco turned toward the blackboard, and quietly slipped away – leaving him lecturing to a single person as if he was addressing a full room. In my mind, I imagined, and imagined still, that Franco continued lecturing to an empty room after the last holdout finally departed.

Subsequently, some of the older graduate students told me that this was an annual event at MIT.

By Dwight Jaffee[3]

During my Ph.D. student days at MIT, 1964 to 1968, I was considered among the "Franco Boys." This was a group of students and MIT visitors working together on what was called the Federal Reserve Econometric Model project. The visitors group included Albert Ando, who had been Franco's student at Carnegie and then went on to a long career at the University of Pennsylvania; Harold Shapiro, who later became President at both Michigan and Princeton; and Robert Rasche, who has been at the St. Louis Fed for many years.

Each of us would meet with Franco every week or two to discuss the progress on our project/thesis. You would wait outside his office until he called you in. As you walked in, you could see him rapidly scanning the paper that you had given him earlier – he clearly had not looked at it until that moment. After maybe one minute, he would look up and say something like: "This all looks fine, but here on page 21, something does not look right … ."

Invariably, he picked on the weakest link of the paper's argument. As I was leaving MIT, I finally asked him for the secret. The answer, of course, was "experience." In that same parting chat, I asked him how he could write as many papers as he did. His answer was, "Dwight, as you, too, will learn, the problem becomes how NOT to write them." My own experience has confirmed both these insights.

Things Italian were of course always evident with Franco. He used to drive this tiny Fiat Spyder convertible to/from MIT – we worried in a car crash there would be nothing left. There was always a rotating group of visiting Italian students, a number of whom have gone on to the highest levels in the Italian government and the Central Bank. Franco's favorite hotel in Rome, ironically, was the Hotel Boston, and he always seemed unhappy with Italian politics. Personally, it also turned out that my wife (of Italian background) grew up on Clark Street in Belmont across from the Modiglianis.

I cannot end without recalling the great fondness all the students and visitors had for Serena as well. Franco always had strong opinions on US politics (as well as Italian), but he always noted that what he could or could not say in public had to be approved by Serena.

By Larry Meyer[4]

I left MIT in the summer of 1969 to take a position as Assistant Professor at Washington University in St. Louis. Franco had been very active in promoting me for this position. When I left I had completed two chapters for my dissertation and was starting on the third. The economics department at Washington University let me know that I was expected to complete my dissertation within a year to remain in good standing. After immersing myself in writing lectures, I found myself half-way into the second semester without having made any further progress on my dissertation. I called Franco and told him I had an idea for a change in the title for my dissertation. I was thinking of calling it "*Two* Essays on Monetary Policy" He said that was fine with him and so I was done!

The next adventure was my dissertation defense. First, I called the third person on the Committee and he said (without reading the final draft) it was OK with him if it was OK with number 2 and Franco. I called number 2 and he said it was OK with him (also without reading it) if was OK with Franco. Everyone deferred to Franco. So I was off to see Franco.

My "dissertation defense" began at about 9 am in the morning. I was nervous but ready to defend. We met in Franco's office. He got up, went to the blackboard, and asked if I would mind if we started by talking about a problem he was having with a paper he was writing. About three hours later, he said we should take a break for lunch.

After lunch, I was really ready to defend. But Franco said there was actually a second paper he was working on that perhaps deserved some discussion. About an hour later, I told Franco that this was the last day to complete my dissertation and I still had to write an abstract, get a cover at the bookstore, etc. At that point, he extended his hand to congratulate me and said, "Well, in that case you're done! Congratulations."

And that's how I got to be a Ph.D. in economics.

Appendix C Overview on Modigliani's Works

Economic contributions

Modigliani pondered economic theory and policies for more than 50 years. His intellectual horizon spanned macroeconomics, money and banking, econometrics, industrial organization, and finance during that timeframe. His best-known contributions are extensions of the Keynesian research program in the areas of liquidity preference and the life-cycle consumption function, to such an extent that the concepts have become identified with him. He evolved the Modigliani-Miller (M&M) hypothesis in finance that took its initial spur from the Keynesian investment concerns.

He was the progenitor of the NAIRU (Non Accelerating Inflation Rate of Unemployment) concept in economics that currently pervades intermediate macroeconomics textbooks. Modigliani was also a precursor to the modern rational expectation hypothesis. For his "pioneering studies of saving and of financial markets" he was awarded the Nobel Prize for Economics in 1985. The approach we take in this overview is first to discuss his methodological contribution, and afterwards, to discuss his significant theories and postulates.

Modigliani follows a positive view in predicting and explaining economic reality.[1] His works have one foot in theory and the other in applications. Frequently, his empirical works show up in the form of regression analysis. But he also appeals to realism, as when he disavowed Robert Barro's theory on the ground that people do not generally think that they and their children are one, and, therefore, reason that they must save for their children's future.

At an early stage in his career, Modigliani joined with Grunberg (1954) to set a positive methodology for research on expectations. Their purpose was to investigate the claim that "In reacting to the *published prediction* of a future event, individuals influence the course of events and thereby falsify the prediction."[2] Modigliani observed that some predictions are *not published*, i.e., they are not *divulged*. Those possible predictions he called "private" predictions. Such possible private predictions can be stated logically: $O(t).L\supset.O'(t)$, where O represents observations on the variables of the system, L represents laws that we use to transform observation statements O to a new set of observation statements O'. The transformation process occurs over time, t.

One major point made about the implications of Modigliani's methodology for economic prediction is that it is "internally consistent." The model is consistent when its true values are ascertained. The implicative symbolic, $\supset$, is true when both O and O' are "true,", both are false, or when O is false and O' is true. What is novel about Modigliani's contribution to the expectations hypothesis is not that something "happens because you expect it,"[3] but that "prediction itself becomes a variable of the system."[4] To explain, a statement may be added to O, augmenting it to say O^*. The new statement will be governed by certain laws that would also augment L to L*. Because the model is "internally consistent," O' will also be augmented to O'^*. This is realized in economic applications by saying that future prices depend on future demand. But future demand is dependent on expected prices. We, therefore, need to explain expected prices. For Modigliani, expected prices depend on current prices and public predictions. Private forecasters can augment their forecasts by adapting to published information.

Modigliani was also involved in clarifying the role of anticipatory data on economic behavior. This effort falls in the genre of "the role of expectations and plans in economic activities."[5] The study followed a planning paradigm, exploring the way businesses use anticipated supply, demand, and production conditions to make decisions. The model Modigliani built is based on the Hicksian paradigm[6] in which everything is dated in order to move from static to dynamic changes, and businesses follow best alternatives.[7] Modigliani found that businesses do not follow their best course of action over their planned horizon. He advocated that under certainty, a "single-value" rather than a "strategic" expectation model is preferable. This implies that "plans had almost no binding effects on future operations."[8] He realized that "single-value expectations are not entirely reliable ... more reliable information about the future can be acquired only at the cost of devoting scarce resources to this task."[9] However, where subjective uncertainty prevails, "some anticipations may have to be represented by subjective (joint) probability distributions, or analogous devices; and some plans may have to be represented by strategies, or schedules, expressing future actions as functions of later information."[10]

Modigliani used a simple Keynesian model where income is disaggregated into consumption and investment to illustrate prediction using anticipatory data. The model assumes that a consumption function can be fitted to non-anticipatory data. The investment function, however, may be determined from anticipatory data, i.e., information on investment plans.[11] Modigliani's position is that anticipatory data provides a bridge for our lack of present knowledge to make quantitative forecasts.[12]

Economic contributions

Keynesian model

Modigliani's early contribution was to put the Keynesian model on a classical foundation. Hicks, Kaldor, and others preceded him in starting that effort. Hicks' work set out "a classical theory in form similar to that in which Mr. Keynes set out his own theory,"[13] which became the IS-LM framework for Keynesian macroeconomic analysis. Kaldor was able to convince "Pigou that he was wrong to believe that a cut in money wages could increase the level of unemployment independently of a fall in the rate of interest."[14] Modigliani wanted "to examine to what extent the novel results of the *General Theory*, including its explanation of 'equilibrium' unemployment, could be traced to the unorthodox assumption of wage rigidity."[15] While he found that the model of Keynes rested mainly on the wage rigidity assumption, he came to realize a major role for the liquidity trap concept. Modigliani expounded his Keynesian ideas mainly with the Hicksian IS-LM apparatus.

Modigliani embraced Keynesian economics in his PhD dissertation on "Liquidity Preference and the Theory of Interest and Money" at the New School for Social Research in 1944. He did a major updating of this model in 1963, "The Monetary Mechanism and its Interaction with Real Phenomena,"[16] as well as in his last published work while alive, "The Keynesian Gospel According to Modigliani."[17]

In his Keynesian model, he sorted out the roles of liquidity preference and rigid wages. The model has equations on the real side of the economy that determine real output, and equations on the monetary side that determine the money value of output, and one equation that brings the two sides together. Modigliani's brand of liquidity preference does not require the concept of rigid wages to explain unemployment. Underlining the idea is that the price of money is anything that can be exchanged for it, therefore, the future price of money is the discount rate $R_t = \frac{1}{1 + r_t}$. Operationally, the rate of interest, r, increases in tight money situations as people hold more cash by liquidating assets. The consequences are to lower investment and saving, which in turn lower income and employment. The demand for money will then decrease to equal its supply. Tight monetary policy, therefore, implies a "rate of interest" to "output" adjustment, which contrasts with the classical view that implies a "rate of interest" to "price of all goods" adjustment. In the process, policy makers would supply an adequate quantity of money or fix the appropriate interest rate.

Stabilization policies

Using his brand of the Keynesian model, Modigliani was concerned with the big question as to whether the economy can be controlled by simple rules, as the monetarists advocated, or through discretionary policy, as he advocated. He thought that the growth in the M1 money supply, the most liquid form of money, destabilizes income through the wide swings in the velocity of money. Discretionary policies appeared more suitable to him because by the 1980s the United States Federal Reserve was able to use intermediate targets to achieve its goal of a final nominal income, even though velocity was varying.[18]

Stabilization issues also focused on the appropriate discretionary policy for shocks to the economy such as the OPEC oil crisis in the 1970s. At issue is how to find an optimal path that unemployment must take in order to bring inflation to its long-run target level. Modigliani evolved several ideas to characterize this process. One idea was the NIRU,[19] the non-inflationary rate of unemployment, where the inflation rate is expected to fall as long as the actual unemployment rate does not fall below a critical level. We may imagine that a level to which inflation can fall will be stable. When that level of prices is reached, a level of output and employment will be attained. In other writings, Modigliani referred to that level of output as NIRO,[20] meaning a non-inflationary rate of output. NIRU and NIRO have dynamic implications for optimal policy measures. Calculating the expected rate of inflation on some weighted average of past prices is one way to achieve the optimality. Its simplest form is that the expected price, p^* is equal to the price in the last period, p_{t-1}. The difference between actual price and expected price, $p-p_{t-1}$, will be some function of the unemployment rate, and NIRU will be a solution to that function.[21] In the NIRU model, it is possible to find turnpike-like solutions. An efficient turnpike path would be for the economy to move straight down on a vertical line anchored on the long-run rate of unemployment for an inflation rate above its critical level. Another turnpike path would be for the economy to veer off to where the short run Phillips Curve (PC) cuts the long run PC curve, before the inflation rate achieves its critical level. The NIRU and NIRO concepts manifest themselves in the standard macroeconomic textbooks as NAIRU, the non-accelerating inflation rate of unemployment.

Savings and consumption hypothesis

After WWII much emphasis was placed on the reconciliation of the observation that the average propensity to consume exceeded the marginal propensity to consume. Many attempts were made to reconcile these two propensities. Modigliani set out to revise the Keynesian consumption function that depended only on absolute income by introducing a peak level income variable in the past to explain savings behavior.[22] Given a trend in the saving-income ratio, the difference between actual and previous peak income would explain cyclical variations around that trend. When actual income is low relative to peak income, savings are depressed. During boom periods, savings would rise until the previous peak level is achieved, then consumption would leap upwards, reconciling the marginal and average propensities.

Modigliani later added a classical foundation to this theory that led up to his life-cycle hypothesis (LCH). The LCH of savings holds that people smooth out their consumption over a lifespan. Borrowing more by younger age cohorts, saving more by prime working age cohorts, and drawing down savings by retirement age cohorts, does this. In terms of the neoclassical paradigm, the individual maximizes lifetime utility, constrained by lifetime income and wealth. As Modigliani stated, consumers can expect a lifetime income based on their labor income, assets, or bequests. In other words, consumers receive income, Y, up to the end of their working life, N. They accumulate savings during their working years, and consume, C, uniformly during their lifetime, $L>N$. Since lifetime consumption must equal lifetime income, assuming no bequests, we can express $CL = NY$, or $C = (N/L)Y$, in which case the terms in parentheses represent the marginal propensity to consume. Fitting the LCH to labor income and net assets, A, the equation $C = .766Y + .073A$ reconciled some anomalies during the post- WWII period. Also, "The fact that wealth enters importantly in the short-run consumption function means that monetary policy can affect aggregate demand not only through the traditional channel of investment but also through the market value of assets and consumption."[23]

The LCH was extended to many other areas of applications, of which two stand out – the burden of national debt and managing social security. In considering the national debt issues, the question has arisen as to whether life-time is finite or infinite. Modigliani thought that the model was practical only from a finite point of view, whereas Robert Barro advocated an infinite horizon.[24] To fathom the logic, assume a game between government and individual taxpayers. The government incurs a debt. Taxpayers may react by saving more now because they or their heirs will be taxed in the future to pay off the debt. The increase in saving will give them the wherewithal to pay off the debt, or in case they die, for their heirs to pay off the debt through bequests. Modigliani questioned whether the infinite horizon assumption is credible, and whether the people do save for bequests. He examined the government deficits and argued that the evidence for Barro's argument was lacking.

Modigliani extended the LCH to Social Security problems from the point of view of treating Social Security as private savings. As a saving, Social Security Taxes (SST) will add to the wealth variable in the LCH model. Modigliani wanted to treat Social Security savings as a mandatory or compulsory activity, somewhat like the forced savings concept. The approach broadens the definition of wealth, and changes some of its consequences. On the one hand, it may reduce the saving-income ratio, as people count on their SS as savings for the future. On the other hand, it may encourage early retirement. Modigliani thought that the two consequences might cancel each other out.[25]

M&M hypothesis

The Modigliani and Miller hypothesis (M&M) also evolved from Modigliani's thinking on Keynesian economics. For Keynesians, the rate of interest is the cost of investment funds. The idea of cost of investment funds can easily be analyzed in terms of a mix of debt and equity. The invariance principle pertains to this idea since one method of financing can expand only at the expense of the other, leaving the value of the firm unaffected. This initial realization led to the now famous M&M hypothesis. Initially, the M&M was proposed without taxes, dividends, and bankruptcy. In later analyses these variables point out conditions under which the invariance condition would be upheld.

In practice, the value of an unleveraged firm, a firm with equity but no debt, could be estimated by dividing the firm's earnings before taxes and interest (EBIT) by a weighted average cost of capital, ρ. If EBIT is \$5,000 and ρ is 10 per cent, the value of the firm from the so-called net operating income (NOI) approach is \$50,000. Suppose that the firm wants to acquire some debt. It can sell some bonds (D) on which it will have to pay some interest (I), which is a tax-deductible expense. If we use the NOI approach, we would not account for this interest deduction, so the value will still be the same. But the corporate tax rate (t_c) will change the value of the firm. If the corporate tax rate is 50 per cent, a dollar of debt raises the firm's market value by 50 cents.

The FRB-MIT-Penn-SSRC model, 1969–1995

Several of Modigliani's theoretical thoughts went into the creation of an international econometric model, which was used by the Federal Reserve Board, until it was reformulated in 1995. The model rested on Modigliani's Keynesian contributions, modified by later research that facilitated better predictions. The model had a real sector that was influenced by fiscal policies, and a financial sector that mainly linked with the real sector through monetary policy. The financial sector is the largest through unborrowed reserve requirements, and the discount rate drives the short-term money rate of interest and the nominal money supply. The response from a change in unborrowed reserves to GNP works through lags and is subject to some delayed effects. As with other large scale models, the FRB-PENN-SSRC was respecified to accommodate new expectation elements in order to pick up conditions such as supply and demand shocks.

Post-Keynesian views

Modigliani communicated with other post-Keynesians, who were determined to see Keynes from other than a neoclassical point of view. He co-authored two articles with the preeminent leader of the neoclassical school, Paul Samuelson, that has generated much research in the area of long-term rates of return. One of the co-authored articles critiques the Pasinetti theorem, which states: "The equilibrium rate of profit is determined by the natural rate of growth divided by the capitalists' propensity to save."[26] This conclusion is derived from a basic differential equation that expresses changes in the profit-income ratio as a difference between the saving-income and investment-income ratios. Samuelson and Modigliani's dual Pasinetti theorem makes the inverse of the naïve accelerator, i.e, income-capital ratio, equal to the growth in population divided by the workers propensity to save. The confluence of the primal and dual methodologies has elevated the analysis to a high level of generality in the determination of the distribution of wages and profits in the economy.

Division of this work

We can divide a cake fairly if one person cuts and the other accepts or rejects. We start by giving the master the knife. Modigliani cut six collected volumes of his articles in professional journals. In Volume I, he started with an article published in 1976, only because it summarized his thinking on macroeconomics at that time. He aimed for a topical discussion of his works covering his interest in Keynesian economics, its applications, and policy issues. In his 2001 *Adventures*, he divided the cake spatio-temporally, ordering his contributions geographically–America, Italy, and Europe. But he also enlisted the help of methodology.

Modigliani's writings can be arranged by topic or publication date. Furthermore, we can rank the topics by order of importance. In 1986, one appraiser provided the following: the life cycle hypothesis, the Modigliani-Miller theorem, the basic Keynesian macroeconomic model, and production concerns in managerial economics.[27] This hierarchical ranking of topics has merits and demerits. It considers Modigliani's important works to be those that earned him the Nobel Prize. Modigliani, however, thought that his contributions had a "unifying thread: a propensity to swim against the current by challenging the self-evident orthodoxies of the moment."[28] Therefore, our preference is to focus on a time and topic presentation of his works.

Chapter 1 Modigliani's Early Life and Influences

Before we focus on the topics from the general introductory point of view, leaving the more scientific aspects for the individual chapters, we review Modigliani's formative years, ascendance of Mussolini to power in Italy and the settlement of Modigliani and his wife in the United States.

Chapter 2 Modigliani and Keynesian Economics

Many people approach Keynesian economics for a quick fix for economic crises. Ordinarily, the economy will take care of itself in the long run through market forces, according to the classical economists. But when things go awry with the macroeconomic machine, policy makers need to replace a cog, or give the engine a push, or a helping hand, Keynesian economics provides that kind of intervention. Modigliani invested a lifetime of research into the Keynesian apparatus. He created a Keynesian model that was turned into a large-scale econometric model of the Federal Reserve Bank. His life-long teachings steadfastly upheld the Keynesian view that was challenged by Keynes' teachers, and is now challenged by their disciples.

The materials for Modigliani's Keynesian framework started with his PhD dissertation in 1944 at the New School for Social Research, titled "Liquidity Preference and the Theory of Interest and Money." That dissertation established Modigliani as a model builder in the realm of interpreting Keynesian economics, delineating the proper role of wage rigidity and liquidity preference in the Keynesian model, and elevating monetary policy to a pedestal for controlling the economy. The model was upgraded and expanded during his lifetime to accommodate anomalies and new ways of thinking.

Chapter 3 The Gospel of Keynesian Reality: Development and Application of Modigliani's Model, 1944–2003, The Realm of Stabilization Policies

Volume I of Modigliani's *Collected Papers* starts with a debate in the 1970s between Milton Friedman, the monetarist, and himself, the Keynesian. Friedman exclaimed: "We are all Keynesians now!" Modigliani reciprocated, "We are all monetarists now!"[29] We can only imagine that some spectators also exclaimed, "Not in our backyard!" for this sort of agreement can only occur under a new school of thought. Anyway, the debate did take place, and the place was a new grassy knoll, one where the grass can be cut by both blades of the scissors – demand side and supply side. The name of the new game was stabilization policies.

Some related materials for stabilization policies are found in Volumes III, IV, and V of his *Collected Papers*. Part II, Volume III is called "Stabilization Policies," and Part III covers International Monetary Systems, focusing on Special Drawing Rights (SDRs). To stabilize the SDR, Modigliani had proposed to use price indexes for globally traded commodities. The title of Volume IV of his *Collected Papers* is "Monetary Theory and Stabilization Policies." Part I of Volume V addresses "the effectiveness of simple minded rules versus discretion to stabilize the economy."[30] This brand of Keynesian economics was developed interactively with theory, applications, amendments, and extensions occurring at different times.

Essentially, Modigliani's concerns with stabilization were derived from his primary interest in liquidity preference and wage rigidity. Liquidity preference is usually discussed in the context of the money market, and wage rigidity in the labor market. In the money market, a change in the interest rate will lead to a change in demand for money. Equilibrium will be reestablished if wages are flexible. This chapter is built around financial markets, investment, and prices, where Modigliani is best seen as an inventor and as a model builder.

Chapter 4 The Life Cycle Hypothesis (LCH)

Keynes was the first to initiate research into the way people spend their money. He expounded his doctrine first in his *General Theory*. It took the form of a great "psychological law" that revealed great insight into how the mass of people save when they act in groups, or as members of a nation. The Keynesian consumption function was chock-full of research materials, forming the basis for the award of two Nobel Prizes, one to Milton Friedman, and the other to Modigliani.

Modigliani's original works on consumption and savings comprise Volume II of his *Collected Papers*. As with his first volume, the second volume opens with a summary essay of his reflections some 20 years after he first advanced the hypothesis. Essentially, his concerns with LCH are based on microeconomic foundations. Its foundations are "the classical postulates of utility maximization applied to decision horizon consisting of the household's life cycle."[31] The purpose is to explain some puzzling behavior of saving.

The core outline of this chapter includes Keynes' law of saving, depicting savings as an increasing proportion of income; Milton Friedman's paradigm of saving, indicating short-run cycles and long-run stability of saving to income ratio, concerns reconciling short and long-run discrepancies in consumption behavior; and Modigliani's contribution to the overall puzzle.

Modigliani explained that his gateway for finance was his concern over the Keynesian investment function.[32] Because Keynes' system is considered short-run, and change in capital stock, which is investment, is the definition of the long-run, Keynes' ideas about investments were swept under the rug. Some use his remark: "in the long run we are all dead" to supersede his thoughts on investment. But later analysis found important nuggets in his views on the instability of the marginal efficiency of capital, and the influence of interest rates as the cost of capital. While Harrod-Domar originated a growth model incorporating the accelerator theory of investment with the tax multiplier, it was

Modigliani who first conceived the idea about the relationship between the cost of finance and the way debt or equity in a firm finances its investment.

Chapter 5 Modigliani and Miller's (M&M) Hypothesis

In this chapter, exploring the Modigliani-Miller (M&M) theorem that revolutionized thinking in corporate finance, we see the formation of a new historic approach to the finance narrative in the literature. Its outline starts with how Modigliani came to this theorem, continues with the collaboration with Miller, and then their parting over the subject. Modigliani revisited the subject later and had expressed the desire just before he died to further pursue work on this theorem.

Chapter 6 Forecasting: The MPS Model

Modigliani was also an accomplished econometrician in every sense of the word. Funded by the Board of Governors of the Federal Reserve Banks (FRB) and the Social Science Research Council (SSRC), Modigliani was the leader in founding of the MIT-Penn-SSRC (MPS) econometric model in the late 1960s. The MPS was one of the early large-scale econometric models in the U.S. It was modified and substantially enlarged frequently to meet the needs of economic challenges such as supply and demand shocks during the 1970s. One of its abiding features is its Keynesian outlook, but from its inception it also integrated new tools into the equation.

At the time the MPS was born, the adaptive expectation hypothesis was in vogue. Modigliani had also pioneered early versions of the rational expectation hypothesis, which was not amenable to applications until much later. Meanwhile, other changes such as competition in the global economy demanded improved specifications for better forecasting results. The MPS was, therefore, replaced with the FRB/US model in 1996.

This chapter includes the less known development of post-Keynesian economics that led to the "The Dual Pasinetti Theorem" advanced by Modigliani and Samuelson. At the heart of this discussion is Modigliani's preoccupation of how to integrate or extend traditional economic analysis to the theory of value and distribution. This brand of economics proceeds with two strides. The short stride version follows the economics of Keynes. The longer stride goes to the heart of the definitions of terms such as capital and profits that could be considered unsettled questions in a growth environment. For this Modigliani integrated neoclassical economics into his Keynesian thought.

Conclusion

Modigliani extended and polished his works over his career. The Keynesian apparatuses he evolved were tailored to several foreign countries, mainly European. Collaborating with his past students, who occupied major positions in central banks and other financial institutions, he evaluated the performances of the international economies against his models. In one of his last published papers, he used data for the European countries to illustrate the Keynesian framework.

The works we present of Modigliani are both deep and broad. His penetrating mind poured onto economic matters starting with his PhD dissertation that set what Samuelson called the Model-T version of Keynesian economics research. As his model degenerated over time, he turned them back into progressive research with new thoughts and specifications. He was able to go to the heart of many subjects related to consumption, investment, and monetary aspects to find some novel ideas. The fruits of his research have helped to make the Keynesian paradigm practical.

Notes

Preface

1. D. J. Wolpe, *Floating Takes Faith* (Springfield, NJ: Behrman House, 2005), p. 116.
2. For an insightful look at the role played by the wives of scientists, see I. I. Mitroff, T. Jacob, and E. T. Moore's article, "On the Shoulders of Spouses of Scientists" in *Social Studies of Science* 7 (1977), pp. 303–327.
3. Ibid., p. 106.
4. H. Gardner, *Creating Minds: An Anatomy of Creativity Seen through the Lives of Freud, Einstein, Picasso, Stravinsky, Eliot, Graham and Gandhi* (New York: Basic Books, 1992), pp. 44–46.
5. Observers of the scientific enterprise note that joint authorship is increasing. J. M. McDowell and M. Melvin, "The Determinants of Co-Authorship: An Analysis of Economics Literature," *The Review of Economics and Statistics* 65, no.1 (1983) pp. 155–160. Also, A.H. Barnett, R. W. Ault, and D. L. Kaserman, "The Rising Incidence of Co-authorship in Economics: Further Evidence," *Review of Economics and Statistics*, 70 no.3 (1988) 539–593. Edmund Burke insightfully remarked: "In my course I have known, and, according to my measure, have co-operated with great men; and I have never yet seen any plan which has not been mended by the observations of those who were much inferior in understanding to the person who took the lead in the business" in *Reflections on the Revolution in France* (London: Penguin, 1986), p. 83. This is what I had to say about collaboration at a seminar held at the Centre Detudes Interdisciplinaires Walras-Pareto, University of Lausanne: "There is a tendency to overglamorize the lone wolf scientists working with limited resources and arriving at astounding results. There are those who argue that eminent scholars are so individualistic that they are by temperament, wholly unsuited for work in any research group." Einstein used to say, "I am a horse for a single harness." R. S. Root-Bernstein, *Discovering* (Cambridge, MA: Harvard University Press, 1989), pp. 382–397. The author, a biochemist and a recipient of the prestigious MacArthur Prize Fellowship (1981–1986), attempts to unearth the blueprint for scientific discovery. He cites approvingly what several other scientists consider to be the "truths" of scientific progress. It is that the most important breakthroughs come in ill-equipped laboratories with limited funds and simple techniques. As an example he tells of Otto Hahn who, in 1938, used "apparatus that fit on a desktop" to split the atom. M. Szenberg, "Editing the Life Philosophies Series of the 1930's Generation of Eminent Economists" in *Editing Economics and Economists as Editors*, P. Bridel, ed. (Geneve and Paris: Droz, 1992), pp. 320–322.
6. M. Szenberg, ed. *Passion and Craft, Economists at Work*, with a Foreword by Paul A. Samuelson (Ann Arbor, MI: University of Michigan Press, 1999), p. 140.

7. F. Modigliani, "Ruminations on My Professional Life," in W. Breit and R.W. Spencer, eds. *Lives of the Laureates* (Cambridge, MA: The MIT Press, 1995), p. 139.

Chapter 1 Modigliani's Early Life and Influences

1. F. Modigliani, 2001.
2. Ibid., blurbs on the cover.
3. http://nobelprize.org/economics/laureates/1985/index.html.
4. W. Breit and R. W. Spencer, 1995, pp. 139–163.
5. Aristotle, 1961, p. 54.
6. F. Modigliani, 1988, pp. 145–158.
7. F. Modigliani and S. L. Cao, 2004, pp. 145–170.
8. P. A. Samuelson, 1999, p. XI.
9. J. Hadamard, 1945, p. 47.
10. W. A. Barnett and R. M. Solow, 2000, p. 223.
11. H. Neisser and F. Modigliani, 1953.
12. W. A. Barnett and R. Solow, 2000, p. 239.
13. F. Modigliani, 1986, p. 215.
14. E. R Tannenbaum, 1972, p. 9.
15. T. H. Geer, 1968. p. 519.
16. B. Mussolini., 1923, p. 5.
17. Ibid., p. 16.
18. Ibid., p. 39.
19. R. Ulich, 1961, p. 188.
20. J. M. Keynes, 1979, p. 80.
21. T. H Geer, op. cit., 1968, p. 521.
22. Mussolini, op. cit., p. xi.
23. T. H. Geer, 1968, p. 523.
24. Ibid., p. 527.
25. F. Modigliani, 2001, p. 13.
26. F. Modigliani,1986a, p. 215.
27. This attitude is reminiscent of Janusz Korczak, a dedicated Jewish doctor to destitute children, who managed both a Catholic as well as a Jewish orphanage in Warsaw before the Second World War. Korczak defended children's rights in courts, as well as in his famous books. He chose to die together with the two hundred Jewish orphans in the death camp Treblinka, rather than save himself. www.korczak.com/Biography/kap-1who.htm. Also, http://en/wikipedia.org/wiki/Janusz_Korczak.
28. F. Modigliani, 2001, p. 2.
29. S. Freud, 1964, p. 34.
30. F. Modigliani, 2001, p. 2.
31. Ibid., 2001, p. 9.
32. P. Neville, 2004, pp. 125–135.
33. Ibid., 2004, p. 151.
34. Ibid., 2004, p. 116.
35. R. J. B. Bosworth, 2002, p. 342.

36. F. Modigliani, 1995, p. 141.
37. R. J. B. Bosworth, 2002, p. 288.
38. F. Modigliani, 1995, p. 141.
39. F. Modigliani, 1986a, p. 217.
40. W. A. Barnett and R. M. Solow, op. cit., p. 223.
41. F. Modigliani, op. cit., 1995, p. 142.
42. In the matter of marriage, Modigliani provides the best prescription for a happy marriage: "Our love was kindled by long talks about what we thought of life ... our ideas and values matched perfectly." F. Modigliani, op. cit, 2001. Also, their families knew each other intimately starting with their great grandmothers. An ancient Talmudical text says it all, "Like should marry like."
43. Ibid., p. 143.
44. F. Modigliani, op. cit, 1986a, p. 219.
45. F. Modigliani, op. cit., 2001, pp. 67–68.
46. It is instructive to note that the same fate befell Paul A. Samuelson despite winning the David A. Wells Prize for his *Foundations of Economic Analysis* (Harvard Economic Studies, Vol. 80, 1947). In both cases Burbank's anti-Semitism played a role in denying them a faculty position at Harvard. It is no wonder that Samuelson describes Burbank as standing for "everything in scholarly life for which I had utter contempt and abhorrence." See M. Szenberg, A. Gottesman and L. Ramrattan *Paul Samuelson On Being an Economist*, with a Foreword by J. Stiglitz. (New York: Jorge Pinto Books, 2005), 23–24. In the index to his *Adventures*, Modigliani refers to him as Professor Burbank, without spelling his first name. Also, he is the only person referred to as "professor" which indicates Modigliani's similar feelings of contempt for him.
47. F. Modigliani, op. cit., 2001, p. 53.
48. P. A. Samuelson, 1987, p. 30.
49. R. D. Parke, 2004, pp. 1–24.
50. "Lay" analysis is the title of one of Freud's works.
51. P. A. Samuelson, op. cit., p. 30.
52. W. A. Barnett and R. M. Solow, op. cit., covered all these disagreements.
53. Personal correspondence 2006.
54. P. A. Samuelson, op. cit., p. 29.
55. Personal correspondence 2006.
56. Personal correspondence 2006.
57. Personal telephone conversation 2006.

Chapter 2 Modigliani and Keynesian Economics

1. J. M Keynes, 1936, p. 372.
2. J. M. Keynes, 1987, p. 24.
3. R. K. Vedder and L. E. Gallaway, 1997, p. 1.
4. A. Kramer, 1984, p. 116.
5. J. M. Keynes, 1987, pp. 296–297.
6. J. M. Keynes, 1987, p. 299.
7. P. Samuelson, 1987, p. 29.
8. F. Modigliani and L. Papademos, 1980, p. viii.
9. F. Modigliani, Vol. 1, 1980, pp. 23–68.

10. Ibid., pp. 69–97.
11. Ibid., pp. 3–22.
12. Ibid., p. 20.
13. F. Modigliani, 2005.
14. W. A. Barnett and R. M. Solow, 2000, p. 227.
15. J. M. Keynes, 1936, p. 246.
16. A. O'Sullivan, 2003, p.132.
17. J. M. Keynes, 1936, p. 249.
18. Keynes, 1936, p. 135.
19. Ibid., p. 248.
20. Ibid., p. 248.
21. Ibid., p. 249.
22. J. M. Keynes, 1987, p. 1.
23. Ibid., p. 3.
24. Ibid., p. 18.
25. Ibid., p. 15.
26. Ibid., p. 27.
27. Ibid., p. 16.
28. A. C. Pigou, 1952, p. v.
29. Ibid., p. 9.
30. J. M. Keynes, 1936, p. 6.
31. J. M. Keynes, 1987, p. 54.
32. Ibid., p. 54.
33. J. R. Hicks, 1984, p. 186.
34. J. M. Keynes, 1936, p. 5.
35. R. K. Vedder and L. E. Gallaway, 1997, p. 1.
36. J. R. Hicks, 1937, p. 186.
37. P. A. Samuelson, 1941, p. 545.
38. R. Harrod, 1934, p. 129.
39. T. K. Rymes, 1989, p. 177.
40. J. R. Hicks,1936, pp. 238–253.
41. Ibid., p. 238.
42. Ibid., p. 239.
43. Ibid., p. 243.
44. J. M. Keynes, 1987, p. 72.
45. Ibid., p. 26.
46. J. R. Hicks, 1936, p. 245.
47. Ibid., p. 246.
48. Ibid., p. 187.
49. J. R. Hicks, 1939, pp. 62–77.
50. J. R. Hicks, 1984, pp. 218–219.
51. J. M. Keynes, 1987, p. 79.
52. A. Lowe, 1965, p. 229.
53. J. M. Keynes,1987, p. 83.
54. Ibid., p. 83.
55. Ibid., p. 71.
56. Ibid., p. 73.
57. Ibid., p. 80.
58. F. Modigliani, Vol. 1, 1980, p. 26.

59. F. Hahn,1985, p. 56.
60. J. M Keynes, 1936, p. 3.
61. A. Lowe, 1965, p. 227.
62. F. Modigliani, Vol. 1, 1986, p. 73.
63. J. M. Henderson and R. E. Quandt, 1971, p. 24.
64. D. Gale, 1982, pp. 8–9.
65. J. M. Keynes, 1936, p. 41.
66. F. Modigliani, 1944, p. 47.
67. D. Patinkin, 1949, p. 1.
68. H. G. Johnson, 1970, pp. 18–19.
69. D. Patinkin, 1948, pp. 135–154.
70. W. J. Baumol, 1972, p. 370.
71. F. Hahn, 1985, p. 61.
72. F. Modigliani, Vol. 1, 1986, p. 83.
73. D. Patinkin, 1961, p. 107.
74. F. Modigliani, Vol. 1, 1986, p. 89.
75. Ibid.
76. F. Modigliani, 1944, p. 69.
77. D. Patinkin, 1948, p. 153.
78. F. Hahn, 1985, p. 60.
79. G. Rubin, 2004, p. 191.
80. Ibid., p. 194.
81. Ibid., p. 210.
82. Ibid., p. 211.
83. F. Modigliani, Vol. 1, 1980, p. 46.
84. M. Morishima, 1977, p. 154.
85. A. C. Pigou, 1952, p. 61.
86. F. Modigliani, 2005, p. 343.
87. J. R Hicks, 1937, p. 191.
88. F. Modigliani, Vol. 1, 1980, pp. 53–54.
89. J. M. Keynes, 1936, p. 214.
90. P. A. Samuelson, 1941, p. 548.
91. P. A. Samuelson, 1969, p. 175.
92. F. Modigliani, Vol. 1, 1980, p. 26.
93. Ibid., p. 28.
94. Ibid., p. 27.
95. Ibid., p. 32.
96. Ibid., p. 37.
97. Ibid., p. 38.
98. Ibid., p. 40.
99. Ibid., pp. 41–42.
100. F. Modigliani, Vol. 1, 1990, p. 43.
101. F. Modigliani, 1980, pp. 69–107.
102. S. Fischer, 1987, p. 230.
103. Ibid., p. 235.
104. A. Leijonhufvud, 1982, p. 100.
105. G. Rubin, 2004, p. 206.
106. A. Leijonhufvud, 1982, p. 327.
107. M. Morishima, 1977, p. 154.

108. A. Leijonhufvud,1982, p. 335.
109. P. A. Samuelson, 1986, p. 277.

Chapter 3 The Gospel of Keynesian Reality, Development and Application of Modigliani's Model, 1944–2003, The Realm of Stabilization Policies

1. J. M. Keynes, 1963, p. 187.
2. H. Hoover, 1952, p. 19. It is worth noting that Irving Fisher used his knowledge of economics, finance, and mathematics to invest in the stock market. He shared his techniques with his fellow Yale faculty members who accumulated a fortune. However, with the stock market crash he not only lost 10 million dollars in 1930, but also his home. Fisher's Yale colleagues who followed his investment strategies became impoverished as well.
3. Ibid., p. 20.
4. J. M. Keynes, 1963, pp. 142–143.
5. Ibid., p. 154.
6. Ibid., p. 161.
7. Ibid., p. 169.
8. Ibid., p. 177.
9. J. Tobin, 1987, p. 6.
10. Ibid., pp. 9–11.
11. L. Papademos and F. Modigliani, 1990, p. 412.
12. Ibid., p. 413.
13. J. Tobin, 1987, pp. 52–53.
14. P. Samuelson, Vol. 5, 1986, p. 276.
15. A. Lowe, 1965, p. 277.
16. P. Samuelson, 1986, p. 286.
17. Ibid., p. 287.
18. J. E. Stiglitz and B. Greenwald, 2003, p. 188.
19. J. Tobin, 1987, p. 443.
20. P. A. Samuelson and R. M. Solow, 1960, p. 177.
21. F. Modigliani, 1986a, p. 6.
22. F. Hahn and R. Solow, 1995, p. 2.
23. J. B. Taylor, 1993, pp. 4–5.
24. R. Dornbusch, et. al, 2004, p. 193.
25. F. Modigliani, 1944, p. 52
26. Ibid., pp. 53–54.
27. F. Modigliani, Vol. 1, 1980a, p. 91.
28. Ibid., p. 93.
29. Ibid., p. 95.
30. Ibid., pp. 96–97.
31. Ibid., p. 4.
32. F. Modigliani, Vol. 4, 1989a, p. x.
33. F. Modigliani, 1986a.
34. F. Modigliani, Vol. 1, 1980, p. 143.

35. Ibid., p.145.
36. F. Modigliani, 1986a, p. 8.
37. Ibid., p. 11.
38. Ibid., p. 18.
39. F. Modigliani, Vol. 4, 1989a, p. 44.
40. Ibid., p. 86.
41. Ibid., p.150.
42. Ibid., p. 145.
43. Ibid., p. 147.
44. Ibid., p. 197.
45. Ibid., p. 187. The propositions that we formulated to capture Modigliani's discussion on stabilization policies, were also covered in his Raffaele Mattioli Lectures published in 1986.
46. F. Modigliani, Vol. 4, 1989a, p. 192.
47. F. Modigliani, 1986a, p. 20.
48. F. Modigliani, Vol. 3, 1980c, p. 189.
49. Ibid., p. 222.
50. F. Modigliani, Vol. 4, 1989a, pp. 175–176.
51. F. Modigliani, 1986a, p. 21.
52. Ibid., p. 20.
53. F. Modigliani, Vol. 4, 1989a, p. 159.
54. F. Modigliani, Vol. 1, 1980a, p. 7.
55. B. T. McCallum, 1979, pp. 57–58.
56. W. A. Barnett and R. Solow, 2000, p. 235.
57. P. A. Samuelson, 1986, p. 839.
58. F. Modigliani, Vol. 3, 1980c, p. 472.
59. K. J. Arrow, 1986, p. S394.
60. F. Modigliani, Vol. 4, 1989a, p. 159.
61. F. Modigliani, Vol. 1, 1980a, p. 8.
62. Ibid., p. 6.
63. B. T. McCallum, 1979, p. 70.
64. S. M. Sheffrin, 1983, p. 55.
65. Ibid., pp. 56–57.
66. F. Modigliani, Vol. 2, 1980b, pp. 442–443.
67. Ibid., pp. 458–459.
68. Ibid., p. 51.
69. R. Dornbusch, et al., 2004, p. 339.
70. P. A. Samuelson, 1986, p. 280.
71. F. Modigliani, Vol. 2, 1980b, p. 459.
72. P. A. Samuelson, 1986, pp. 280–281.
73. F. S. Mishkin, 1996, p. 36.
74. F. Modigliani, Vol. 2, 1980b, p. 60.
75. Ibid., p. 460.
76. Ibid., p. 463.
77. Ibid., p. 416.
78. Ibid., p. 419.
79. Ibid., p. 423.
80. Ibid., p. 423.
81. F. Modigliani, 1989b, Vol. 5, p. 93.

82. Ibid., p. 94.
83. Ibid., p. 96.
84. R. Barro, 1974, pp. 1095–1117.
85. F. Modigliani, Vol. 5, 1989b, p. 118.
86. Ibid., p. 117.
87. Ibid., p. 99.
88. Ibid., p. 101.
89. H. Neisser and F. Modigliani, 1953, p. vi.
90. R. Dornbusch, et al., 1985, p. 243.
91. Ibid., p. 263.
92. Ibid., p. 244.
93. F. Modigliani, Vol. 3, 1980c, p. 324.
94. Ibid., p. 325.
95. F. Modigliani, Vol. 5, 1989b, p. 21.
96. F. Modigliani, Vol. 3, 1980c, p. 325.
97. Ibid., p. 326.
98. R. Dornbusch, et al., 1985, p. 263.
99. F. Modigliani, Vol. 3, 1980c, p. 341.
100. F. Modigliani, 1986a, p.179.
101. F. Modigliani, 1986, p. 203.
102. W. A. Barnett and R. Solow, 2000, p. 398.
103. F. Modigliani, Vol. 6, 2005, p. 358.
104. Ibid., p. 356.
105. F. Modigliani, 1986a, p. 171.
106. Ibid., pp. 200–201.
107. Ibid., p. 201.
108. F. Modigliani, 2003, p. 4.
109. Ibid., p. 5.
110. V. E. Morgan, 1965, pp. 181–182.
111. R. F. Harrod, 1969, p. 153.
112. H. G. Johnson, 1971, p. 59.
113. Ibid., pp. 60–61.
114. J. M. Keynes, 1971, p. 63.
115. B. Snowdon and H. R. Vane, 1999, pp. 243–244.
116. Ibid., p. 251.
117. S. Fischer 1977, pp. 191–205.
118. B. Snowdon and H. R. Vane, 1999, p. 249.
119. F. S. Mishkin, 1996, p. 36.
120. B. Snowdon and H. R. Vane, 1999, p. 244.
121. E. M. Gramlich, 2004.
122. B. Snowdon and H. R. Vane, 1999, p. 251.
123. R. Solow, 1998, p. 26.
124. B. Friedman, 1979.
125. S. Fischer, 1977.
126. F. Modigliani, Vol. 3, 1980c, p. 188.
127. B. T. McCallum, 1979, p. 58.
128. M. Friedman and R. Friedman, 1998, p. 229.
129. F. Modigliani 1980, Vol. 3, p. 140.
130. F. Modigliani, 2001, p. 172.

131. F. Modigliani 1980, Vol. 3, p. 141.
132. Ibid., p. 143.
133. Ibid, p. 157.
134. F. Modigliani, 1989, Vol. 4, p. 205.
135. F. Modigliani, 2001, p. 125.
136. Ibid., pp. 128–129.
137. F. Modigliani, 1989, Vol. 4, p. 357.
138. F. Modigliani et al., Manifesto, 1998.
139. F. Modigliani, 2005, Vol. 6, p. 340.
140. F. Modigliani et al., 1998, p. 1.
141. F. Modigliani, Vol. 1, 1980, pp. 379–223.
142. Ibid., pp. 253–281; 356–361.
143. Ibid., p. 382.
144. Ibid., p. 384.
145. F. Modigliani, Vol. 4, p. 356.
146. Ibid., p. 358.
147. Ibid., p. 278.

Chapter 4 The Life Cycle Hypothesis

1. J. M. Keynes, 1936, p. 94.
2. A brief survey is provided by C. G. F. Simkin, 1968, p. 49.
3. P. A. Samuelson, Vol. 5, 1986, p. 664.
4. J. M. Keynes, 1936, p. 96.
5. Ibid., pp. 127–128.
6. F. Modigliani, Vol. 2, 1980a, p. 420.
7. S. Kuznets, 1946, p. 119.
8. A. Smithies, 1945, p. 6.
9. F. Modigliani, Vol. 2, 1980a, p. 8.
10. Ibid., p. 11.
11. F. Modigliani, Vol. 2, 1980a, pp. 413–420.
12. F. Modigliani, Vol. 2, 1980b, pp. 371–443.
13. F. Modigliani, Vol. 2, 1980a, p. 413.
14. Ibid., p. 414.
15. J. L. Mosak, 1945, pp. 25–53.
16. A. Smithies, 1945, pp. 1–14.
17. Also, Paul A. Samuelson incorrectly predicted in the *New Republic* greater unemployment following the end of World War II. Samuelson referred to this prediction as his "sad experience." See M. Szenberg, et al., 2005, p. 75.
18. F. Modigliani, Vol. 2, 1980a, p. 416.
19. F. Modigliani, Vol. 2, 1980b, p. 379.
20. F. Modigliani, Vol. 2, 1980a, p. 417.
21. F. Modigliani, 1947, p. 425.
22. W. Leontief, 1947, pp. 441–442.
23. L. R. Klein and S. Ozmucur, 2005.
24. F. Modigliani, 1986a, pp. 125–126.
25. Ibid., p. 127.
26. Ibid., p. 127.

27. Ibid., p. 128.
28. L. R. Klein and S. Ozmucur, 2005, p. 8.
29. F. Modigliani, Vol. 6, 2005, pp. 3–45.
30. Ibid., p. 5.
31. R. Dornbusch, et. al., 2004, p. 345.
32. F. Modigliani, Vol. 2, 1980a, pp. 323–381.
33. F. Modigliani in Fischer et al., 1987, p. 7.
34. Ibid., pp. 7–8.
35. Ibid., p. 7.
36. F. Modigliani, Vol. 5, 1989, p. 25.
37. Ibid., p. 26.
38. F. Modigliani, 2001, p. 60.
39. Ibid., pp. 61–62.
40. F. Modigliani,1980a, Vol. 2, p. 293.
41. E. Brumberg, 1953.
42. F. Modigliani, Vol. 6, 2005, pp. 47–78.
43. Ibid., p. 54.
44. Ibid., Appendix.
45. Ibid., p. 48.
46. F. Modigliani, 1980a, Vol. 2, p. 329.
47. Ibid., p. 331.
48. Ibid., p. 353.
49. Ibid., p. 361.
50. Ibid., p. 364.
51. Ibid., p. 367.
52. Ibid., p. 410.
53. H. S. Houthakker, 1965, pp. 212–224.
54. F. Modigliani, 2005, Vol. 6, pp. 48–51.
55. Ibid., p. 32.
56. Ibid., p. 32.
57. R. Goldsmith, 1955, p. 22.
58. R. Stone and W. M. Stone, 1959, p. 2.
59. F. Modigliani, Vol. 2, 1980a, pp. 328–329.
60. C. W. J. Granger, 1999, pp. 42–43.
61. D. Romer, 1996, p. 318.
62. R. J. Barro, 1989, p. 156.
63. M. Flavin, 1981, pp. 974–1009.
64. J. Y. Campbell and N. G. Mankiw, 1989.
65. R. E. Hall and F. S. Mishkin, 1982, p. 461.
66. R. P. Mariger,1987, p. 533.
67. T. Japelli, 1990, p. 219.
68. F. Modigliani, 1987, p. 13.
69. F. Modigliani and C. Steindel, 1977, pp. 175–209.
70. Ibid., p. 183.
71. Ibid., p. 196.
72. The statement titled "Economists' Statement Opposing the Bush Tax Cuts" was released on Monday, 10 February, 2003 at a 10:00 a.m. press conference in the Holeman Lounge of the National Press Club in Washington, DC.
73. F. Modigliani, 1987, p. 14.

74. Ibid., p. 16.
75. Ibid., p. 20.
76. Ibid., p. 22
77. F. Modigliani, 2001, p. 79.
78. F. Modigliani, *Adventures* 2001, p. 70.
79. W. A. Barnett and R. M. Solow, 2000, p. 239.
80. F. Modigliani, 2001, p. 52.
81. J. S. Duesenberry, 1967, p. 45.
82. Ibid., p. 90.
83. [3] F. Modigliani, 1987, p. 32. [1] F. Modigliani, 2005, p. 376.
84. Ibid., p. 93.
85. Ibid., p. 94.
86. R. J. Barro, 1974.
87. F. Modigliani, 2005, p. 376.
88. R. E. Hall and J. B. Taylor, 1997, p. 284.

Chapter 5 Modigliani and Miller's (M&M) Hypothesis

1. F. Modigliani, 1980, Vol. 3, pp. 4–5.
2. Ibid., p. 6.
3. W. A. Barnett and R. M. Solow, 2000, p. 233.
4. F. Modigliani and M. Miller, 1954, p. 271.
5. J. B. Williams, 1997, pp. 72–73.
6. Ibid.
7. W. A. Morton, 1954, p. 442.
8. Ibid.
9. F. Modigliani, 1989, Vol. 5, p. 443.
10. W. A. Barnett and R.M. Solow, 2000, p. 223.
11. D. Durand, 1952, p. 216.
12. F. Modigliani, 1989, p. 149.
13. F. Modigliani, 1980, Vol. 3, p. 13.
14. F. Modigliani, 1980, Vol. 3, p. 10.
15. Ibid., pp. 10–11.
16. H. Varian, 1987, p. 55.
17. F. Modigliani 1980, Vol. 3, p. 11.
18. J. C. Van Horne, 1998, p. 256.
19. F. Modigliani, 1980, Vol. 3, p. 21.
20. R. Dornbusch, et al., 1987, p. 32.
21. J. C. Van Horne, 1998, p. 256.
22. R. Dornbusch, et al., 1987, p. 32.
23. F. Modigliani, 1980, Vol. 3, p. 12.
24. Ibid., p. 13.
25. Ibid.
26. Ibid., p. 22.
27. Ibid., p. 30.
28. F. Modigliani, 1988, pp. 151–152.
29. Ibid., p. 152.

30. M. Miller, 1977, p. 267, and 2002, p. 442.
31. M. Miller, 1977, p. 267.
32. J. C. Van Horne, 1998, pp. 263–64.
33. F. Modigliani, 1980, Vol. 3, p. 42.
34. Ibid.
35. Ibid.
36. Ibid., p. 53.
37. Ibid., p. 56.
38. Ibid.
39. R. Dornbusch et al., 1985, p. 37.
40. Ibid., p. 41.
41. F. Modigliani, 1989, Vol. 5, pp. 257–258.
42. J. Weston and T. E. Copeland, 1986, pp. 597–598.
43. J. E. Stiglitz, 1969, p. 788.
44. M. E. Rubinstein, 2003, p. 202.
45. T. J. Sargent, 1979, p. 157.
46. A. A. Robichek and S. C. Myers, 1966, p. 6.
47. F. Milne, 1995, p. 21.
48. P. Dubey, et al., 1994, p. 64.
49. J. E. Stiglitz, 1969, pp. 784–793.
50. M. E. Rubinstein, 2003, p. 3.
51. F. Modigliani, 1989, Vol. 5, p. 304.
52. Ibid., p. 305.
53. Ibid., p. 310.
54. F. Modigliani, 1986, p. 62.
55. Ibid., p. 63.
56. Ibid.
57. Ibid., p. 64.
58. M. Miller, 2002, pp. 421–422.
59. S. N. Neftci, 2000, p. xxv.
60. Ibid., pp. 27–28.
61. J. E. Stiglitz, 1969, p. 784.
62. F. Milne, 1975, pp. 166–168.
63. F. Modigliani and M. Miller, 1969, p. 592.
64. W. L. Baldwin and T. J. Velk, 1968, pp. 39–43.
65. W. F. Sharpe, 1970, p. 13.
66. M. Magill and M. Quinzii, 1996, p. 421.
67. F. Modigliani and M. Miller, 1969, p. 592.
68. J. Becker, 1978, pp. 65–68.
69. M. E. Rubinstein, 1973.
70. L. Modigliani,1997, p. 2.
71. F. Modigliani, 2005, Vol. 6, p. 290.
72. Ibid.
73. F. Modigliani, 1988, p. 150.
74. D. Romer, 1996, p. 387.
75. M. Miller, 2002, p. 434.
76. J. Tobin, 1985, p. 241.
77. Ibid., p. 247.
78. J. E. Stiglitz, 1979, p. 784.

79. M. Miller, 2002, p. 425.
80. F. Modigliani, Vol. 3, 1980, p. 60.
81. M. Miller, 2002, p. 444.
82. F. Modigliani, 1998, p. 154.
83. M. Magill and M. Quinzii, 1996, pp. 422–425.
84. Ibid., p. 422.
85. Ibid., p. 425.
86. F. Milne, 1995, pp. 166–168.
87. P. Dubey, et. al., 1994, pp. 1–37.
88. M. Magill and M. Quinzii, 1996, pp. 422–425.

Chapter 6 Forecasting: The MPS Model

1. H. Neisser and F. Modigliani, 1953.
2. H. Brems, 1956, p. 351.
3. H. Neisser and F. Modigliani, 1953, p. vi.
4. Ibid., p. 6.
5. Ibid., p. 75
6. F. Modigliani, 2001, p. 99.
7. Ibid., p. 100.
8. F. Brayton, et al., 1997, p. 2.
9. F. Modigliani, 2001, p. 100.
10. Ibid., p. 101.
11. F. Modigliani, 1980, Vol. 1, p. 116.
12. Ibid., p. 115.
13. M. Intriligator, 1983, p.206.
14. A. Ando, 1977, pp. 534–546.
15. F. W. Mc Elroy, 1978, pp. 1–23.
16. C. Christ,1991, pp. 1–17.
17. P. Cagan and F. Schwartz, 1987, p. 194.
18. A. Ando and F. Modigliani, 1975, p. 525.
19. Ibid., p. 543.
20. F. W. McElroy, 1978, p. 4.
21. C. Christ, 1991, pp. 257–289.
22. A. Ando, F. Modigliani, and R. Rasche, 1972, pp. 543–598.
23. A. Ando, 1977, p. 544.
24. F. Modigliani, et al., 1970, p. 203.
25. Ibid.
26. Ibid., p. 175.
27. Ibid., p. 203.
28. F. Modigliani, 1980, Vol. 1, p. 277.
29. P. Cagan and A. J. Schwartz, 1987, p. 183.
30. F. Modigliani, 1980, Vol. 1, p. 309.
31. Ibid.
32. Ibid., p. 317.
33. Ibid., p. 323.
34. Ibid., p. 334.
35. Ibid., p. 339.
36. F. De Leeuw and E. M. Gramlich, 1968, pp. 16–17.

37. R. Rasche and H. T. Shapiro, 1968, p. 126.
38. F. De Leeuw and E. M. Gramlich, 1968, p. 21.
39. R. Rasche and H. T.Shapiro, 1968, p. 126.
40. F. De Leeuw and E. Gramlich, 1968, p. 37.
41. Ibid., p. 25.
42. F. Modigliani and C. Steindel, 1997, pp. 175–209.
43. Ibid., pp. 200–201.
44. A. Zellner and S. C. Peck, 1984, pp. 141–157.
45. Ibid., p. 143.
46. Ibid., p. 146.
47. Ibid., p. 151.
48. Ibid., p. 153.
49. A. Ando, 1981, p. 333.
50. F. Brayton and E. Mauskopf, 1985, p.170.
51. Ibid., p. 174.
52. F. Modigliani, 1980, Vol. 1, p. 128.
53. L. Papademos and F. Modigliani, 1990, p. 405.
54. P. Cagan, 1956, pp. 23–117.
55. P. Cagan, 1973, pp. 3–4.
56. R. Solow, 2002, p. 73.
57. Ibid., p. 74.
58. L. Papademos and F. Modigliani, 1990, p. 415.
59. F. Modigliani, 1989, Vol. 4, p. 158.
60. E. M. Gramlich, Edward M, Fed Speech, March 26, 2004.
61. Modigliani 1980, Vol. 3, p. 193. The constant term is reported as –1.02 in Modigliani, 1989, Vol. 4, p. 182. It is not clear also how the coefficient of lagged inflation jumped from 0.68 to 0.82 in the latter.
62. F. Modigliani, 1989, Vol. 4, p.184.
63. Ibid., pp. 184–185.
64. Ibid., p. 179.
65. Ibid., Table 1, p. 186; Table 2, p. 189.
66. Ibid., Table 3, p. 192.
67. Ibid., p. 193.
68. F. Modigliani, 1980, Vol. 3, p. 194; F. Modigliani, 1989, Vol. 4, p. 185.
69. F. De Leeuw and E. Gramlich, 1968, pp. 11–40.
70. Ibid., p. 29.
71. Ibid.
72. R. Rasche and H. T. Shapiro, 1968, pp. 143–144.
73. R. C. Fair, 1986, pp. 1987–1988.
74. C. R. Nelson, 1972, pp. 902–917.
75. Ibid., p. 910.
76. E. Mauskopf, 1990, pp. 985–1009.
77. B. McCallum, 1979, pp. 57–73.
78. A. Ando, 1974, pp. 541–571.
79. B. McCallum, 1979, p. 60.
80. Ibid., p. 63.
81. Ibid., p. 65.
82. A. Zellner, 2002, p. 11.
83. F. Brayton, et.al, 1997, p. 227.
84. Ibid., pp. 238–239.

85. K. J. Arrow, 1984, p. 266.
86. P. Cagan, 1981, pp. 170–172.
87. K. J. Arrow, 1984, p. 265.

Appendix A A Question of Identity

1. S. E. Luria, p. 3.
2. Ibid., p. 4.
3. J. Malamud, pp. 1–3.
4. E. Goodheart, pp. 255–256. It is worthy of note that the anti-fascist, Arendt was a student and the lover of the Nazi philosopher, Martin Heidegger for 40 years, till his death in 1976. She was instrumental in his rehabilitation after WWII. [http://www.heartfield.pwp.blueyonder.co.uk/love.htm]. Also, of interest is the fact that Theodor Herzl, founder of political Zionism at the end of the 19th Century, wanted to propose to the Pope "Help us against the anti-semites and I will start a great movement for the free and honorable conversion of Jews to Christianity." M. H. Goldberg, p. 4.
5. D. J. Wolpe, 2005, p. 17.
6. Y. Avner, p. 21. When the celebrated Italian journalist Oriana Fallaci asked Golda Meir whether she was religious, she responded "Me religious? Never! Only my grandfather was religious, but those were the days when we lived in Russia. In America we observed the festivals, but went to the temple very seldom. I only went for the High Holy Days to accompany my mother. You see, to me being Jewish means being proud to be part of a People that has maintained its distinct identity for more than 2,000 years, with all the pain and torment inflicted on it." Y. Avner, August 10, 2007, p. 25.
7. R. Pinsky adds that his grandfather was "married to a Methodist woman, his third wife. He had a Christmas tree, did not go to school. But if you tried to tell him he was not Jewish he would punch you in the nose." E. Brawarsky, p. 34. The grandfather, despite being a bar-man, understood that there is a difference between identity, heritage, and belief.
8. F. Modigliani, 2001, p. 105.
9. M. Klein, p. 7. In a newly published book, R. Goldstein tells us that Spinoza "waited until both his parents had passed away before he revealed his heresy ... " He continued to attend services in the synagogue everyday for a year reciting Kaddish mourning his parents. Spinoza's God was the one to which Einstein felt closest ... God was the equivalent of nature, playing no role in the day to day affairs of mankind. S., Lipman, *The Jewish Week*, (June 23, 2006). In other words, besides acknowledging one's responsibility to mankind and "one's particular origins, [one] carries a special regard for and responsibility to one's parents and grandparents." R. Ben, p. 32.
10. F. Modigliani, 2001, p. 253.
11. It is important to note that in his autobiography, Modigliani is silent about his mother after her return to Rome in the 1940s, with the end of World War II. He doesn't even mention her death. When I probed this lacuna, the answer I received from a family member was "She was religious." I was also told that the children of Giorgio, his older brother, are prominent members of the Rome Synagogue.

Appendix B Selected Personal Vignettes

1. William A. Barnett is Oswald Distinguished Professor of Macroeconomics, University of Kansas, and editor of *Macroeconomic Dynamics*.
2. Alan S. Blinder is the Gordon S. Rentschler Memorial Professor of Economics at Princeton University and Co-Director of Princeton's Center for Economic Policy Studies, which he founded in 1990. He served as Vice Chairman of the Board of Governors of the Federal Reserve System from June 1994 until January 1996.
3. Dwight Jaffee is Willis Booth Professor of Banking and Finance, Haas School of Business, University of California, Berkeley.
4. Larry Meyer serves on the Board of the National Bureau of Economic Research, is a Senior Advisor to the G-7 Group, and a Fellow of the National Association of Business Economists. He also served as a member of the Board of Governors of the Federal Reserve from 1996 until 2002.

Appendix C Overview on Modigliani's Works

1 F. Modigliani and E. Grunberg, 1954, pp. 465–466.
2. Ibid., p. 465.
3. W. A. Barnett and R. M. Solow, 2000, p. 235.
4. F. Modigliani and E. Grunberg, 1954, p. 466.
5. F. Modigliani and K. J. Cohen, 1961, p. 3.
6. J. R. Hicks, 1946, p. 115.
7. F. Modigliani and K. J. Cohen, 1961, pp. 4–18.
8. Ibid., pp. 10–11.
9. Ibid., p. 19.
10. Ibid., p. 78.
11. Ibid., p. 93.
12. Ibid., p. 152.
13. J. R. Hicks in M. G. Mueller, 1969, p. 138.
14. F. Targetti and A. P. Thirlwall, 1989, p. 4.
15. F. Modigliani, Vol. 1, 1980, pp. xi-xii.
16. Ibid., pp. 69–97.
17. F. Modigliani, Vol. 6, pp. 327–359.
18. F. Modigliani, Vol. 5, 1989, p. x.
19. F. Modigliani, Vol. 3, 1980, p. 189.
20. Ibid., p. 222.
21. F. Modigliani, Vol. 4, 1989, pp. 175–176.
22. F. Modigliani, 1947, 1949.
23. F. Modigliani, 1986, p. 712.
24. R. J. Barro, 1974.
25. F. Modigliani, Vol. 5, 1989, pp. 3–34.
26. L. Pasinetti, 1976, p. 276.
27. P. J. K. Kouri, 1986, pp. 311–334.
28. M. Sarnat, 2004, pp. iv-vi.
29. F. Modigliani, 1980, p. 3.
30. F. Modigliani, 1980, p. x.
31. F. Modigliani, 1980, p. xiv.
32. W. A. Barnett and R. M. Solow, op. cit., p. 233.

Bibliography

Allen, R. G. D., *Macro-Economic Theory*, (London: St Martin's Press, 1968).

Ando, A. and F. Modigliani. "The Life Cycle Hypothesis of Saving: Aggregate Implications and Tests" *American Economic Review* 53, no. 1, (March, 1963), 55–84.

Ando, A., F. Modigliani, and R. Rasche, "Equations and Definitions of Variables for the FRB-MIT-PENN Econometric Model, November, 1969," in *Econometric Models of Cyclical Behavior* Vol.I, B. G. Hickman, ed., (New York: Columbia University Press, 1972).

Ando, A., "Some Aspects of Stabilization Policies, the Monetarist Controversy, and the MPS Model," *International Economic Review*, Vol. 15, No. 3, (Oct., 1974), 541–571.

Ando, A., and F. Modigliani, "Some Reflections on Describing Structures of Financial Sectors," in *The Brookings Model: Perspective and Recent Developments*, G. Fromm and L. Klein, eds., (Amsterdam: Elsevier, 1975).

Ando, A., "Theoretical and Empirical Basis of Macroeconometric Models," in *Large-Scale Macro-Econometric Models: Theory and Practice*, J. Kamenta and J. B. Ramsey, eds., (Amsterdam: North-Holland, 1981).

Arrow, K. J., *Individual Choice Under Certainty and Uncertainty*, (Cambridge, MA: The Belknap Press of Harvard University Press, 1984).

Arrow, K. J., "Rationality of Self and Others in an Economic System," *The Journal of Business*, Vol. 59, No. 4, Part 2: *The Behavioral Foundation of Economic Theory* (Oct., 1986), S385-S399.

Atkinson, A. B. and L. E. Ohanlan, "Are Phillips Curves Useful for Forecasting Inflation?" *Federal Reserve Bank of Minneapolis Quarterly Review*, Vol. 25, No. 1, (Winter, 2001), 2–11.

Avner, Y., "The More Things Change, the More They Stay ... " *Jewish Herald* July 28, 2006., 21–22.

Baldwin, W. L. and T. J. Velk, "Uncertainty of the Income Stream in the Modigliani Miller Model," *Quarterly Review of Economics and Business*, (Winter, 1968), 39–43.

Barnett, W. A. and R. M. Solow, "An Interview with Franco Modigliani," *Macroeconomic Dynamics*, Vol. 4, (2000), 222–256.

Barro, R. J., "Are Government Bonds Net Wealth?," *Journal of Political Economy*, Dec.,(1974), 1095–1117.

Barro, R. J., ed., *Modern Business Cycle Theory*, (Cambridge, MA: Harvard University Press, 1989).

Baumol, W. J., *Economic Theory and Operation Analysis*, 3rd edn (Englewood Cliffs N.J: Prentice-Hall, 1972).

Becker, J., "General Proof of Modigliani-Miller Propositions I and II sing Parameter-Preference Theory," *The Journal of Financial and Quantitative Analysis*, Vol. 13, No. 1 (March, 1978), 65–69.

Ben, R., "On Being Jewish in a Secular World," *Midstream*, (March/April 2006), 31–32.

Bosworth, R. J. B. *Mussolini*, (London: Hodder Arnold, 2002).

Brayton, F. and E. Mauskopf, "The Federal Reserve Board MPS Quarterly Econometric Model of the US Economy," *Economic Modeling*, Vol. 2, Issue 3, (July, 1985), 170–292.

Brayton, F. and P. Tinsley, "A Guide to FRB/US," Version 1.0, Oct 1996, Federal http://www.federalreserve.gov/pubs/feds/1996/199642/199642pap.pdf.

Brayton, F., E. Mauskopf, D. Reifschneider, P. Tinsley, and J. Williams, "The Role of Expectation in the FRB/US Macroeconomic Model," *Federal Reserve Bulletin*, (April, 1997), 227–245.

Brayton, F., A. Levin, R. Tyron and J. C. Williams, "The Evolution of Macro Models at the Federal Reserve Board," Feb 7, 1997. http://www.federalreserve.gov/pubs/feds/1997/199729/199729pap.pdf

Brawarsky, S., "The Poetry of Memory" *The Jewish Week*, (2006).

Breit, W. and R. W. Spencer, eds, *Lives of Laureates*, (Cambridge, MA: The MIT Press, 1995).

Brems, H., Book review of *International Incomes and International Trade: A Quantitative Analysis*, by H. Neisser and F. Modigliani, (Urbana IL.: University of Illinois Press, 1953) in *The Review of Economics and Statistics*, Vol. 38, No. 3 (Aug., 1956), 351–353.

Brumberg, E., "Utility Analysis and Aggregate Consumption Function: An Empirical Test and It Meaning," Ph.D. dissertation, Johns Hopkins University, 1953.

Cagan, P., "The Monetary Dynamics of Hyperinflation," in *Studies In the Quantity Theory of Money*, M. Friedman, ed., (University of Chicago Press, 1956).

Cagan, P., "Controls and Monetary Policy, 1969–1973," in *A New Look at Inflation: Economic Policy in the Early 1970s*, P. Cagan, M. Estey, W. Fellner, G. Haberler, and C. E. McLure, Jr., eds., (Washington, DC: American Enterprise Institute, 1973).

Cagan, P., "Financial Futures Markets: Is More Regulation Needed?," *Journal of Future Markets*, Vol. 1, 1981, 169–190.

Cagan, P. and A. J. Schwartz, "How Feasible is a Flexible Monetary Policy?" in *Money in Historical Perspective*, A. J. Schwartz, ed., (University of Chicago Press, 1987).

Campbell, J. Y. and N. G. Mankiw, "Consumption, Income, and Interest: Reinterpreting the Time Series Evidence," *NBER Macroeconomics Annual*, 1989.

Christ, C. F., "Pitfalls in Macroeconomic Model Buildings," in *Economic Models, Estimation, and Socioeconomic Systems: Essays in Honor of Karl A. Fox*, T. K. Kaul and J. K. Sengupta, eds., (Amsterdam: Elsevier Science Publishers, 1991).

De Leeuw, F. and E. Gramlich, "The Federal Reserve-MIT Econometric Model," *Federal Reserve Bulletin*, Vol. 54, No. 1, (Jan., 1968), 11–40.

Dimand, R. W., *The Origins of the Keynesian Revolution*, (Stanford University Press, 1988).

Dornbusch, R., S. Fischer, and J. Bossons, *Macroeconomic and Finance: Essays in Honor of Franco Modigliani*, (Cambridge, MA: The MIT Press, 1985).

Dornbusch, R., S. Fischer, and J. Bossons, *Macroeconomics and Finance: Essays in Honor of Franco Modigliani*, (Cambridge, MA: The MIT Press, 1987).

Dornbusch, R., S. Fischer and R. Startz, *Macroeconomics*, (New York: McGraw-Hill, 2004).

Dubey, P., J. Geanakoplos, and M. Shubik, *Default in General Equilibrium Model with Incomplete Markets*, Cowles Commission Discussion Paper #773, 1994 version.

Duesenberry, J. S., *Income, Saving, and the Theory of Consumer Behavior*, (Cambridge, MA: Harvard University Press, 1949).

Duesenberry, J. S., *Income, Savings and the Theory of Consumer Behavior*, (Oxford University Press, 1967).

Durand, D., "Cost of Debt and Equity Funds for Business: Trends and Problems of Measurement" in NBER, *Conference on Research in Business Finance*, New York 1952, 215–247.

Fair, R. C., "Evaluating the Predictive Accuracy of Models," in *Handbook of Econometrics*, Vol. III, Z. Griliches and M. D. Intriligator, eds., (Amsterdam: Elsevier, 1986).

Fischer, S., "Long-Term Contracts, Rational Expectations, and the Optimal Money Supply Rule," *The Journal of Political Economy*, Vol. 85, No. 1, (Feb., 1977), pp. 191–205.

Fischer, S., "1944, 1963, and 1985," in *Macroeconomics and Finance: Essays in Honor of Franco Modigliani*, R. Dornbusch, S. Fischer, and J. Bossons, eds., (Cambridge MA: The MIT Press, 1987).

Flavin, M., "The Adjustment of Consumption to Changing Expectation about Future Income," *The Journal of Political Economy*, (Oct., 1981), 974–1009.

Freud, A., *The Writings of Ann Freud, Volume I: Introduction to Psychoanalysis, Lectures for Child Analysts and Teachers: 1922–1935*, (New York: International University Press, 1974).

Freud, S. *Leonardo da Vinci and a Memory of His Childhood*, (New York: W. W. Norton & Co., 1964).

Friedman, B., "Optimal Expectations and the Extreme Information Assumptions of Rational Expectations Macromodels." *Journal of Monetary Economics*, Vol.5, (Jan., 1979), 23–41.

Friedman, M. *A Theory of the Consumption Function*, (Princeton University Press, 1957).

Friedman, M., "The Role of Monetary Policy," *American Economic Review*, Vol. 58, (Jan., 1968), 1–17.

Friedman, Milton and Rose Friedman, *Two Lucky People*, (University of Chicago Press, 1998).

Gale, D., *Money: In Equilibrium*, (London: Cambridge University Press, 1982).

Geer, T. H., *A Brief History of Western Man*, (New York: Harcourt Brace Jovanovich, 1968).

Goldberg, M. H., *The Jewish Connection*, (New York: Bantam Books, 1976).

Goldsmith, R., *A Study of Saving in the United States*, (Princeton University Press, 1955).

Goodheart, E., *Confessions of a Secular Jew* (NewYork: The Overlook Press, 2001).

Gramlich, E. M., "Remarks by Governor Edward M. Gramlich," Wharton Public Policy Forum Series, Philadelphia, Pennsylvania, Apr., 22, 1999. [http://www.federalreserve.gov/BOARDDOCS/SPEECHES/1999/ 199904222.htm].

Gramlich, E. M., "Remarks by Governor Edward M. Gramlich: At the Federal Reserve Board Models and Monetary Policy Conference," Washington, DC: March 26, 2004. [http://www.federalreserve.gov/BoardDocs/speeches/2004/20040326/]

Granger, C. W. J. *Empirical Modeling in Economics: Specification and Evaluation*, (London: Cambridge University Press, 1999).

Grunberg, E., and F. Modigliani, "The Predictability of Social Events," *Journal of Political Economy*, Vol. 62, No. 6. (Dec., 1954), 465–478.

Gurley, J. and E. Shaw, *Money in a Theory of Finance*, (Washington DC: The Brookings Institution, 1960).

Hadamard, J., *The Psychology of Invention in the Mathematical Field*, (New York: Dover Publications, 1945).

Hahn, F. and R. Solow, *A Critical Essay on Modern Macroeconomic Theory*, (Cambridge, MA: The MIT Press, 1995).

Hall, R. E., "Stochastic Implications of the Life Cycle-Permanent Income Hypothesis: Theory and Evidence," *The Journal of Political Economy*, (Dec., 1978), 971–987.

Hall, R. E., and F. S. Mishkin, "The Sensitivity of Consumption to Transitory Income: Estimates from Panel Data on Households," *Econometrica*, Vol. 50, No. 2, (March 1982), 461–481.

Hall, R. E., and J. B. Taylor. *Macro Economics*, (New York: W. W. Norton & Co., 1997).

Harrod, R. F. *Money*, (London: St. Martin's Press, 1969).

Heins, A. J., and C. M. Sprenkle, "A Comment on the Modigliani-Miller Cost of Capital Thesis," *American Economic Review*, (Sept., 1969), 590–592.

Henderson, J. M. and R. E. Quandt. *Microeconomic Theory: A Mathematical Approach*, (New York: McGraw-Hill, 1971).

Hicks, J. R., "Mr. Keynes' Theory of Employment," *The Economic Journal* 46, no. 182, (June., 1936), 238–253.

Hicks, J. R., *Value and Capital: An Inquiry into Some Fundamental Principles of Economic Theory*, (Oxford University Press, 1939).

Hicks, J. R., *Value and Capital*, (Oxford University Press, 1946).

Hicks, J. R., "IS-LM—An Explanation," *Journal of Post-Keynesian Economics* (Winter, 1980–1981). Reprinted in *The Economics of John Hicks*, (Oxford: Basil Blackwell, 1984), 216–229.

Hicks, J. R. "Mr. Keynes and the Classics," *Econometrica*, 1937, 147–159, Reprinted in *The Economics of John Hicks*, (Oxford: Basil Blackwell 1984).

Hicks, J. R., *The Economics of John Hicks*, Dieter Helm, ed., (Oxford: Basil Blackwell, 1984).

Holt, C. C., F. Modigliani, J. F. Muth and H.A. Simon, *Planning Production, Inventories and Work Force*, (Englewood Cliffs, NJ: Prentice Hall, 1960).

Hoover, H., *The Memoirs of Herbert Hoover: The Great Depression 1929–1934*, (New York: Macmillan, 1952).

Houthakker, H. S., "On Some Determinants of Saving in Developed and Underdeveloped Countries," in E. A. G. Robinson, ed., *Problems in Economic Development*, (London: Macmillan, 1965), 212–224.

Intriligator, M. D., "Economic and Econometric Models," in *Handbook of Econometrics*, Vol. I, + Z. Griliches and M. D. Intriligator, eds., (Amsterdam: North-Holland, 1983), 182–216.

Jappelli, T., "Who is Credit Constrained in the U.S. Economy?" *The Quarterly Journal of Economics*, Vol. 105, No. 1, (Feb., 1990), 219–234.

Johnson, H. G., *Essays in Monetary Economics*, 2nd edn., (London: George Allen and Unwin University Ltd., 1970).

Johnson, H. G., *Macroeconomic and Monetary Theory: Lectures in Economics I.* (London: Gray-Mills Publishing., 1971).

Kaldor, Nicholas., "Letter," in *John Maynard Keynes: The General Theory and After, Part II, Defense and Development*, Donald Moggridge, ed., (Royal Economic Society, 1973).

Keynes, J. M., *Essays in Persuasion*, (New York: W. W. Norton, 1963).
Keynes, J. M., *The Collected Writings of John Maynard Keynes: Volume 4, A Tract on Monetary Reform*, E. Johnson and D. Moggridge, eds., (London: The Royal Economic Society, 1971).
Keynes, J. M., "A Tract on Monetary Reform," in *The Collected Writings of John Maynard Keynes*, Vol. 4, (London: Macmillan, 1971).
Keynes, J. M., *The General Theory and After, Part II, Defense and Development*, Donald Moggridge, ed., (London: Royal Economic Society, 1973).
Keynes, J. M., *The General Theory of Employment, Interest and Money*, (London: Macmillan, 1936).
Keynes, J. M., *The General Theory and After: Part II: Defense and Development*, vol. XIV, Donald Moggridge, ed., (London: Cambridge University Press, 1987).
Klein, L. R. and S. Ozmucur, "The Wealth Effect: A Contemporary Update," paper presented at the New School University, 2005.
Klein, M. ed., *Modigliani Beyond the Myth*, (New Haven: Yale University Press, Jewish Museum, 2004).
Kouri, P. J. K., "Franco Modigliani's Contribution to Economics," *Scandinavian Journal of Economics* 88, No. 2 (1986), 311–334.
Kramer, A., *Conversations with Economists*, (Lanham: Rowman and Littlefield Publishers, 1984).
Kuznets, S., *National Product Since 1869*, (National Bureau of Economic Research, 1946).
Leijonhufvud, A., *On Keynesian Economics and the Economics of Keynes*, (Oxford University Press, 1982).
Leontief, W., "Comment" in *Studies in Income and Wealth, No. 11*, (New York: International Bureau of Economic Research, 1949), 441–442.
Lowe, A., *On Economic Knowledge*, (New York: Harper and Row, 1965).
Luria, S. E., *A Slot Machine, A Broken Tube* (NewYork: Harpes & Row, 1984).
Magill, M. and M. Quinzii, *Theory of Incomplete Markets*, (Cambridge, MA: The MIT Press, 1996).
Malamud, J., "My Father is a Book," *Threepenny Review* (Summer, 2003).
Mariger, R. P., "A Life-Cycle Consumption Model with Liquidity Constraints: Theory and Empirical Results," *Econometrica*, Vol. 55, No. 3, (May, 1987), 533–557.
Mauskopf, E., "The Transmission Channels of Monetary Policy: How Have They Changed?," *Federal Reserve Bulletin*, Vol. 76, No. 12, (Dec., 1972), 985–1009.
McCallum, B. T., "Monetarism, Rational Expectations, Oligopolistic Pricing, and the MPS Econometric Model," *The Journal of Political Economy*, Vol. 87, No. 1, (Feb., 1979), 57–73.
McElroy, F. W., "A Simple Method of Causal Ordering," *International Economic Review*, Vol. 19, No.1, (Feb., 1978), 1–23.
Meade, James E., "The Outcome of the Pasinetti-process: A Note," Economic Journal, Vol. 76, 1966, 161–165.
Miller, M. H., "Debt and Taxes," *Journal of Finance*, Vol. 32, No. 1, Papers and Proceedings of the Thirty-Fifth Annual Meeting of the American Finance Association, Atlantic City, New Jersey, September 16–18, 1976, (May, 1977), 261–275.
Miller, M. H., *Selected Works of Merton H. Miller: A Celebration of Markets* Vol. II, (University of Chicago Press, 2002).

Milne, F., "Choice Over Asset Economies: Default Risk and Corporate Leverage," *Journal of Financial Economics*, Vol. 2, (1975), 165–185.

Milne, F., *Financial Theory and Asset Pricing*, (Oxford: Clarendon Press, 1995).

Mishkin, F. S., "The Channels of Monetary Transmission: Lessons for Monetary Policy," *Banque De France Bulletin Digest*, No. 27, (March, 1996), 33–44.

Modigliani, F., "Liquidity Preference and the Theory of Interest and Money," *Econometrica* 12, No.1, (Jan., 1944), 45–88.

Modigliani, Franco, "Fluctuations in the Saving-Income Ratio: A Problem in Economic Forecasting," *Social Research*, Vol. 14, No. 4, (Dec., 1947), 413–420.

Modigliani, F., "Fluctuations in the Saving-Income Ratio: A Problem in Economic Forecasting," *Studies in Income and Wealth*, 11 (1949), 371–443.

Modigliani, Franco and Emile Grunberg, "The Prediction of Social Events," *The Journal of Political Economy*, Vol. 63, No. 6, (Dec., 1954).

Modigliani, Franco and Kalman J. Cohen, *The Role of Anticipations and Plans in Economic Behavior and Their us in Economic Analysis and Forecasting*, (Urbana, IL: The University of Illinois, 1961).

Modigliani, F., *The Review of Economic Studies*, Vol. 33, No. 4, (Oct., 1966), 303–306.

Modigliani, F., "Monetary Policy and Consumption: Linkages via Interest Rate and Wealth Effects in the FMP Model," *Consumer Spending and Monetary Policy: The Linkages*, F. Modigliani, et al. eds., (Federal Reserve Bank of Boston, 1971), 61–62.

Modigliani, F., "The General Theory of Employment Interest and Money under the Assumptions of Flexible Prices and of Fixed Prices," (Dissertation, New School, 1944).

Modigliani, F., *The Collected Papers of Franco Modigliani, Vol. 1, Essays in Macroeconomics*, A. Abel and S. Johnson, eds., (Cambridge, MA: The MIT Press, 1980).

Modigliani, F., "Fluctuations in the Saving-Income Ratio: A Problem in Economic Forecasting," *Social Research*, Vol. 14, No. 4 (Dec., 1947), in F. Modigliani, *Collected Papers of Franco Modigliani*, Vol. 2, A. Abel, ed., (Cambridge, MA: The MIT Press, 1980).

Modigliani, F., "Fluctuations in the Saving-Income Ratio: A Problem in Economic Forecasting" in F. Modigliani *Collected Papers of Franco Modigliani*, Vol. 2, A. Abel, ed., (Cambridge, MA: The MIT Press, 1980).

Modigliani, F., *The Collected Papers of Franco Modigliani, Vol. 2, The Life Cycle Hypothesis of Savings*, A. Abel and S. Johnson, eds., (Cambridge, MA: The MIT Press, 1980).

Modigliani, F., *The Collected Papers of Franco Modigliani, The Theory of Finance and Other Essays, Vol.3*, A. Abel, ed., (Cambridge, MA: The MIT Press, 1980).

Modigliani, F., "Reply" to "Fluctuations in the Saving-Income Ratio: A Problem in Economic Forecasting" in *Collected Papers of Franco Modigliani*, Vol. 2, A. Abel., ed., (Cambridge, MA: The MIT Press, 1980), 443.

Modigliani, F., "The Monetarists Controversy or, Should We Forsake Stabilization Policies?," *The American Economic Review* 67, no. 2 (March, 1977), in *Collected Papers of Franco Modiglian, Essays in Macroeconomics, Vol. 1*, A. Abel ed., (Cambridge, MA: The MIT Press, 1980), 3–22.

Modigliani, F., "The Monetary Mechanism and its Interaction with Real Phenomena," *Review of Economics and Statistics* 45 (Feb., 1963): 79–107. Reprinted in *Collected Papers of Franco Modigliani*, Vol. 3, A. Abel, ed., (Cambridge, MA: The MIT Press, 1980), 69–97.

Modigliani, F. and L. Papademos. "Optimal Demand Policies against Stagflation," in *The Collected Papers of Franco Modigliani*, Vol. 3, A. Abel, ed., (Cambridge: The MIT Press, 1980), 198–219.

Modigliani, Franco, *Collected Papers of Franco Modigliani*, Vol. 2, A. Abel. ed., (Cambridge, MA: The MIT Press, 1986), originally published as "Fluctuation in the Saving-Income Ratio: A Problem in Economic Forecasting," in *Studies in Income and Wealth, No. 11*, (New York: International Bureau of Economic Research, 1949).

Modigliani, F., *The Debate Over Stabilization Policy*, (New York: Cambridge University Press, 1986).

Modigliani, F., "Life Cycle, Individual Thrift, and the Wealth of Nations," in *Macroeconomics and Finance: Essays in Honor of Franco Modigliani*. R. Dornbusch, S. Fischer, and J. Bossons, eds., (Cambridge MA: The MIT Press, 1987).

Modigliani, F., "MM–Past, Present, Future." *The Journal of Economic Perspectives* 2, No. 4, (Autumn, 1988), 145–158.

Modigliani, F., *The Collected Papers of Franco Modigliani, Monetary Theory and Stabilization Policies, Vol. 4*, S. Johnson and A. Abel, eds., (Cambridge MA: The MIT Press, 1989).

Modigliani, F. *The Collected Papers of Franco Modigliani, Savings, Deficits, Inflation, and Financial Theory*, Vol. 5, A. Abel and S. Johnson, eds., (Cambridge, MA: The MIT Press, 1989b).

Modigliani, Franco, Jean-Paul Fitoussi, Beniamino Moro, Dennis Snower, Robert Solow, Alfred Steinherr and Paolo Sylos Labini, "An Economist's Manifesto on Unemployment in the European Union," *BNL Quarterly Review*, No., 206, September 1998, pp. 1–22,

Modigliani, Franco, *Collected Papers of Franco Modigliani*, Vol. 6, (Cambridge, MA: The MIT Press, 2005).

Modigliani, F. *Adventures of an Economist*, (New York: Texere, 2001).

Modigliani, F. "The Keynesian Gospel According to Modigliani," *The American Economist* 47, no. 1, (Spring 2003), 3–24, reprinted in *Collected Papers of Franco Modigliani*, Vol. 6, (Cambridge, MA: The MIT Press, 2005), 327–359.

Modigliani, F. and C. Steindel, "Is a Tax Rebate an Effective Tool for Stabilization?," *Brookings Papers on Economic Activity*, No. 1, (1977), 175–209.

Modigliani, F., R. Rasche and J. P. Cooper, "Central Bank Policy, the Money Supply, and the Short-Term Rate of Interest," *Journal of Money, Credit and Banking*, Vol. 2, No. 2, (May, 1970), 166–218.

Modigliani, F. and K. J. Cohen, *The Role of Anticipation and Plans in Economic Behavior and their use in Economic Analysis and Forecasting*, (Urbana IL: The University of Illinois, 1961).

Modigliani, F. and L. Papademos. "Monetary Policy for the Coming Quarters – The Conflicting Views," in *The Collected Papers of Franco Modigliani*, Vol. 4, S. Johnson and A. Abel eds., (Cambridge, MA: The MIT Press, 1989), 155–201.

Modigliani F. and S. L. Cao, "The Chinese Saving Puzzle and the Life-Cycle Hypothesis," *Journal of Economic Literature*, 42 (March, 2004), 145–170.

Modigliani, L., "The Time for Risk Measurement is Now," in Morgan Stanley*: U.S. Investment Research, U.S. Strategy*, Feb., 12, 1997. http://www.morganstanley.com/institutional/primebrokerage/modig4.pdf

Morgan, Victor E., *A History of Money*, (New York: Penguin, 1965).

Morishima, M., *Walras's Economics*, (London: Cambridge University Press, 1977).

Morton, W. A., "The Structure of the Capital Market and the Price of Money." *American Economic Review*, Vol 44, No. 2, (May, 1954), 440–457.

Mosak, J. L., "Forecasting Postwar Demand III," *Econometrica*, Vol. 13, (Jan., 1945).

Mueller, M. G. *Readings in Macroeconomics*, (New York: Holt, Rinehart and Winston, 1969), 25–53.

Mussolini. B., *Mussolini: As Revealed in his Political Speeches* (November 1914-August 1923), B. Bernardo.ed., (London: J. M. Dent & Sons, 1923).

Neftci, S. N., *An Introduction to the Mathematics of Financial Derivatives*, ed., (New York: Academic Press, 2000).

Neisser, H. and F. Modigliani. *National Incomes and International Trade: A Quantitative Analysis*, (Urbana, IL: University of Illinois Press, 1953).

Nelson, Charles R., "The Prediction Performance of the FRB-MIT-PENN Model of the U.S. Economy," *The American Economic Review*, Vol. 62, No. 5, (Dec., 1972), 902–917.

Neville, P., *Mussolini*, (London: Routledge, 2004), 125–135.

O'Sullivan, A. *Urban Economics*, (New York: McGraw Hill, 2003).

Papademos, Lucas and Franco Modigliani, "The Supply of Money and the Control of Nominal Income," in *Handbook of Monetary Economics*, Vol. I, B. M. Friedman and F. H. Hahn, eds., (Amsterdam: North-Holland, 1990), 399–494.

Parke R. D., "The Society for Research in Child Development at 70: Progress and Promise," *Child Development*, 78, (Jan. / Feb., 2004), 1–24.

Patinkin, D., "Relative Prices, Say's Law, and the Demand for Money," *Econometrica*, 16, (April, 1948), 135–154.

Patinkin, D., "The Indeterminacy of Absolute Prices in Classical Economic Theory," *Econometrica* 17, (Jan., 1949), 1–27.

Patinkin, D., "Financial Intermediaries and the Logical Structure of Monetary Theory: A Review," *The American Economic Review* 51, (March, 1961), 95–116.

Phelps, E. S., "Money-wage Dynamics and Labor Market Equilibrium," *Journal of Political Economy*, Vol. 76, (July–Aug., 1968), 678–711.

Pigou, A. C., *Unemployment*, (New York: Henry Holt, 1914).

Pigou, A. C., *The Theory of Unemployment*, (London: Macmillan, 1933).

Pigou, A. C., *Lapses from Full Employment*, (London: Macmillan., 1945).

Pigou, A. C., *Employment and Equilibrium*, (London: Macmillan., 1952).

Ramrattan, L. and M. Szenberg, "Franco Modigliani: 1918–2003, In Memoriam," *The American Economist*, Vol. XLVIII, No. 1, (Spring, 2004), 3–8.

Rasche, R. and H. T. Shapiro, "The F.R.B.-M.I.T Econometric Model: Its Special Features," *The American Economic Review*, (May, 1968), 123–149.

Rebecca, G., *"Betraying Spinoza: The Renegade Jew Who Gave Us Modernity,"* Schocken Books, (NewYork: 2006).

Robichek, A. A. and S. C. Myers, "Problems in the Theory of Optimal Structure," *The Journal of Financial and Quantitative Analysis*, Vol. 1, No. 2 (June, 1966), 1–35.

Romer, D., *Advanced Macroeconomics*, (New York: McGraw-Hill, 1996).

Rubin, G., "Patinkin on IS-LM: An Alternative to Modigliani," *History of Political Economy* 36, Annual Supplement (2004), 190–216.

Rubinstein, M. E., "A Mean-Variance Synthesis of Corporate Financial Theory," *The Journal of Finance*, Vol 28, No 1, (March, 1973), 167–181.

Rubinstein, M. E., "Great Moments in Financial Economics: II. Modigliani-Miller Theorem," *Journal of Investment Management*, (Spring, 2003).

Rymes, Thomas K., *Keynes' Lectures: 1932–35: Notes of a Representative Student,* (Ann Arbor, MI: University of Michigan Press, 1989).

Samuelson, P. A. and R. M. Solow, "Analytical Aspects of Anti-Inflation Policy," *The American Economic Review*, Vol. 50, (May, 1960), 177–194.

Samuelson, Paul A., "The Evaluation of 'Social Income: Capital Formation and Wealth," in F. A. Lutz and D. C. Hague, eds., *The Theory of Capital Proceedings of a Conference held by the International Economic Association,* (London: Macmillan, 1961).

Samuelson, Paul A., *The Collected Scientific Papers of Paul A. Samuelson,* Vol. 4, Hiroaki Nagatani and Kate Crowley, eds., (Cambridge, MA: The MIT Press, 1977).

Samuelson, P. A., "The 1985 Nobel Prize in Economics," in R. Dornbusch, S. Fischer, and J. Bosson, *Macroeconomics and Finance: Essays in Honor of Franco Modigliani* (Cambridge, MA: The MIT Press, 1987).

Samuelson, P. A., "Extirpating Error Contamination Concerning the Post-Keynesian Anti-Pasinetti Equilibrium" *Oxford Economic Papers* 43, No. 2 (April, 1991), 177–186.

Samuelson, P. A., "Foreword" in *Passion and Craft, Economists at Work,* M. Szenberg ed., (Ann Arbor, MI: University of Michigan Press, 1999).

Samuelson, P. A., "Professor Pigou's Employment and Equilibrium,' *The American Economic Review*, 31, (Sept., 1941), 545–552.

Samuelson, P. A., "What Classical and Neoclassical Monetary Theory Really Was," *Monetary Theory*, R. W. Clower ed., (London: Penguin, 1969), 175.

Samuelson, P. A., *Collected Scientific Papers,* Vol. 5, K. Crowley ed., (Cambridge, MA: The MIT Press, 1986).

Samuelson, P. A., "The 1985 Nobel Prize in Economics," in *Macroeconomics and Finance: Essays in Honor of Franco Modigliani*, R. Dornbusch, S. Fischer, and J. Bossons eds., (Cambridge, MA: The MIT Press, 1987).

Samuelson, P. A., "Franco Modigliani Memorial Service." Presented at Sloan School of Management, MIT, December, 2003.

Sargent, T. J., *Macroeconomic Theory*, (New York: Academic Press, 1979).

Sarnat, M., "Franco Modigliani (1918–2003)," Editorial, *Journal of Banking & Finance* 28 (2004).

Sharpe, W. F., *Portfolio Theory and Capital Markets,* (New York: McGraw-Hill, 1970).

Sheffrin, S. M., *Rational Expectation,* (New York: Cambridge University Press, 1983).

Simkin, C. G. F., *Economics at Large,* (London: Weidenfeld and Nicolson, 1968).

Smithies, A., "Forecasting Postwar Demand: I," *Econometrica,* Vol. 13, No. 1, (Jan., 1945), 1–14.

Snowdon, B. and H. R. Vane, *Conversations with Leading Economists,* (Northampton: Edward Elgar, 1999).

Solow, R. M., *Monopolistic Competition and Macroeconomic Theory,* (New York: Cambridge University Press, 1998).

Solow, R. M., "'Analytical Aspects of Anti-Inflaton Policy' after 40 Years," in *Paul Samuelson and the Foundations of Modern Economics,* K. Puttaswamaiah, ed., (Somerset N.J: Transaction Publishers, 2002), 71–78.

Stebbing, L. Susan, "A Modern Introduction to Logic," (New York: Harper TorchBooks, 1961).

Stigler, G. J., Review of "Lapses from Full Employment," *The American Economic Review* 36, (Dec., 1946), 927–928.

Stiglitz, J. E., "A Re-Examination of the Modigliani-Miller Theorem" *The American Economic Review* 59, No. 5, (Dec., 1969), 784–793.

Stiglitz, J. E., "On the Irrelevance of Corporate Financial Policy," *The American Economic Review*, Vol., 64, No. 6, (Dec., 1974), 851–866.

Stiglitz, J. E. and B. Greenwald, *Toward a New Paradigm in Monetary Economics*, (New York: Cambridge University Press, 2003).

Stone, R. and W. M. Stone, *The Marginal Propensity to Consume and the Multiplier, A Statistical Investigation*, (New York: Kraus Reprint Coorporation, 1959).

Sutch, R. and F. Modigliani, "The Supply of Money and the Control of Nominal Income" in *Handbook of Monetary Economics, Vol. I*, B. M. Friedman and F. H. Hahn, eds., (Amsterdam: North-Holland Publishing Company, 1990).

Szenberg, M., A. Gottesman, and L. Ramrattan, eds. *Paul Samuelson, On Being an Economist*, with a Foreword by J. Stiglitz, (New York: Jorge Pinto Books, 2005).

F. Targetti and A. P. Thirlwell eds., *The Essential Kaldor*, (New York: Holmes and Meier, 1989).

Tannenbaum, E. R., *The Fascist Experience: Italian Society and Culture, 1922–1945*, (New York: Basic Books, 1972).

Taylor, J. B., *Macroeconomic Policy in a World Economy: From Econometric Design to Practical Operation*, (New York: W. W. Norton & Company, 1993).

Tobin, J. *Essays in Economics: Theory and Policy*, (Cambridge, MA: The MIT Press, 1985).

Tobin, J. "Economic Stabilization Policies in the United States," in *Policies for Prosperity: Essays in a Keynesian Mode*, P. M. Jackson, ed., (Cambridge MA: The MIT Press, 1987), 439–453.

Tobin, J., *Essays in Economics: Macroeconomics*, (Cambridge, MA: The MIT Press, 1987).

Ulich, R., *The Education of Nations: A Comparison in Historical Perspective*, (Cambridge, MA.: Harvard University Press, 1961).

Van Horne, J. C., *Financial Management and Policy*, (Englewood Cliffs, NJ: Prentice Hall, 1998).

Varian, H. R., "The Arbitrage Principle in Financial Economics," *The Journal of Economic Perspectives*, Vol. 1, No. 2, (Autumn, 1987), 55–72.

Vedder, R. K. and L. E. Gallaway. *Out of Work*, (New York University Press, 1997).

Weston, J. F., and T. E. Copeland, *Managerial Finance*, (New York: The Dryden Press, 1996).

Wolpe, D. J., *Floating takes faith* (Springfield, NJ: Behrman House).

Williams, J. B., *The Theory of Investment Value*, (Burlington, VT: Fraser Publishing, 1997).

Zellner, A., "My Experience with Nonlinear Dynamic Models in Economics," in *Studies in Nonlinear Dynamics & Econometrics*, Vol. 6, Issue 2, (2002), 1–16.

Zellner, A. and S. C. Peck, "Simulation Experiments with a Quarterly Macroeconometric Model of the U.S. Economy," in *Basic Issues in Econometrics*, A. Zellner ed., (University of Chicago Press, 1984).

Index